A New Testament

Guide to the Holy Land

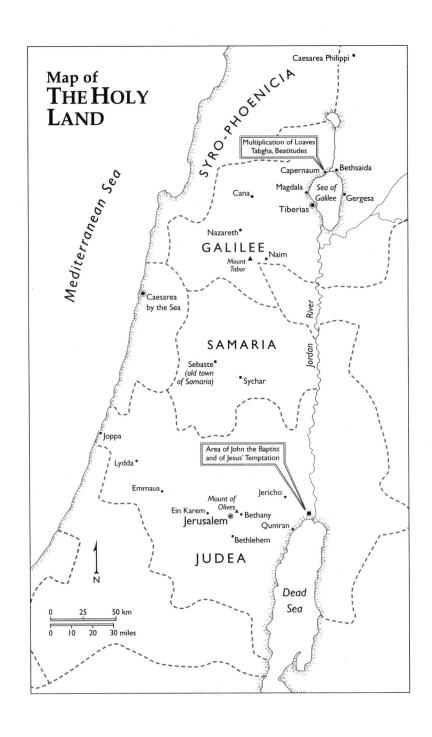

Map of
THE HOLY
LAND

Caesarea Philippi •

SYRO-PHOENICIA

Mediterranean Sea

Multiplication of Loaves
Tabgha, Beatitudes

Capernaum • • Bethsaida
Magdala • *Sea of*
Cana • *Galilee* • Gergesa
Tiberias •

Nazareth •

GALILEE
Naim •
Mount ▲
Tabor

◉ Caesarea
by the Sea

Jordan River

SAMARIA

Sebaste •
(old town • Sychar
of Samaria)

• Joppa

Area of John the Baptist
and of Jesus' Temptation

Lydda •

Emmaus •
Jericho •
Mount of
Olives ▲
Ein Karem • ◉ • Bethany
Jerusalem ◉ Qumran •

• Bethlehem

JUDEA

↑
N

Dead
Sea

| 0 | 25 | 50 km |
| 0 | 10 | 20 | 30 miles |

A New Testament

Guide to the Holy Land

SECOND EDITION

J O H N   J .   K I L G A L L E N ,   S . J .

an imprint of
Loyola Press

Chicago

JESUIT WAY

an imprint of

Loyola Press
3441 North Ashland Avenue
Chicago, Illinois 60657
1-800-621-1008

Cover and interior design by Lisa Buckley

Cover illustration: detail from *The Calling of the Apostles Peter and Andrew*, Duccio di Buoninsegna, Samuel H. Kress Collection, Photograph © 1997 Board of Trustees, National Gallery of Art, Washington

Library of Congress Cataloging-in-Publication Data
Kilgallen, John J.
A New Testament guide to the Holy Land/John J. Kilgallen.—2nd ed.
        p.   cm.
    Includes bibliographical references and indexes.
    ISBN 0-8294-1041-4
    1. Israel—Guidebooks. 2. Christian shrines—Israel. 3. West Bank—Guidebooks. 4. Christian shrines—West Bank. 5. Bible. N.T. Gospels—Geography. I. Title.
DS103.K53   1998
225.9'1—dc21   97-47704
                                                                  CIP

98 99 00 01 02 / 10 9 8 7 6 5 4 3 2

Contents

PART ONE

GALILEE AND SAMARIA

List of Illustrations

Foreword

Wwhat a pleasure it is to see this second edition of *A New Testament Guide to the Holy Land.* I was director of Loyola Press when the first edition appeared. I had been Fr. Kilgallen's Jesuit Provincial Superior before that and I knew of the tours of the Holy Land that he had led on his summer vacations from the Pontifical Biblical Institute in Rome. Like others of his friends and students, I had asked him why he didn't write a book along those lines for other pilgrims to the biblical sites. *A New Testament Guide to the Holy Land,* first published in 1987, was the result.

It was a marvelous book: simple, direct, informative, and quietly inspirational without being "preachy." Friends to whom I gave it as a gift when I heard they were going on a Holy Land tour came back praising the "added dimension" it had given their visits to biblical sites. Others, like myself, who have never been to the Holy Land, have found in the book a new and enriching context for their reading of the Scriptures.

This second edition improves upon the first in a variety of ways. There are new illustrations, additional maps, a glossary, and a very helpful but brief reading list. The strengths of the original, however, remain undiluted.

Fr. Kilgallen wears his scholarship lightly. He is not out to impress the reader with his own knowledge but to help him or her better understand both the Holy Land and the Scriptures. His eminently readable text is plain and straightforward, yet his knowledge not only of the holy places but particularly of the New Testament shines out on every page. Readers who have never been to the Holy Land and have no plans to go there will still learn much in this book about the Gospels and the letters of St. Paul.

In short, the additions to this "tenth anniversary" edition have only served to make a wonderful book more helpful. I rejoice to see it back in the bookstores again.

Daniel L. Flaherty, S.J.

Introduction

The first edition of this book was published over ten years ago and represented a reworking of lectures given earlier to students at the Holy Land sites. Continued demand for this kind of guide to the New Testament sites, my own further visits to Israel and meditations there, and a more comprehensive application of the New Testament (e.g., Pauline thought) to these sites—all of these have led me to write what I believe to be a better guide to the New Testament sites in the Holy Land.

My goal in this second edition is the same as that of the first: to help the pilgrim understand what the New Testament has to say about a particular site, and to enter into a better understanding of the New Testament itself. In other words, I am not here interested in presenting what others, e.g., the Fathers of the Church, or theologians, or Saints, or later writers, might think that these sites mean; I am interested only in what the New Testament thinks they mean. I use the discussion of these sites as an opportunity to develop for the reader some of the main ideas which preoccupied the evangelists and moved them to write their Gospels.

That the visitor or pilgrim may be more satisfied with this book, I have added what I thought to be sufficient geographical, historical, and archeological data. Such additional data may not answer all of one's questions, and for this inadequacy I apologize. For anyone seeking more information, I have added a list of recommended further readings (pp. 283-84).

I hope that this volume will be easy to carry and inexpensive, so I did not quote the biblical texts about which I write. I assume that the reader will have a New Testament. I also trust that the visitor will read the appropriate New Testament passages in close association with this book; ultimately, those passages and the holy sites deserve our fullest attention and memory.

I present the holy sites in a certain geographical order: first, Galilee and its environs, and then Jerusalem and its environs. But visits to Israel do not have to start in Galilee and end in Jerusalem, so I include an index of the sites and themes. I add, too, indexes of subjects and biblical texts and a list of important dates and periods.

I have assumed that the reader can find on his or her own each of the sites treated in this volume. Thus, I have avoided in this book what is always the most chancy enterprise: trying to guess where a person is staying so that I can plot out for him or her how to get to a particular door of a shrine, which door may well be no longer in use! Rather, I am confident that the pilgrim will reach the desired site, read the appropriate New Testament passages, and then the appropriate comments about that site in this volume.

In describing this book I have presumed that it will be used at the site it speaks about. I had never thought of the book being used while one is at home, either in preparation for a trip to Israel or in reflection on a trip already made there—or even for personal enrichment, whether or not one ever goes to Israel. Yet I have heard from people who have used the book in one of these less expected ways that it has proved very helpful to them, and so I note that this book can well serve many readers as well as actual pilgrims to holy sites in the land of Israel.

Is my book meant to be spiritually uplifting? Yes, but primarily indirectly. It operates on the assumption that deeper understanding of what God has told us about the events of Jesus' life in Israel can develop our spirituality. The better one comprehends the Word of God, the better, I hope, one will cherish Jesus and his Father. As St. Ignatius of Loyola advises his retreatant, "I ask for what I desire. Here it will be to ask for an intimate knowledge of our Lord."

May the One who made and still makes the sites holy and who breathes meaning into the New Testament also live more fully in the lives of those who visit his places in search of him.

Table of Abbreviations

Acts	Acts	Hg	Haggai
Am	Amos	Hos	Hosea
Bar	Baruch	Is	Isaiah
1 Chr	1 Chronicles	Jas	James
2 Chr	2 Chronicles	Jb	Job
Col	Colossians	Jdt	Judith
1 Cor	1 Corinthians	Jer	Jeremiah
2 Cor	2 Corinthians	Jgs	Judges
Dn	Daniel	Jl	Joel
Dt	Deuteronomy	Jn	John
Eccl	Ecclesiastes	1 Jn	1 John
Eph	Ephesians	2 Jn	2 John
Est	Esther	3 Jn	3 John
Ex	Exodus	Jon	Jonah
Ez	Ezekiel	Jos	Joshua
Ezr	Ezra	Jude	Jude
Gal	Galatians	1 Kgs	1 Kings
Gn	Genesis	2 Kgs	2 Kings
Hb	Habakkuk	Lam	Lamentations
Heb	Hebrews	Lk	Luke

Lv	Leviticus	2 Pt	2 Peter
Mal	Malachi	Rom	Romans
1 Mc	1 Maccabees	Ru	Ruth
2 Mc	2 Maccabees	Rv	Revelations
Mi	Micah	Sg	Song of Songs
Mk	Mark	Sir	Ecclesiasticus (Sirach)
Mt	Matthew	1 Sm	1 Samuel
Na	Nahum	2 Sm	2 Samuel
Neh	Nehemiah	Tb	Tobit
Nm	Numbers	1 Thes	1 Thessalonians
Ob	Obadiah	2 Thes	2 Thessalonians
Phil	Philippians	1 Tm	1 Timothy
Phlm	Philemon	2 Tm	2 Timothy
Prv	Proverbs	Wis	Wisdom
Ps(s)	Psalms	Zec	Zechariah
1 Pt	1 Peter	Zep	Zephaniah

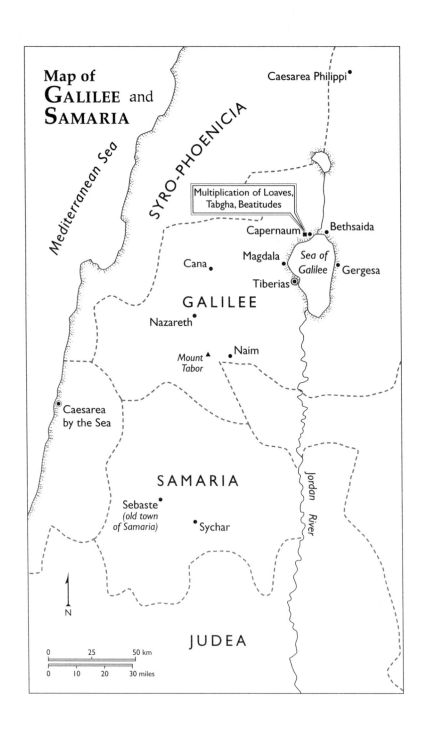

Map of
GALILEE and
SAMARIA

Mediterranean Sea

SYRO-PHOENICIA

Caesarea Philippi •

Multiplication of Loaves,
Tabgha, Beatitudes

Capernaum • • Bethsaida

Magdala • *Sea of Galilee*

Cana • • Gergesa

Tiberias ◎

GALILEE

Nazareth •

Mount Tabor ▲ • Naim

◎ Caesarea
by the Sea

SAMARIA

Sebaste •
(old town of Samaria) • Sychar

Jordan River

↑
N

JUDEA

0	25	50 km
0	10	20	30 miles

Galilee and Samaria

Nazareth

"HE WILL BE CALLED A NAZOREAN."
~MATTHEW 2:23

Nazareth, in the Galilean hills, even now is a small town: modern Upper Nazareth is Jewish, ancient Lower Nazareth is Arab. Arab Nazareth, where the ancient biblical sites are to be found, sits within a few miles of the edge of a cliff, from which one has a wonderful view of the Valley of Esdraelon. Recently evidence has suggested that the town had the distinction of providing some of the thousands of priests who served annually in the Jerusalem Temple.

The Basilica of the Annunciation

The modern visitor to the Basilica of the Annunciation enters on the ground floor and passes through what serves as the parish church of the local Arab Roman Catholic community. There is a staircase from this ground-floor level to the basilica's lower level.

On the lower level of the basilica, all attention is directed to a simple altar placed directly and exactly under the center of the basilica's very high dome. The altar is surrounded on three of its sides by banks of seats which can accommodate about forty people. On the fourth side are the remains of a natural cave which enclose another, grotto-like room, which has its own altar. It is within this grotto-like room that a very old and strong tradition places the visit of the angel Gabriel to Mary; it is here that Mary learned of God's plan for her and here that Mary conceived Jesus.

Nazareth: capital with relief sculpture from the eleventh-century crusader church

This basilica, begun in 1960 A.D. to honor the annunciation to Mary and her conception of Jesus, is at least the fourth church or basilica on this site. We know that a church was built here in the early decades of the Byzantine Empire, enclosing a mosaic that recalls a deacon named Conon of the early second century A.D. Just walk up to the grille which serves to protect the grotto-like structure, but do not pass through the grille; rather, walk to the left along the grille till you come to a mosaic in the floor. It is this mosaic which tells of Deacon Conon, no doubt a testimonial to his devotion to this holy site. The famous grotto-like room is entered by passing through the grille. Clearly we can assume that the Byzantine basilica enclosing the Conon mosaic was built over a site that had been venerated for its sacredness for many decades before him; indeed archeological diggings have uncovered many graffiti written in this area to honor Jesus and Mary by early pilgrims to Palestine who were searching for the holy places.

The Byzantine basilica was eventually destroyed, but centuries later the Crusaders took it on themselves to build another and larger church to commemorate the sacred events of the annunciation and conception of Jesus. Finished about 1100 A.D., the crusader church lasted only about one hundred and fifty years. Then in 1620 the Franciscans arrived in Nazareth and about 1730 finally won permission to build a modest church on this site. This small church was destroyed to make way for the striking twentieth-century basilica which we can enjoy today.

Each of these churches, Byzantine, crusader, Franciscan, and modern, encloses the sacred grotto of the Annunciation; the newest basilica intentionally encloses remains of the Byzantine/Conon and crusader churches. A knowledgeable guide at the site can point out the remains and outlines of each of these earlier churches.

But let us turn our thoughts and imagination to the Nazareth of the ancient times. What can we say about Nazareth in general and about its relationship with the New Testament in particular?

The name Nazareth seems to come from a Hebrew word which means both *to blossom* and *to guard*. To some, therefore, Nazareth is the town which guards, from its position in the hills of Galilee, the vast plain of Esdraelon which stretches below it to the south; even today, from the platform surrounding the Basilica of the Annunciation, we can catch sight of this plain. But to others, Nazareth, always a small town in the first century A.D., is better understood to symbolize the beauty of the Galilee flowers and, more practically to be the place which, as archaeology has shown, served for many centuries before Christ as the storage place for the bountiful grain harvested in Galilee. Even today, in the Church of St. Joseph, about fifty yards from the Basilica of the Annunciation, we can visit ancient caves which served as granaries for Jesus' predecessors in Nazareth.

Imaginatively, we should place ourselves within the Basilica of the Annunciation and face southward; we should picture ourselves standing on the hill overlooking the wonderful Plain of Esdraelon, standing among little houses which run along the brow of the hill and overlook the great plain. On this hill, among these houses called Nazareth, would be found the house in which Mary lived. Tradition says that adjacent to this house would have been something in part like a garden; it would be in this area next to the house that the Angel Gabriel spoke to Mary. It is this small area which all four of the churches have tried to protect, embellish, and honor.

The Old Testament said nothing about Nazareth. It is the New Testament which attributes so much to this small town. Given its unimportance in Old Testament promises and hopes for salvation sent by God, it is not surprising that Nathaniel retorted to those who spoke of Jesus of Nazareth as the Messiah: "What good can possibly come from Nazareth?"

Nathaniel's question, reported by John (1:46), was echoed in the same Gospel when people in Jerusalem discussed whether or not Jesus was the Messiah. Some believed that the Messiah should come from David's family and from David's town, Bethlehem; for these people Jesus did not qualify since he was known to be from Nazareth. Others believed that the origin of the Messiah would simply be unknown; Jesus, of course, admitted that he was from Nazareth, and so disqualified himself for those people as well.

Indeed, both Matthew and Luke, for their parts, made it clear that Jesus was born in Bethlehem; thus they can argue that Jesus, though hailing from Nazareth, was born in David's town, Bethlehem, and so can be called Son of David, a first step to show that Jesus was the Messiah promised as a son to David.

But for all the unimportance of this small town, Nazareth bursts on the consciousness of millions and millions of people, for it is the site of two precious periods of Jesus' life, that of his conception and childhood, and that of his adult, preaching life. Let us look at each of these two moments.

Annunciation to Mary
~ LUKE 1:26–38 ~

Luke tells us of the visit of the Angel Gabriel to Mary in Nazareth. *Gabri* means *my strength* and *el* means *God;* thus, *Gabriel* means *my strength is God.* The function of the angel is to announce the beginning of the most important phase of God's plan to save all people. Gabriel had already appeared in Israel's history as the interpreter of Daniel's dreams, in the Book of Daniel (8:16–26 and 9:21–27). Now he appears to Mary, to say that this is the time when God is going to give to the world what Daniel and so many Old Testament figures had so ardently hoped for.

The same Gabriel had, six months earlier and about eighty miles south, announced another phase of this same divine plan: the role of a child miraculously conceived by Elizabeth and to be named John. This child would serve the divine plan in this way: filled with the Holy Spirit from his conception, he would eventually be a prophet like Elijah and would, as Elijah was expected to do, prepare the Israelite people to meet their God coming to them. Eventually, John would understand that part of his preparation of the people to meet God was a baptism in which the baptized or repentant Israelite would enjoy forgiveness of sins, a forgiveness which was meant to be an experience of salvation.

Nazareth: Basilica of the Annunciation

Now the Angel Gabriel described for Mary the role of the child she would miraculously conceive. Her child should be called *Jesus*, a name popularly said in Jesus' time to come from the Hebrew word meaning *to save*. A fitting name for this child! His role was described by the Old Testament image we find in the second book of Samuel (7:12–16): Jesus would sit on the throne of David his father, a throne which will endure forever. Jesus, in other words, will be the king or Messiah that God had promised to Israel through David. Thus, this child Jesus will grow into the person who, in Israelite tradition, was the unique intermediary between God and Israel. The king, the Messiah, represented the needs and hopes of Israel to God, and in turn, he was the one through whom God channeled his blessings: wisdom, power, protection, prosperity. It is this function, representative to God and channel from God, which Jesus would carry out in the divine plan of salvation.

Mary's question about how the conception of Jesus would take place—"I have no sexual relations with men"—was the means of revealing a crucial truth about Jesus. Through the Holy Spirit's coming upon her and through the power of the Most High, this child was to be conceived. From the role of the Spirit and of the Most High (who are not described here as having sexual intercourse with Mary) we are to draw two inescapable conclusions: Jesus is holy because he is caused by the Holy Spirit, and he is Son of God because he is caused by God, the Most High. Thus, though the precise way God influenced Mary remains mysterious, we are to conclude that the result of God's influence means Jesus is God's son. It is not that Jesus is the Son of God because God calls him to be his son; he is the Son of God because God in some mysterious way produced Jesus as a father produces a son.

To be the son of God in this way means that Jesus has the qualities of his Father, as a son would have the qualities of his father. These qualities are not given to Jesus later, but belong to him in his very conception. In brief, whereas many prophets and great men and women of Israel experienced the influence of God and of God's Spirit in their lives, and whereas John the Baptizer experienced the presence of the Holy Spirit once he was conceived, Jesus was—although in an unexplained way— the product of God and of God's Spirit, as a son is the product of a father. This statement means that Jesus is revealed here to owe his very existence and identity to God through his human mother, Mary; in this way, Jesus is totally unique among human beings. To explain Jesus' origins this way is to say that no other explanation for his character, for his qualities during his public life, will suffice. What we will hear and see Jesus say and do in the rest of the Gospel and in the Acts of the Apostles is in great measure due to the fact that Jesus was produced, fathered by God and by no one else. In this way Jesus is, among many called *son* or *sons of God*, truly and uniquely the Son of God.

Jesus means to *save*. One cannot stress too much the emphasis Luke places in his infancy stories on the reality of the divine plan of salvation. Jesus is certainly to be revealed as the one and only saviour of the world, but even he must be seen as part (though the most spectacular part) of the great plan of God which has intermittently been revealed already in the Old Testament. The plan stretches far beyond the public life of Jesus in Palestine—indeed Luke indicates that this divine plan stretches to the end of time and to the ends of this world. All of the experiences of salvation—before, during, or after the human life of Jesus—are seen as parts of a comprehensible order or plan. Even today one can find one's place in this plan.

One should note that the first image by which Jesus is described by Luke is fully realized only after the public life of Jesus is over; that is, Jesus never becomes king, Messiah of Israel, during his public life, but takes the position of king only after his resurrection and ascension. This fact means that other images of Jesus will be more appropriate to his life, words, and deeds in Galilee and Jerusalem. Ultimately, however, we are to remember that Jesus is destined to be at the right hand of the Father, the proper position of the beloved King Messiah, the intermediary between God and mankind. When Jesus seated himself at God's right hand after his ascension, he fulfilled what David and all Israel prayed would come to pass; Jesus was, because he was Son of God from conception, greater than all the figures of the Old Testament, and once enthroned beside his Father, he shows himself clearly to be Lord or Master even of David.

The beautiful description of Gabriel's encounter with Mary is called the Annunciation because what seems to dominate the story is the announcing of who Jesus, Mary's son, really is. There is, however, another element to the story, which is very significant, but does not belong to a simple story of announcement. Luke will not let the story finish until Mary gives her memorable words: "Behold the servant of the Lord, be it done to me as the Lord wishes." This element of Luke's story makes one think that we have here not only a story revealing Jesus' meaning, but a story which also shows a sending of Mary and which waits for her free obedience to God. Mary becomes for many interpreters the ideal companion of God, ready to do his will, however clear or unclear, and however daunting that will might seem to be. No matter how great the difficulties and uncertainties of her sending, her trust is greater than them all; with that expressed, the story of the Annunciation can, and does, end.

Once the angel leaves Mary in Nazareth, Luke tells of Mary's haste to help her relative Elizabeth who was already six months pregnant with John. Clearly, Mary is pregnant when she first meets with Elizabeth, so we can presume that the conception of Jesus took place most likely right after Mary had said her "yes" to God. At this moment God mysteriously becomes a human being; no longer would God be content to send human beings as his emissaries or representatives to bring his offer of reconciliation and forgiveness. God now somehow comes himself, to offer us forgiveness, to die so that the just punishment of sin need no longer be ours to pay; God came to live a human life and thus instruct us by example (and not just teach us by his word) above all else what is the truly good, holy, happy, and noble way to live human existence.

Such is part of the significance of this site of Nazareth—indeed overwhelming for the mind, so joyous and freeing for the spirit. We know now the profound meaning of this child; the rest of the Gospel and Luke's Acts of the Apostles will reveal just how this Son of God, this Son of David, and this obedience of Mary all played out for the good of all of us.

Annunciation to Joseph
~ MATTHEW 1:18–25 ~

The Gospel of Matthew does not tell us where Joseph received his dream and all of its information—a dream which proved to be truly an annunciation to Joseph. Tradition assumes that this dream took place in the town where Joseph and Mary lived, at a site very near to the Basilica of the Annunciation, indeed, on the very same grounds as the basilica.

The angel's words to Joseph had their practical point; they were to prevent an impending mistake by Joseph. Joseph, after noticing that Mary, his intended bride, was pregnant, got ready to divorce her. (The engagement to marry was, in these days, a legal action, and the breaking of the legal bond a real divorce; it called for a document which explained this divorce, without which Mary would not be recognized to be free of her engagement and so, if she attempted marriage with another man, would be considered an adultress and worthy of being stoned to death.)

The angel meant to stop Joseph from this divorce action and he did it by the explanation he gave regarding this pregnancy. He explained that the child Mary carried had, in some mysterious way, God as his Father, and not some human being. Indeed, this child would be called Jesus, a name which means *God saves through him*, reveals the role the child should play as an adult, and thus explains why God intervened to cause this child to be conceived. Joseph, then, should not divorce Mary, but proceed to be her husband and the one to rear this Son of God.

Matthew knew, as eyewitness and as author of the rest of his story, all the "savings" Jesus did, all those miracles by which Jesus saved people from sorrow, pain, death. But, when Matthew pinpoints the saving character of Jesus, he concentrates on Jesus' saving us from our sins; this salvation, and not physical salvation, is Jesus' greatest contribution to us and our complete happiness.

Matthew himself, true to his way of reflecting on events, recalled the Old Testament, in this case the prophet Isaiah's words: "a virgin will conceive and bear a son; they shall call him *God with us*" (Is 7:14), for God assures us that through this child God is with us. Did Isaiah really know about and speak about the conception of Jesus? Matthew does not mean to say that Isaiah did actually foresee this birth of Jesus around 6 B.C.; Isaiah was speaking about another child of his own time, who would be an instrument of God for the peace and protection of Israel. But Isaiah's words are, as Sacred Scripture, the words of God; Matthew knew this, and understood that God was speaking about Jesus, even if God's prophet Isaiah did not understand the words to refer to Jesus. Since Matthew knows how truly God is with us through Jesus, he took God's words, which Isaiah spoke and understood in one way, and indicated that these words of God were truer than Isaiah ever expected: they were really speaking about Jesus. It is this truth that Matthew affirms when he writes that Jesus is the fulfillment of Isaiah's ancient words about a wonderful child.

The annunciations to Mary and Joseph come to us from Luke and Matthew. Matthew emphasized in his own way, as Luke did in his own way, that the degree to which God was with us through Jesus can only be explained by professing God as, in some mysterious fashion, the real and only Father of Jesus. So strong was Matthew's conviction about this explanation and his desire to profess it, that he stated again, at the close of his chapter 1, that Mary had intercourse with no man before Jesus was born. Thus, Luke and Matthew begin their stories to us about Jesus with the profound belief that Jesus is, as no one else is, the Son of God. It is only by knowing that God is Jesus' Father that one can truly understand the person we will read about in the rest of the Gospels, and especially how Jesus could be called the One who will save us from our sins.

Childhood of Jesus
~ LUKE 2:39–40, 51–52 ~

The childhood of Jesus is not described in the Gospels. We can only let our imaginations wander a bit, as we stand in the town where Jesus grew up, to estimate what life for him must have been like with a mother like Mary and a father like Joseph. Luke twice tells us that Jesus "grew" or "progressed steadily." When Luke says this for the first time, Jesus is only forty days old, having come back from Jerusalem and the Temple where, according to the Law of Moses, he had to be presented to God (and where Mary had to be purified after giving birth). This description, that Jesus grew physically and spiritually, in wisdom about life and with the grace of God, means to cover all Jesus' young years, not only the first one or two. It also means to say that God for his part, and Mary and Joseph for their parts, helped the young Jesus to find his way through the years of youthfulness.

The second time Luke refers to Jesus' growth is the moment when Jesus, having been found in the Jerusalem Temple by his parents, returns to this town of Nazareth to continue his teen years, into his twenties and early thirties. Jesus is noted for his obedience to his parents, and for his spiritual and physical and psychological maturing.

The Gospels tell us nothing of the particulars of these many years; we can only guess at them. But it seems reasonable to say, looking backwards from what we know of the adult Jesus, that God must have watched over Jesus as a child and a young man, and that the influence of Jesus' parents on him, as his first teachers in all things, must have been profound and very positive. Indeed, the character of Jesus the adult is not just the result of his being Son of God; it is the result as well of the care his parents took in raising him, educating him, being examples for him, loving him. Jesus' later brilliance in expounding the teachings of his Old Testament traditions can be traced to the care with which he was taught his religion from his earliest years, and to the convictions he grew to embrace, which were urged upon him by his parents.

It was right here in this part of Israel where that maturation of Jesus took place, which we experience and admire in the accounts of his public life.

The Choice of Nazareth
~ MATTHEW 1:19–23 ~

Nazareth is the home of Jesus, Mary, and Joseph, but it became that only for a very particular reason. Herod the Great had tried to have Jesus killed in Bethlehem. An angel warned Joseph to take his family out of Bethlehem to escape the swords of Herod's troops; Joseph chose to go southward, into Egypt, where many Jews had lived since the time of the Babylonian victory over Jerusalem in 587 B.C. At the death of Herod the Great (about two years after Jesus was born), Joseph, under the direction of an angel in still another dream, was told he could go home safely. Joseph, it seems, preferred to go back to the Jerusalem area, perhaps to Bethlehem (only a few miles south of Jerusalem), but the successor of Herod the Great, Herod's son Archelaus, was rumored to be no less cruel than Herod the Great himself, so Joseph went northward into the territory of a more moderate ruler. Thus, Joseph chose to live under another son of Herod the Great, Antipas, who would prove to be the one to condemn John the Baptizer to death and, with Pilate, would try Jesus for a capital crime. Joseph chose the territory of Herod Antipas, that is, he chose Galilee (the top third of Israel)—and within the boundaries of Galilee Joseph settled, with his family, in Nazareth.

Matthew, however, was especially interested in telling of Joseph's settling in Nazareth because the town's name helped to reveal Jesus' identity. How did the town's name do this? Once Joseph is described as settling in Nazareth, Matthew notes that the Old Testament had said about a special person that "he shall be called a Nazorean" (Mt 2:23). One can immediately hear the similarity between "Nazareth" and "Nazorean"; the town makes one think of this special person, this Nazorean.

What does Nazorean mean? Scholars say it can mean either "dedicated" or "a shoot from the trunk of a tree." Whichever meaning one takes (and we are not sure which meaning Matthew himself preferred—or did he think that both were apt?), Matthew is asking us to remember that to "come from Nazareth" means either "to be dedicated" or "to be a shoot from the trunk of a tree." That is, when I think of Jesus of *Nazareth*, I remember that he is "Jesus the dedicated one," and "Jesus, a shoot from the trunk of a tree, i.e., Jesus a descendant from the family tree of David, his ancestor."

Actually, to be honest, there is no actual, single sentence anywhere in the Old Testament that reads "he shall be called a Nazorean." What Matthew has done is put into the form of one sentence the sense of much of the Old Testament, that there would come a special person who would be Son of David, who would be profoundly dedicated to God. In this way, Matthew again professes to his reader that Jesus is the completion of the Old Testament hopes and promises. Even the name of his home town, although apparently not important, helps us to understand better who Jesus is.

Adulthood of Jesus: the programmatic episode
~ LUKE 4:16–30 ~

This town of Nazareth had a significant part to play in the life of the adult Jesus, too. Whereas one of Luke's major sources of infomation, the Gospel of Mark, indicated that Jesus' preaching career in Galilee was headquartered about twenty-five miles away at Capernaum, Luke chose to set the tone for the entire public life of Jesus by narrating a story which is situated in Nazareth. This story is called by many scholars today the *programmatic episode* of Luke's Gospel. By reviewing its elements we shall see why the story is called "programmatic."

The Gospel of Luke tells of Jesus' coming home to Nazareth very early in his preaching career. Since it was the Sabbath, Jesus went to the synagogue. Near the modern Basilica of the Annunciation is an actual ancient synagogue where we can imagine what Jesus' visit to Nazareth's synagogue must have been like. The few details of the story that Luke tells accurately describe the way the synagogue service would have been run. Jesus, as a visitor that day, would be asked to read a section of the Jewish Scriptures and offer a comment on his reading.

Jesus' choice of a scriptural passage was a section from the prophet Isaiah (61:1–2). Here the prophet described an unnamed person who was anointed by God, which means that he was Messiah; *Messiah* and *Christ* come respectively from the Semitic and Greek terms for *anointed*. Because he was anointed by God, this person received God's Holy Spirit. Why was he anointed and filled with the Spirit? So that he might bring good news, proclaim liberty and sight, set free; all his acts could be summed up by saying, as Isaiah did, that this person was to proclaim a time of favor from God. The time of reunion with God, the time of healing and freedom that comes from reconciliation with God and forgiveness—that time was here.

In the Nazareth synagogue, Jesus identified himself as this anointed one of Isaiah. As such, he indicated that the longed-for favor of God would be given through him. "This text is being fulfilled today," Jesus said. Jesus dispensed the good news, liberty, sight, freedom. This citation from Isaiah was very important to Luke. Other descriptions of Jesus are true to the person and total mission of Jesus—Lord, Savior, King, Light to the Gentiles, Glory of Israel, Son of God, the Holy One—and Luke depended on them to help the reader to grasp the essence of Jesus. As far as Jesus' active life in Galilee was concerned, his preaching, teaching, and healing, the quotation from Isaiah 61 was the best terminology by which Luke could sum up and introduce the reader to what would happen in Jesus' public life in Galilee. With the rest of Jesus' public life in mind, Luke gave the reader the outlines of the program which Jesus would follow in succeeding chapters.

It is important to note how much the Isaian quotation stresses the preaching of the anointed one: *announcing* good news, *proclaiming* liberty and sight, *proclaiming* the year of favor. Jesus would work many miracles, but Luke, like so many other New Testament writers, was anxious to affirm that the blessing given to all Christians is not an assurance that Jesus will intervene in our lives to work miracles, but is rather the abiding wisdom of Jesus' mind. Teaching, the early Christians learned, was in the long run more valuable than miracles.

But the program which Luke wanted to anticipate was not fully described by Isaiah's words, for there is more to the story of Jesus' life than teaching and miracles—and so there is more to the story of Jesus' visit to Nazareth's synagogue. The initial reaction to Jesus' identification of himself as the anointed of God and to the implication that the year of God's favor was now here—the initial reaction of the people was favorable.

Within minutes, however, doubts began to rise: the signal of these doubts was the apparently innocent question about Jesus' origins. Apparently innocent, for its true meaning is a suggestion that Jesus' background—born of Mary and Joseph and growing up here in Nazareth in a most ordinary way—indicated that Jesus should not claim any distinction for himself, that his words might sound pretty, but he surely should claim no unique relationship to God for himself. Indeed, what in the past thirty years in Nazareth suggested that Jesus was anything but an ordinary Jew, pious but ordinary?

In a very few moments, then, the climate changed. Jesus recognized this change and immediately proceeded to condemn his fellow Israelites and Nazarenes. His condemnation revolved around the axiom that a prophet is not honored in his own country. Jesus now draws two examples from Israel's past to show both that great prophets have been rejected by Israel and what Israel can expect when its prophets are rejected.

In the time of the greatest of Israel's prophets, Elijah (who lived about nine hundred years before Jesus), the heavens were shut for over three years, so that no rain fell on Israel; this was a punishment for sin. Yet, when God was punishing Israel, he did work miracles, but not for Israel—God worked a miracle through Elijah for a foreigner, a widow from north of Israel; God did nothing of the kind for Israel, who had sinned and turned against the prophet, the representative of God.

And in the time of Elisha, who succeeded Elijah as Israel's chief prophet, God cured a leper from Syria, but would not cure any leper in Israel. Such was the reaction of God to the Israelites who sinned and rejected his prophet. The lesson was not misunderstood by Jesus' listeners; indeed, Luke intended the meaning of Jesus' words to be applied not only to Jesus' own contemporaries, but also the Jews of succeeding generations who would not accept the preaching about Jesus and thus would lose the favor of God which would be conferred, strangely enough, on Gentiles.

So Jesus warns the Nazarenes that their negative evaluation of him is dangerous; they are rejecting one sent by God. Jesus' likening the Nazarenes to those who did not listen to Elijah and Elisha angers the Nazarenes; they do not believe in him and so they lead Jesus out of Nazareth to throw him to death off the edge of a cliff. Jesus, Luke says, does not permit this death, but at the end walks through their midst. We have in this one Nazareth story the four elements which outline the program of the rest of the Gospel. At first, Jesus will be marvelled at by many, even accepted by many. Second, there will come a time of anger at him and rejection. Third, there will arrive the moment of putting Jesus to death. Finally, there will be Jesus' "escape," that is his resurrection, when Jesus escapes from the clutches of death.

This episode of chapter 4 of Luke is more important than others because it introduces the entire work of Jesus and the ultimate rejection by many in Israel of his person and his work. This story in Luke also reflects what other Gospels narrate: the reluctance of Jesus' own relatives and of his fellow Nazarenes to accept him. Perhaps it is too trite to say that "familiarity breeds contempt"; the doubts about Jesus are due to causes other than simple familiarity. Yet clearly we should face the degree of rejection offered Jesus by his own townspeople; it is remarked by all the synoptic gospels. So unresponsive were these Nazarenes that the scarcity of healing Jesus did in Nazareth was put down to their disbelief in him. They probably never even brought their sick to him—what a loss!

In this reflection on Nazareth, we have talked about the sites which make it famous: the Basilica of the Annunciation, the nearby Church of St. Joseph, built in 1914 A.D. on the remains of granaries predating Jesus' time in Nazareth, and the synagogue not far from the basilica, to be found by walking through the marketplace of Nazareth. Two other places of interest are Mary's Fountain and the Church of St. Gabriel, next to one another at the northeast end of the main road running through Nazareth. So popular a place is the town in which Jesus was conceived and reared, however, that there are yet other very interesting places to be discovered in Nazareth. All of this interest and development in a village unmentioned until the time of Jesus is its own mute witness to the significance of what happened here—a happening which all the meditation in the world will never fully understand, a happening for which we can be eternally grateful. To make us like him, he became one of us. Strange, wonderful proof of how far love will go.

Cana

"Do whatever he tells you."

~John 2:5

About four miles north by northeast of Nazareth is the traditional site of the wedding that Jesus, Mary, and Jesus' disciples attended in Cana of Galilee, as John's Gospel reports. Here, too, according to the same Gospel, Jesus met the court official whose son lay ill in Capernaum; Jesus assured the official that his son would recover, and, as predicted, the official, on returning to Capernaum, found that his son was cured—just at the hour when Jesus gave his assurance. Finally, this village was the original home of Nathaniel, one of the Twelve, a Galilean brought to Jesus by Philip (Jn 1:45–51). Nathaniel said the famous words, "Can anything good come from Nazareth?" Since each of these three events, all found only in the Gospel of John, are of some importance in the development of the Fourth Gospel, let us pause for a moment to consider each of them.

Nathaniel
~ John 1:45–51 ~

The prologue of John says "In the beginning was the Word, and the Word was with God, and the Word was God . . . And the Word became flesh and dwelt among us . . ." and then tells of the witness John the Baptizer gave at Bethany (see pp. 112-13) concerning Jesus (Jn 1:35–36). This witness moves two of John's disciples to visit Jesus; their visit convinces them that they have found the Messiah, the one of whom Moses wrote in the Law and the prophets spoke. One of these two disciples of John was a man named Andrew, a brother of Simon Peter; the two brothers were originally from Bethsaida, but currently lived in Capernaum. (If one thought of the Sea of Galilee as a clock face, one would put Bethsaida at about one o'clock and Capernaum just before eleven o'clock.) The day after meeting Simon Peter, Jesus met another person from Bethsaida; this was Philip, who in turn found Nathaniel of Cana (Jn 1:45).

It is hard for interpreters to explain thoroughly the encounter between Jesus and Nathaniel (Jn 1:47–51). Nathaniel certainly moved very quickly, psychologically speaking, from scepticism about this Jesus to confessing him to be Son of God and King of Israel. Granted that Jesus told Nathaniel that he had seen Nathaniel under a fig tree before he even knew that Jesus existed, still it seems quite an abrupt psychological change on Nathaniel's part to give so speedily and surely to Jesus titles which are quite profound in their meaning and usually associated with hard-earned faith. Indeed, these two titles, Son of God and King (Messiah) of Israel, are the two titles which the Gospel writer hoped his reader would embrace most avidly after reading the entire Gospel. Nathaniel seems to have achieved this goal within three verses—only to be one of those who ran away when Jesus was captured in the Garden of Gethsemani. But rather than bring up further difficult aspects of this story, let us try to offer an interpretation which makes good sense of the entire Johannine report.

First, Nathaniel's act of faith or confession of Jesus' identity was a model for later Christians to imitate. Not that we always move as speedily as Nathaniel did, but ultimately we are to confess Jesus to be Son of God and Messiah, as did this man from Cana.

Second, Nathaniel not only confessed the appropriate titles, but also raised a major objection to acceptance of Jesus as Messiah; the Messiah was either to come from Bethlehem, that is from the line of David who was associated with Bethlehem, or from a place unknown to any human being. Jesus came from Nazareth, so Nathaniel reasoned: why should anyone believe that he was the Messiah?

Third, Jesus called Nathaniel an "Israelite who was incapable of deceit." We suspect that in saying this Jesus is contrasting Nathaniel and the Patriarch Jacob whose other name was Israel. At issue is the "deceitfulness" or honesty of each man. Indeed, the ancient founder of Israel was at times deceitful (cf. Gn 27 and 30: 25–43). Jesus seems to be saying that here is another person, this time one of the Twelve Apostles who founded the Christian Church. This person will not be like the ancient Patriarch, but will be honest, truthful. Honest and truthful when and about what? In his witnessing to Jesus, and about the asounding and profound mystery that God worked in Jesus. By contrasting Nathaniel and Jacob, then, Jesus claims that it is his Twelve who can be trusted to found the community based always on truthful witness to God and about Jesus.

Fourth, Nathaniel's confession of Jesus as King and Son of God rested on Jesus' superior knowledge of Nathaniel and his character before Jesus and Nathaniel ever met. Here, too, the figure of Nathaniel is used to teach a lesson for all. Nathaniel was correct in concluding from Jesus' vision of him under a fig tree that Jesus must be a King (Messiah), Son of God; that people should have drawn these conclusions from the signs Jesus works in the rest of the Gospel is a major argument of the Gospel as a whole and so was very appropriately introduced here. Again, John was not interested in showing *how* one moves psychologically from a work of Jesus to belief in him; John wanted only to state, in an abbreviated story form, *that* the signs Jesus worked should lead, if one is logical, to a swift confession of him as Son of God and King of Israel.

Finally, the sign (Jesus' seeing him under the fig tree) which led Nathaniel to belief in Jesus would be surpassed in importance and greatness; one example of a "greater and more important sign" will be the raising of Lazarus from the dead (see pp. 144–47). But Jesus' saying that there are things *greater* than his marvelous vision of Nathaniel under the tree leads Jesus to speak of something *greater* than even the raising of Lazarus from the dead: the reader was to think of Jesus as the very Temple of God.

Jesus says that Nathaniel would see angels ascending from and descending upon the Son of Man. This must be a reference to an event earlier in the life of Jacob than Jacob's struggle with the angel of God. Sometime before this struggle, Jacob had passed a night during which he dreamt of angels descending to and ascending from a special place; the dream included what became known as Jacob's Ladder—by this ladder the angels ascended and descended (Gen 28:10–19). When Jacob awoke from this dream, he identified the holy site of the angels as the site on which he had his dream. He also thought of this site as the dwelling place of God since angels hovered about it. God has, in other words, a residence on earth as well as a dwelling place in the heavens. Jacob gave this holy place a name: Bethel, or House of God. *Beth* means *house of* and *el* means *God*. Here, then, at Bethel was the beginning of the holy shrine in Israel, the place where God was believed to have dwelt before he took up residence in the House or Temple of Jerusalem.

To this scene of actions involving Jacob and Bethel Jesus now refers. Jesus indentified himself as the new shrine, the new residence, the new House of God, because from him ascend and to him descend the angels. Later, Jesus would tell the Samaritan woman at the well dug by Jacob, that there would come a time when people would worship neither on the Samaritan mountain of worship, Gerizim, nor on the Israelite mountain of worship, Zion or Jerusalem (see pp. 96-98). Jesus alone would be the Temple of God; in him would God dwell, and the key to true worship of God would be acceptance of Jesus as the one in whom mysteriously dwells God himself.

The story of Nathaniel capsulized several important points John also made here and throughout his Gospel. That Nathaniel, as a human and private person, weakened eventually in his commitment to Jesus was immaterial to John; John was interested in showing in brief that Jesus' signs should lead us all to confess the deepest identity of Jesus, the very Presence of God. The story about Nathaniel, then, is really a thinly disguised argument, in story form, to encourage the reader to confess Jesus to be King and Son of God, and to be the Presence of God himself; signs show this, as does the witness of Jesus' earliest and constant companions.

Wedding at Cana
~ JOHN 2:1–12 ~

The episode in John's Gospel which follows immediately on Jesus' meeting with Nathaniel of Cana describes the marriage feast of Cana. In a sense this story is easy to understand. Jesus anticipated the needs of a couple who would be embarrassed when the wedding wine ran out; the miracle did not involve healing, but helped people in a true need. But other considerations make the story a bit more difficult to understand and make us look for possibly a deeper purpose here than just the presentation of the merciful wonder-worker.

Cana: Church of the Miracle of Water and Wine

Mary brought the need of the wedding couple to Jesus' attention. Jesus' response to Mary's hint in her words, "They have no wine," is startling and puzzling if not disconcerting: "Woman, what is this to you and to me? My hour has not yet come." What could this possibly mean, and what bearing does it have on a story in which Jesus proceeded to do anyway what he thought objectionable?

Once again we are in a particularly Johannine situation: John loved to take an ordinary story and draw from it a deeper significance, even if it were somewhat at odds with the tenor of the story from which it was drawn. Here Jesus was trying to signal a very important fact: the happiness, symbolized by the plenitude of wine that he can miraculously produce, would be fully realized for those who believe in him only after his "hour," that is, after his death and resurrection. That is to say, Mary's request for wine was received at a deeper level than that of mere wine for a particular wedding feast of a few hours; it was interpreted as a request for the fullness of happiness that the Messiah was to bring and that was to last forever. Jesus sees in Mary's request a desire not just for wine but for all that Jesus' power could bring to human beings. Would he not give all this happiness now? Would not his mercy move him to give it now?

In story form John has Jesus affirm that this marvelous giving of the Messianic gifts would begin only after Jesus' hour, with the gift of the Holy Spirit; Jesus' hour, I repeat, was the terrible time of his suffering and death, and John wants to state from the outset of his Gospel that Jesus is the Messiah, but will not begin to give his gifts until the public life of Jesus is over. It was hard to have the Messiah in the midst of the people and still not have his gifts until after he has died—just as it is hard to have Jesus in our midst and still not have the fullness of happiness we know he can give us, and will give us only after we die.

So Jesus' words to his mother, in which he seemed uninterested in working a miracle, really do not mean that; what they do mean is that, if Jesus works miracles (and he will, once the Gospel gets underway), the reader is to understand that Jesus is the Messiah of God for Israel, even if he brings the cherished gifts of the Messiah only after his entire public life is over. John is inserting into a miracle story a caution about what to expect from Jesus' public life; the gravity of the warning is reflected in Jesus calling his mother "woman." By addressing her with this title he is speaking to her, not in her capacity as an individual person who is his mother, but in her capacity as representative of the church, of the believers, who are here instructed to perceive the true meaning about Jesus, while realizing that he did not come to give the Messianic gifts, but to manifest God's love and ask for love in return.

The wedding miracle also gives us the opportunity to think about Jesus' signs. They are more than just a manifestation of power. Signs worked by Jesus reveal that he is from God; they also reveal other profound truths about him. For instance, in the raising of Lazarus to life, Jesus showed great power, but the raising to life was meant to show that Jesus could raise to the fullness of life which we call heaven, to a life with God forever—this degree or kind of life is not what Lazarus received from Jesus when Jesus raised him from the dead (see pp. 144-47). The turning of water into wine was a great manifestation of power, it is true; but the miracle also revealed Jesus to be the one who will make real for us the great Messianic kingdom of God with all the blessings we could ever want, and more. John always hoped, as he presented the miracles of Jesus, that we readers could go beyond just the show of physical power to see the greater eternal good Jesus can and will bring us, to see the true greatness of Jesus to be not just wielder of momentary power, but Son of God, the source of everlasting life.

The Gospel of John also tells the reader that through this sign Jesus revealed his glory to his disciples. The glory of Jesus was a quality usually reserved for the Resurrection when the relationship between Jesus and his Father was most visible and nothing could obscure it; it was then that Jesus most fully shared in the glory of God. But the cause for glory was expressed throughout the life of Jesus; it involved the use of divine power by which are overcome elements from which human beings cannot save themselves. When that power was used, we saw the reason for glorifying the one who used that power. The cause for glorifying Jesus, however, was also that profound meaning about him which a sign or miracle revealed. Thus Jesus was glorified for his power to work this or that miracle, but he was also glorified as one who gives life in its deepest sense, as one who gives sight in the deepest sense, as one who gives the water and bread, the sustenance, of life in the deepest sense, and as the one who would provide the wine of the Messianic banquet—another metaphor for that deepest happiness that God can give a human being. Finally, Jesus is glorified for the love he reveals behind his doing good for others. This love is just below the surface of every miracle, every sign; it is most visible, most impressive, in Jesus' dying for us. Strangely, the moment when Jesus seems most unlikely to be from God is the moment when he most clearly manifests God's undying love for us—if we can only see it all clearly.

Ultimately, John noted that Jesus' disciples believed in him. By this statement, John meant that Jesus' disciples were convinced that Jesus was from God and that on the basis of this conviction they would leave all to follow him. At this moment, what made sense to them was that Jesus somehow represented God. That they have a faith that would stand up to trials is not said; John was more interested in showing that the disciples gave the response which should logically follow from a miracle, a sign, a revelation of Jesus' meaning and glory.

At Cana, then, Jesus did not simply work a miracle. As far as John was concerned, to report this miracle was to link Jesus inextricably with his Father and to reveal him as Son of God; to open the meaning and identity of Jesus was to touch on the essence of his glory. Jesus was the Son of God destined to bring about that time when the Spirit of God could be poured on the world of believers, when the fullness of all that God promised could be ours—through his Son.

Cure of a Court Official's Son
~ JOHN 4:46–54 ~

Two chapters later John told the story of a cure Jesus worked in Cana for a young man who lay helpless in Capernaum. Like miracle-story reports in general, this account told of a sick person, of Jesus' response, and of a cure, and rounded off the story with a reaction from the audience. The details of the miracle story formula are brief and terse, to highlight the wonder Jesus has worked; compared with that, all else was secondary and eventually forgotten, though we may regret now not being able to know any more about these events.

But like many another miracle story, this one enveloped a saying of Jesus, which was all the more important precisely because it seemed out of place. In this story, Jesus, on hearing of the plight of the young man, exclaimed, "If you [plural] do not see signs and wonders, you [plural] would not believe!" Given that the boy's father, probably a Gentile, did seek out Jesus, we wonder why Jesus was so harsh with him. But there was something behind this cry of Jesus which was a strong reprimand because it went far beyond the boy's father. The plural *you* very clearly indicated that Jesus had many people in Galilee on his mind when he gave his criticism.

What is the point of Jesus' criticism? Were not signs and miracles part of his ministry and a way to lead people to believe in him? At least, such seems to be a part of the message of the Gospel of John. There is a certain truth in these objections, yet there is something else here of greater significance. From what we can tell from the entire gospel tradition, and thus not simply from the Fourth Gospel, the central ministry of Jesus was his call to Israelites to return to the Lord God, to repent. This call to repentance in turn inevitably raised the question of Jesus' authority to speak for God. It was at this point that the miracles of Jesus were important, for they substantiated his claim that people must listen to him, that he does represent God; these signs are meant to lead people to God through listening and obeying what God commands through Jesus' words. But the people ought to repent, whether miracles were given them or not. In this framework, Jesus wanted to know why people did not respond to his call to change their lives, why they seemed only to want miracles and more miracles. The point at issue is crucial. What his people wanted was a change of circumstances which would make their lives happier; what Jesus wanted was a change of heart which would make their lives happier. They wanted him only when they wanted a miracle; they did not want what he thought to be true wisdom.

From what we can tell, Jesus never refused a request for a miracle, and many times he worked a miracle without being asked. For all that, he felt that such miracles, which justified his calling people to repentance, were secondary; the message, the call, was the call itself. Those who truly loved and sought out God knew the truth of what Jesus was asking. Their Jewish tradition had already argued this truth for centuries; they knew that, miracles or not, it was God's wisdom which would bring them to happiness. Why, then, Jesus asks, must you be interested only in miracles?

Yes, Jesus worked the miracle for this dying young man; he worked it gladly, and it led the father to accept Jesus' claim that he was from God. Cana, tiny Cana, asks us also to see the wisdom of Jesus' call to return wholeheartedly to the Father of us all. Let us accept Jesus wholeheartedly, for his word is the true wisdom, and to live in union with him is to enter that life which he gives through the gift he gives: the Spirit of God himself.

The Sea of Galilee

"IT IS I; DO NOT BE AFRAID."
~JOHN 6:20

The Sea of Galilee is a heart-shaped body of water, about eleven miles long at its longest and about seven miles wide at its widest. It is called the *Sea of Galilee* because it forms the northeastern part of the territory of Galilee. This body of water is also called the *Sea* or *Lake of Gennesaret* or the *Sea of Chinnereth*, words taken from a Hebrew word meaning harp, for the Sea is also shaped like a harp. It was also known in the New Testament times as the *Sea of Tiberias*, named after the Emperor Tiberias who ruled the Roman world during the public life of Jesus.

At the *Sea of Tiberias* was the town of Tiberias, built by Herod Antipas, son of Herod the Great and stepfather of Salome who won the head of John the Baptizer by her dancing. (If you think of the Sea as a clock face, Tiberias would be at about nine o'clock.) Herod Antipas named the town, which he wished to be the capital of Galilee, after the Roman Emperor, Tiberias Caesar, who, among his other acts, appointed Pontius Pilate to be his representative in the bottom two-thirds of Israel (Samaria and Judea), or Palestine as it was called then. Because Tiberias was built in part over a Jewish cemetery, pious Jews refused to have anything to do with the town, although it became the premier town of the region for trading and fishing. As far as we know, Jesus never entered Tiberias.

Calling the Apostles

~ Matthew 4:18–22; Mark 1:16–20; Luke 5:1–11 ~

This Sea of Galilee, which is about thirty-two miles in circumference, provided a good living for fishermen like Simon and his brother Andrew, for the brothers James and John. It also provided the setting, at least in part, for three types of New Testament events.

Along the shores of the Sea of Galilee Jesus called Simon and Andrew, James and John to follow him; they left all and followed him. The Marcan and Matthean stories of this call are brief so that the reader sees the logical response to the sudden call of the Master: when Jesus says, "Come," the disciple who knows who is calling leaves all to follow immediately; there can be no other logical reply. Life cannot always be lived so logically, but the logic itself is worth underlining, for it shows how different was Jesus from all others who called for one's attention and company. In Luke's version, Simon responded to Jesus once he saw a miraculous catch of fish and it dawned on him who this Jesus might be and how awesome was the calling. But whether we read the Marcan/Matthean description of the call or that of Luke, the point is the same: the truly logical, if not psychological, step to take when the Master says to come is to leave all immediately and follow him. Ironically, that is exactly what will happen at the call at death.

In Matthew, Mark, and Luke the call of Jesus is not only to a sharing of life together with Jesus, but to a "fishing for human beings." This fishing calls for total dedication, for leaving all; not all Christians are called to leave all, but it is clear that Jesus asked some to travel with him and live like him. Why there are these various forms of Christian discipleship is not always clear, but it is there and the living out of these various forms proves the wisdom behind each type of living out the following of Christ.

Calming the Waves

~ Matthew 8:23–27; Mark 4:34–51; Luke 8:22–25 ~

Another type of report about things associated with the Sea of Galilee was made up of two happenings. First, Jesus calmed the waves of the Sea when he and his disciples seemed about to drown in them. Another time,

Jesus walked on these waters. The calming of the waves was another wonderful sign of the dominance the Master had over all elements of the world: spiritual powers (like demons), disease and death, and nature itself. The story of the calming of the waves was told, however, to emphasize the trust the disciples should have in Jesus. Their cry to him, "We are lost," did not reveal a true appreciation of the power or of the love of Jesus for his disciples. The story was told, then, not only to show Jesus' immense power over nature, but also to encourage the reader never to lose heart in the rough waves of life; the power and love of Jesus have been promised to the disciple and Jesus will not fail.

Sea of Galilee: seagull in flight over calm waters

Walking on the Waters
~ MATTHEW 14:22–33; MARK 6:45–52; JOHN 6:16–21 ~

The second story concerned with the Sea of Galilee described Jesus as walking on the waters, as if to go ahead of his disciples to prepare their way to reach the other side. Again, we have a miracle which the gospel writers used to show how the Christian community, often left to row against the tides which threaten it, has a Master of such power and dominance that he can protect and smooth the community's journey, no matter how difficult the trials. In this walk on the water, the mystery of Jesus' identity was placed before the reader; we are expected to ask, "Who is he that can do this?" The hope is that we would find it reasonable to call this Jesus divine. Indeed, if Jesus' act here reminds the reader of anyone, it reminds him of the God of Israel who intervened so mightily and lovingly on behalf of Israel. Most notable was God's protection for forty years, as he led Israel from Egypt to the Promised Land. That is the image behind the scene of Jesus leading his disciples across difficult waters to safety.

Curing the Demoniac
~ MATTHEW 8:28–34; MARK 5:1–20; LUKE 8:26–39 ~

The third event associated with the Sea of Galilee is a bizarre account of a man freed from possession by evil spirits. Since these evil spirits were content to live in the depths of the deepest waters, always a fearsome place in the mind of Israel, they asked Jesus, who was about to send them away from the poor man, to send them back into the waters. Jesus sent them into pigs, animals unpleasant to Jews who were forbidden to eat such an unclean animal. The pigs rushed over the eastern hills of the Sea of Galilee. The story was meant to impress the reader with the power of Jesus, even to the clear dominance of those powers which no human being can control.

The Sea of Galilee holds its own charm, its own mystery, for it is a silent, yet living body of nature which in its own way communicates to anyone who touches it the joy of having carried, if only briefly, the Lord of the Universe, and its Lord. The sea invites contemplation about turbulence and peace, about power exercised out of love and calling for trust. Like so many other voices of Israel, the sea calls for faith in the one whom it carried to his people in distress. It obeyed his voice and his orders and hopes that many others would do so as well—for the ultimate happiness of the entire universe God made.

Capernaum

"THEY CROSSED TO CAPERNAUM
TO LOOK FOR JESUS."
~ JOHN 6:24

Capernaum, which means *town of Nahum*, rests on the northern shore of the Sea of Galilee, about two and one-half miles west of the upper Jordan River which pours into the Sea of Galilee from the Lebanese mountains—from the ancient Mount Hermon—to the north. In the time of Jesus, Capernaum was a small town by our standards, but it was a tax post and money exchange for those coming from the east into Israel on the Way of the Sea; the road that passed by the north end of the Sea of Galilee, headed over to the Mediterranean shoreline and proceeded to Egypt.

Capernaum today offers some very interesting ruins. Probably the most eye-catching are the remains of a fifth-century A.D. synagogue which, many agree, stands on top of a basalt synagogue which goes back to the first century A.D. and was probably the very synagogue that Jesus and his friends attended, where Jesus spoke about himself as the bread of life (Jn 6:59). To the south of the limestone fifth-century synagogue are the ruins of a basalt octagon. This octagon, really three octagons together, shows the base of an octagonal church built here also in the fifth century. This church replaced a fourth-century church on this exact spot. Archaeological diggings have unearthed beneath these two churches graffiti from very early Christian times which tend to identify the area enclosed by these two churches as the house of Peter, who spent much of his adult life with his family in Capernaum.

Capernaum: ruins of a fifth-century A.D. *synagogue*

Looking beyond the octagonal forms, we see traces of many square rooms, some of them separated by narrow lanes. These outlines are considered to be the outline of the city of Capernaum. Its buildings were hardly fancy; the roofs were a combination of tree limbs and a kind of plaster made out of mud, twigs, leaves, and the like, and there was not much room or light in these rooms. But this was the fishing town and tax post Jesus used as his center of activity, when he chose to have a home at all. Unfortunately, Jesus' home town of Nazareth had deep reservations about his relationship with God and ultimately rejected him; Capernaum, after a longer time, followed this attitude of Narareth—and Jesus cursed Capernaum because it refused to repent (Mt 12:23; Lk 10:15).

Call of Matthew

MATTHEW 9:9; MARK 2:13; LUKE 5:27–28 ~

From his post came the tax collector Matthew, to whom Jesus spoke the words, "Come, follow me." Are these words too simple to serve as the only means Jesus used to draw Matthew's attention and loyalty? Yet they are the words which the Lord spoke, and the reader who loves the Lord is the one they are meant to inspire. Jesus was highly criticized for dealing with Matthew and his kind of people; tax collectors drew their salary out of the taxes levied on Israel. One need only a moment to imagine the injustice these tax collectors were rightly accused of. So suspected were these men that they were forbidden by custom to serve as witnesses in a trial; they were absolutely untrustworthy cheats. Jesus once again showed his willingness to distinguish between the sinner and the sin, in the hope that he could save the lost of Israel. His contemporaries followed another model: reject the sinner in the hope that avoidance and criticism would lead to repentance and in the hope that his excommunication would deter others from being so sinful. They could not understand Jesus' approach to the sinner.

Capernaum, called by Matthew "Jesus' own town," was the setting for some very important sayings and cures by Jesus. Throughout the Gospel accounts the reader finds that miracle stories often go beyond the telling of wondrous acts to stress controversial and significant statements of Jesus. In Capernaum Jesus cures a man of an unclean spirit. The miracle was marvelous, but Jesus' command to the spirit not to continue its public acknowledgement that Jesus was the Holy One of God is mysterious—until we realize from the rest of Mark that Jesus was consistently worried that people would identify him *only* as a miracle worker or holy man. Jesus understood his mission to be something quite different from solving the world's hunger for happiness through miracle working or from being praised for his goodness; he came to call sinners to change their lives, and then to die as a criminal, weak and hardly a "holy one." His was a mission which was hard to grasp, since it involved, not wonder-working, but call for repentance, and it involved a cruel death which made Jesus look weak, sinful, and foolish. Yet, such was the mission given him, such was the life he led, and Matthew is just one of those whose conversion showed the value of Jesus' doing what his Father asked of him.

34 ◆ PART ONE GALILEE AND SAMARIA

Cure of the Paralyzed Man
~ MATTHEW 9:2–8; MARK 2:3–12; LUKE 5:18–26 ~

Jesus later cured a man who had for a very long time been paralyzed. When this man had been lowered through a roof made from various bits of shrubbery, mud, and wood, as mentioned in Mark and Luke, Jesus praised the faith of those involved in the man's being lowered to him— and forgave him his sins! Accustomed as later Christians may be to the truth that Jesus forgives sins, we still appreciate the people's bewilderment at Jesus' words of forgiveness. Putting it bluntly, the man hoped for a cure of his paralysis, not forgiveness of sins! That the man wanted a physical cure is here immaterial, of course; the Gospels are accentuating the greater gift, the forgiveness of sins which results from belief in Jesus. Without this forgiveness what good finally is physical well-being?

Certain religious figures nearby took offense because Jesus had taken to himself a power which belonged to God alone. By the end of the story, the paralyzed man was cured and Jesus argued aggressively and persuasively that he indeed had the power reserved to God.

The conclusion of the story is powerful; the miracle is meant to convince the reader that Jesus not only cures, as does God, but also forgives sins, as only God does. The cure and forgiveness help reveal the deepest identity of Jesus and warn the reader that the meaning of Jesus far surpasses the impressive powers of visible physical and mental curing which initially capture the attention of his contemporaries.

Cure on the Sabbath
~ MATTHEW 12:9–14; MARK 3:1–6; LUKE 6:6–11 ~

A third miracle happened in the synagogue of Capernaum. Here Jesus cured the withered hand of an Israelite—and he did it on the Sabbath. Israelite tradition had interpreted the Law of Moses against work on the Sabbath to include miracle working; miracle working was a *work* to be avoided on the Sabbath. The Gospels offer more than one argument against the unreasonableness of thinking that God's law prohibits curing the sick on the Sabbath; but the understanding at the time insisted that God did not want the work of healing to go on on the Sabbath. At an earlier moment Jesus had, in Capernaum, claimed that he was Master of the

Sabbath, that his way of understanding how to keep holy the Sabbath was the right, godlike way to keep the Sabbath holy. Now, in the synagogue he continued to defy the common interpretation, only to have the authorities begin the search for ways to do away with him.

Essentially, Jesus' argument was twofold. First, if the usual understanding of the Law of Moses allowed for care of one's animals on the Sabbath, why could Jesus not care for God's blessed children? Why would a sick person's remaining sick for another day make God's day holy? Second, the Sabbath had, as one of its meanings for Israel, the remembrance of being set free from evil. Is not Jesus acting in accordance with the spirit of the Sabbath when he sets a person free from his or her sickness? Would Jesus rather not be remiss if he did *not* help this Israelite on the day which celebrates freedom from all kinds of slavery?

In Capernaum, then, Jesus claimed a power to forgive sins, an understanding which went against traditional thinking; he also claimed that his was a mission which essentially called for repentance rather than miracle working. Here he also ate with sinners, in the hope that, as with Matthew, he could separate the sinners from their sins. This new entity called *Jesus* was entirely foreign in many respects from the pharisaic way of living the will of God; as a result, Jesus was marked for extermination. Truly, the center of the antagonism Jesus raised to a point that it killed him was his insistence that he was the true representative of God. Indeed, everything in Israel's past was to be reevaluated by him. This claim was what put him on the road to death.

Meaning of Miracles

A further word is in order about the miracles of Jesus at Capernaum. Jesus cured both the paralyzed and the possessed. These cures represent the spectrum of immense power that Jesus enjoyed over all that dominates human beings. Whether it be a question of physical or mental bondage, a word from Jesus set them free—just a word. His domination over what we cannot free ourselves from was so complete and so ever-present that Jesus, in any world of miracle working (and there were others who did work miracles), stood out as supreme in power over inimical and crippling dominance. Whereas to other miracle workers power was given in measure, Jesus' power seems limitless. It is only with the realization that his mission was aimed at something other than physical and mental cures (and even raising from the dead) that we begin to understand why he did not simply change for the good all that crushes human beings physically and mentally.

The miracle working of Jesus was not his main work. But then it is all the more striking that he cured and healed so often. It was as though, while he aimed at winning over human beings to love and obey him, he could not restrain himself, asked or not, from intervening in the grief of others to bring them some measure of peace and health, though they would, he knew, remain subject to the further trials inherent in living in this world. His miracles were, then, a sign of the total concern which defined the love of Jesus for every human being suffering under the domination of forces unleashed in the world, not by God's choosing, but by man's sinning. But Jesus undertook no systematic cleansing of sickness from the world, for his mission was not that; it was to call us to change of heart.

Behind this choice of mission lies a way of thinking which has its beginning at the very start of the Bible.

Through Adam sin and death entered this world and controlled it. Adam had separated himself from Love and the effects of Love, one of which was life; human beings share in that separation, so that *this age* (a semitechnical word for the world which we know to be characterized by corruption and death) was lived under the warring powers of divine Love and Satanic death and corruption. To separate oneself from God was to separate oneself from the health and life originally intended by God to last forever. Jesus' entry into *this age* changed little of the continued dominance of the powers unleashed on us by sin against God. This final solution to removal of these evil powers was conversion away from sin, joined to union with Jesus so that, after death, we can rise to new and complete, unending life. This *new life*, this *entry into the new age* occurs only after death. Though the New Testament argues very well that certain effects of the "age to come" already exist in "this present wicked age," such as God's forgiveness of sins now and his dwelling in us, by and large the structure of the world lies still under the dominance of the powers unleashed by sin, the greatest of which powers is death.

Jesus entered a world dominated by Satan—indeed, Satan was so powerful that he tempted Jesus by promising Jesus all the kingdoms of the world if he would worship Satan. Jesus' miracles did not completely reverse the decline and corruption of our world and of our bodies and minds, but they are signs of what the irrepressible love of God would eventually achieve. What Jesus hinted at in miracle working was a time when, after sin was repaired, God would change all and make all new again. Then there would be no more suffering, for the total person, now a willing and loving friend of God, would enjoy the full effect of God's love. This effect we call *total perfection*. Paul rejoiced in the first step towards perfect happiness when he said we are no longer slaves, but actually children of God. John the Evangelist tried to go even further; he said that now we are children of God, but we cannot even guess what we will be like when we finally emerge from this wicked and corrupting age to be face to face in friendship and intimacy with Goodness and Life itself.

Miracles, then, are acts of new life, and so quicken our hope for the end of the age of corruption and the beginning of what we all feel is the real goal of human existence: perfect happiness. Miracles, however, are only brief and momentary interventions by God, who planned our happiness, not by eliminating it through the public acts of Jesus, but by first asking us to return to him and to form that alliance, that friendship which will eventually bring about our perfection. Till then, we hope, with a hope based on the wonderful deeds of Jesus—especially his own entrance into the *age to come*, where he is the first of us made perfect.

Capernaum never perceived who this Jesus was who worked miracles in it. We must do better than the citizens of Capernaum, for the miracles of Jesus worked at Capernaum suggest the fulfillment of the deepest hopes for happiness we know. The right appreciation of the Wonder-Worker will help us achieve what he ardently hopes we will freely choose. He will in time expel from our experience all the evil forces, especially the evil spirits, allowed into his world by man's free choice to live without God; but then he was concerned to win back that free will, so that all the benefits of friendship with God—health, peace, wholeness, unending life, happiness—can follow.

A Great Miracle

In the Capernaum synagogue, Jesus gave his great discourse about himself as the food of life (see p. 47). He had fed the multitude in a lonely place, then taught them. He would lead them to realize that the deeper, never-ending hunger for life itself is satisfied by the only one designated by God to calm that hunger: Jesus, the food of life. In a visit to this town we can hear again those words of great promise: everyone who eats my flesh and drinks my blood will live—forever.

Multiplication of
the Loaves and Fish

"WHERE COULD ANYONE GET
BREAD TO FEED THESE PEOPLE?"
~ MARK 8:4

The fields that lie along slopes about two miles to the west of
Capernaum are traditionally considered to be the area where Jesus multi-
plied the loaves and the fish for the crowds following him. In the fourth
century, Christians took advantage of the peace the Emperor Constantine
allowed them. They built a chapel to commemorate the multiplication of
the loaves and fish, the only miracle recorded in all four Gospels, and two
other chapels, one in honor of the Sermon on the Mount and the other in
honor of an appearance of Jesus to his disciples after his resurrection (Jn
21). In the fifth century, a larger chapel was built to replace the century-
old small chapel of the loaves and fish; but this larger chapel was itself
soon destroyed through the Persian (614) and Moslem (637) invasions and
never rebuilt. Though the Church of the Multiplication was destroyed in
the seventh century, there are remains, including impressive mosaics, of
the fourth-century chapel. While leaving this chapel area untouched, the
Benedictines have built a lovely, simple, modern church nearby to commemorate the multiplication of loaves and fish.

Here, then, near Capernaum and the northwest shore of the Sea of
Galilee, tradition suggests to us that the famous multiplication occurred.
Let us consider this miracle for a moment, especially in the light of cer-
tain details reported by the Gospels.

Capernaum: modern Benedictine church commemorating the multiplication of loaves and fish

In Mark and Matthew Jesus performed this miraculous multiplication on two different occasions; in Luke and John we have reports of only one multiplication of loaves and fish. Let us consider each of these stories in turn, beginning with Mark, the source for much of what Luke and Matthew have given us.

Mark's Account
~ Mark 6:34–44; 8:1–9 ~

Mark's first story of the loaves and fish has four noteworthy circumstances. First, Mark tells us that multiplication of the loaves followed Jesus' teaching the crowds, teaching that was itself a response to the appearance of the crowd as "sheep without a shepherd." Second, before working this miracle Jesus asked his disciples to provide bread for the crowd; the disciples could not even imagine doing this! We wonder what eventual outcome Mark has in mind here by recording the Apostles' admission of their limitations. Third, twelve baskets were filled with leftover bread and fish (although they had begun with only five loaves and two fishes)—for what purpose? Finally, those who ate the bread numbered about five thousand people; and we wonder what significance this number has beyond simply showing how powerful a miracle Jesus worked.

These four circumstances frame the wondrous multiplication of loaves and suggest the way of thought which Mark wanted us to follow. Since the Eucharist of bread and wine was celebrated at least every Sunday from the earliest times of Christianity to the period when Mark was writing, about 70 A.D., it would not be surprising to find a miracle of Jesus written up to support this eucharistic practice without any distortion of the basic intention of Jesus to feed a hungry crowd before him. Therefore, many scholars suggest that Mark described this miracle of the bread not only to underline the wonder Jesus worked, but also to link it specifically with the Eucharist by which hungry Christians of every time can share in the food provided by Christ. Let us look at this situation more closely.

Since the feeding of the crowd followed immediately on the teaching of those whom Jesus pitied, we are reminded of the deepest structure of the eucharistic celebration: the teaching of Jesus, read and explained, preceded the gift of the eucharistic bread of life. And then the disciples would have to hand on the teaching and provide the eucharistic food; once helpless by themselves to give life to the world, now they, as extensions of Jesus, know how to provide food for so many. And the gathering of the baskets of bread, one for each disciple, reminds us that each of the Twelve would have the task of feeding those who are like sheep without a shepherd. Finally, the number five thousand symbolizes the people of Israel and so suggests that the spiritual feeding of Christians began with the Christians who are part of Israel and faithful to Jesus. Thus, the wonderful feeding of the crowd at the Sea of Galilee became a symbol of that new feeding of the Christian people, as details of the storytelling lead us to understand. The number seven (five loaves and two fishes) represents the nations Israel had to dispossess in order to possess the Promised Land. In other words, seven refers to the Gentiles. The number five represents Israel by referring to Israel's *Torah*, the most holy books of the Old Testament, the first five books of the Scriptures.

Mark reports a second multiplication of loaves that took place before four thousand people outside the confines of Palestine and ended with a collection of seven baskets of fragments. The number seven probably again symbolizes the Gentiles, as the number five symbolizes the people of Israel. Thus this second multiplication appears to complement the first, just as the Gentiles filled out the people of Israel in the Christian community of the first century. Once again, the movement to feed the needy crowd came from Jesus, who was sensitive enough to realize the hunger of the people. His disciples accentuated the wonder of what Jesus would do when they expressed their bewilderment at trying to find a way of feeding all these hungry people. It is because of their union with Jesus that they find the way.

Matthew's Accounts
~ MATTHEW 14:13–21; 15:32–39 ~

The first miracle of the loaves and fish in Matthew has an orientation similar to the corresponding story in Mark; this is no surprise since Matthew drew heavily on Mark as a source. It is also no surprise to realize that Matthew read Mark, agreed with him, and having little to add, simply reproduced the essential lines of Mark because he was impressed by Mark's story. Matthew reduced the story's length by reducing the exchange of words between Jesus and his disciples as they moved towards the miracle. In Matthew's telling of the story, the disciples brought the hunger of the people to Jesus' attention; as in Mark, Jesus suggested that the disciples feed these people—indeed, in Matthew, Jesus strongly implies that the disciples actually have the wherewithal to feed these people. Of course, they do—as long as Jesus first provides them with it!

Matthew's story of a second multiplication of loaves and fish again parallels what Mark gives as Jesus' second miracle of bread. One should note, here and in the previous three stories we have considered, that Jesus "takes the bread, gives thanks [which is the meaning of *eucharist*], breaks the bread and gives it . . ." This sequence of actions is reminiscent of the famous words of the Last Supper and of every eucharistic celebration modeled on the Last Supper. It is possible to think that the miraculous bread to feed thousands was a symbol of Jesus' word of teaching; but Jesus' own association of bread with his body makes us think that the wondrous bread of the multiplication symbolizes the person of Jesus, and not just his word.

Luke's Account
~ LUKE 9:10–17 ~

Luke recounted only one miracle of loaves and fish. But then Luke never shows Jesus going through Gentile, non-Israelite, territory. (It is left to Luke's Acts of the Apostles to trace the offer of God's salvation to lands outside Israel.) It was precisely at the end of a journey through pagan country that Jesus, in Matthew and Mark, worked a second bread miracle for four thousand people, with seven baskets of scraps left over.

Luke's story has essentially the same elements as the Marcan stories; Mark was, we recall, a major source of information for Luke. As did Matthew and Mark, Luke emphasizes the suggestion of Jesus that the disciples care for the hungry crowd; when they confess their inability to do so, Jesus provides the food, but in such a way that the disciples actually administer it. It is interesting that Luke tells his reader that "each one had as much as he wanted." Each one was satisfied. The multiplication of loaves, in Luke's outline, comes just before Jesus' question to the disciples: "Who do people say that I am?" "Who do you say that I am?" By virtue of this juxtaposition of stories, Luke seems to suggest that Jesus

Capermaum: mosaic of loaves and fish in fifth-century chapel

was looking for an answer which would be influenced in a significant way by the multiplication of the loaves and fish. Since both Elijah and his disciple, Elisha, were involved in works of providing food miraculously for people, it is not surprising that Elijah was one of the answers people gave when trying to come up with the identity of Jesus. For Peter, however, the multiplication of loaves supported his conviction that Jesus was nothing less than the Messiah, the Christ, of God. Like an Elijah of the ninth century B.C., Jesus was still greater, because the food he provides is so much greater. In Luke, then, the wondrous bread serves both as symbol of the Eucharist, served by Jesus' ministers, and as help in discovering the identity of Jesus, who gives the bread of life.

John's Account
~ JOHN 6:1–5 ~

John has left an indelible story in the minds of his readers about the miraculous bread. Not only does John tell the story of the multiplication, but he follows it with a major speech of Jesus the next day in Capernaum (Jn 6:22-59); considering the absence from John of any other speech of Jesus about the meaning of bread and wine at the Last Supper, we can accept what Jesus says at the multiplication of loaves as the Johannine account of the eucharistic practice of the Church.

The story of the loaves and fish, as told in the Gospel of John, has the eucharistic overtones we have seen in the Matthean, Marcan, and Lucan stories. Added to these elements are two points typical of Johannine story-telling. Although he asked the disciples where enough food might be found for all these people, Jesus "knew exactly what he would do." Here, as everywhere in John, Jesus was in command of the situation and was not at a loss for word or action—as was befitting his divinity. Second, the people responded to this miracle by attempting to make Jesus king. This move toward kingship was a temptation elsewhere in the Gospel, but such interpretations of Jesus as this one are given in John with the clear intention of showing how far short they fall in their perception of Jesus' deepest identity.

The people who received this wondrous bread were not satisfied; they wanted the power to *do* what Jesus did and thus not be dependent on Jesus. They wanted to do the works of God, miracles. Jesus turned their phrase, "works of God," to his own phrase "work of God." By this turn of phrase he indicated that the only work for God's creatures, God's people, was faith in God; faith in him was the only way they would have the food they sought to create, the life they longed for. In short, they would depend on him, not on themselves, for the life which comes from eating the food of God.

The food of God, however, needs explanation, and so Jesus began his lengthy discussion of the food from heaven. The discourse Jesus gave concerned four points. First, Jesus is the food, for it is only by living off him that one can have and sustain life. Second, living off him does not mean simply obeying his words; it means actually eating his body and drinking his blood. In this way, God draws so close to us that we live by virtue of his intimacy and love, as though he were the very food by which we live forever. This intimacy suggests more than just a union of wills, which exists when one obeys another; this intimacy means *becoming* what one eats and drinks, a becoming which can only be described ultimately as mystical. There is a very profound belief here: our life has a new source, different from that rooted in our parents, a source which alone can make us live forever. This source is only good, and from union with it can come only good, or, in other words, life.

Third, this food by which we live really gives a life which never ends; in this it is different from all other foods, even that manna in the desert, which, no matter how miraculous we esteem it, could give life for only a short time. Jesus is the food that truly is from heaven, where only life unending can be found.

Finally, Jesus carefully taught that to accept him as food of life we must have the calling and grace of God. And further, we must be open to belief that he really is the savior, that he really wants to be our food, that he really can keep us alive and wants to do it through the Eucharist. Unfortunately, this element, this call to faith in himself, must be a regular part of Jesus' discourses to his contemporaries, because by and large, they did not have the predispositions, the openness, the readiness to take him at his word. Indeed, following upon the great discourse about Jesus' readiness to become our food, many disciples refused to walk anymore with him. Jesus always noted that he did his best to reach everyone; if he failed, it was not his fault, but that of his hearer.

Tabgha

About two miles west of Capernaum is an area which was named in Greek after its seven springs of water; the Greek name was *heptapegon*, a word which corrupted into Arabic *ettabgha*. The area is called *et-Tabgha* or *Tabgha* today. Associated with this area is the wonderful appearance of Jesus to his disciples, related in John 21, as these disciples were fishing in the Sea of Galilee. A lovely chapel was built in 1934 on the shore of the Sea of Galilee to commemorate Jesus' words to Peter at the time of this apparition, "Feed my lambs, feed my sheep." Recent though this church is, the site has had, often for centuries at a time, a shrine in place since about 315, to remind visitors of Jesus' moments spent on the shore this day with his disciples.

Jesus after the Resurrection
~ JOHN 21:1–14 ~

John 21 underlines three elements of interest. First, the disciples had scattered to their homes after the death and resurrection of Jesus. Peter and others were from Capernaum and so they returned there and, for want of knowing what to do next, resumed their old trade of fishing. While these men were fishing, Jesus appeared and revealed himself by his wondrous knowledge that, if they would only drop their nets where he suggested, they would find fish for which they had been searching all night long. On recognizing Jesus on the shore, the disciples hurried to him and found him preparing a breakfast. Now came an important moment, contained in a small detail: Jesus ate the fish served for breakfast. By eating this material thing he showed that he was the entire, complete Jesus, body and soul, who had risen from the dead.

To say that the complete Jesus rose from the dead may seem confusing or of little significance. Yet, as was clear from the New Testament efforts to affirm it, the resurrection of Jesus, which included the notion of bodily resurrection, was a concept that had to be struggled for in the first century. Luke 24 emphasizes Jesus' eating with his disciples and thus explicitly states that Jesus could not be simply a phantom or ghost. John 20 tells us that Jesus invited Thomas to touch his scarred hands, feet, and side. In its own way this story also suggests that Jesus has risen with his crucified body. One notices that in Matthew 28, as Jesus met his disciples in Galilee and was about to depart from them, some still doubted; this doubt seems centered about the reality of the resurrection of the body of Jesus; these disciples certainly were seeing something of Jesus, but was this not just a ghost, could it be that he was risen, body and soul? In short, it was possible for some people in this first century and afterwards to make a distinction that satisfied them: Jesus might have risen from the dead in some spiritual sense, and that would account for his being seen in visions, but, they specify, he surely did not rise body and soul from the tomb outside Jerusalem.

In various ways Christians refused to settle for this spiritual understanding of the Resurrection. Their initial argument centered about the fact, visible to anybody who wanted to look, that the tomb in which Jesus had been buried was now empty. The empty tomb did not prove that Jesus rose, but once Jesus showed that he had risen, body and soul, it did support the Resurrection. Another argument involved the teaching of the Old Testament (Ps 15 as echoed in Acts 2:25–31), which indicated that a descendant of David would die, but not stay dead, and that this escape from permanent death involved the body of this person as well as his soul. The third argument Christians used was that, as the story of John 21 affirms, Jesus did, at various times, deliberately do things that showed that he had risen physically as well as in spirit.

There was a very important aspect to the persistent determination of Christians to present Jesus as bodily risen from the dead. In presenting him this way, they first underlined the reality that the Jesus who rose was none other than the Jesus who lived and died before their very own eyes. Thus, not only did the entire Jesus rise, but the identity of the risen one was affirmed to be that of Jesus of Nazareth. Second, contrary to the Greek philosophical way of thinking that happiness was to be achieved by getting rid of one's mortal, changing body, Judaism knew that the entire human being was good, for God had called Adam (source of all human life), body and soul, *good*. God made no distinction between body and soul in his calling Adam good, and so we can expect that the totality of Adam would be saved from death and all other evil when God raises him from death. Thus God would fall short of saving what is good, if he saved only Jesus' soul from death but not his body. Third, Christians perceived the union between Jesus and his followers to be so intimate that the fate of Jesus would be the fate of the believer. The belief that Jesus rose from the dead physically, then, grounds the belief that Christians rise bodily from death. True, Jesus rose so soon after his death that corruption had not entered his body, whereas for others corruption was a very real condition of the deceased body. For all that, people like St. Paul would argue tenaciously that the resurrection of the Christian includes physical resurrection; somehow God would provide a body for the risen Christian, a body which the Christian would know as his own. St. Paul points to the heavens as an example: there the sun has its own body and the star has its own body so that each sun and star may perform its assigned task; in the same way, on earth I have a body fitted for this world, and in heaven I will have a body fitted for that world—whatever the difference between those bodies may be, in heaven and on earth, I will have a body and it will be mine, and will make up the complete me. Another way of looking at this is to note, with St. Paul, how a blossom, with leaves and stem, comes from a seed which, before it was buried in the ground, had only the appearance of a seed. Before it corrupted in the ground, the flower had appeared only as a seed; after the seed corrupted, the flower appears in all its glory. So with us: we have a body here, and we will have a glorified body, suited for heaven, at our being raised from the dead.

Commission of Peter
~ JOHN 21:15–17 ~

The second important element of Jesus' appearance to his disciples on the seashore centers on certain words of Jesus to Peter, the man who had denied knowing Jesus three times in Jerusalem when Jesus was on trial for his life. Now Jesus asked Peter three times whether or not he loved him. Peter affirmed three times that he indeed loved Jesus, and so in a sense made up for the lack of love he showed in Jerusalem. But the more important element of this interchange between Jesus and Peter lies in the command of Jesus which follows each of Peter's three protestations of love. Jesus says, "Feed my lambs," then "Tend my sheep," finally "Feed my sheep." What is the meaning of this triple command?

A centuries-old image of Israel is that of God's flock of sheep. At one point the prophet Ezekiel, under divine inspiration, strongly criticized the authorities or shepherds of Israel because they had cared so poorly for God's sheep, and crowned his criticism by stating that Yahweh would rid himself and Israel of these shepherds and become Israel's sole, responsive, and responsible Shepherd. Not unexpected, then, was the account (Jn 10) wherein Jesus distinguished the true, good shepherd of the flock of Israel from thieves and brigands who care only to make profit off the sheep. Before Jesus, the Good Shepherd, left earth definitively, however,

Looking across the Sea of Galilee from the Primacy of Peter Chapel

he took the opportunity to give Peter the responsibility of tending Jesus' flock, the flock of the new people of God. This responsibility was based on the fact that Peter truly loved the Shepherd and therefore could be entrusted with the care of Jesus' own flock; Jesus was going to entrust his loved ones only to someone who, Jesus knew, loved him above all else. It is love for Jesus that will keep Peter faithful to the flock.

That it was to Peter and to no others that this responsibility was given, here on the shore of the Sea of Galilee accounts for the naming of the little chapel here the Chapel of the Primacy. In other words, Jesus here conferred on Peter a responsibility that made Peter primary among human beings in caring for Jesus' flock; hence, we have the term primacy to sum up this event.

Peter was to *tend* and *feed*. Though these two terms might be simply elements belonging to the metaphor of shepherd used here, many scholars think that they pertain to two distinct and essential elements of Christian life: teaching the will of God and providing the eucharistic food. Thus Peter was asked to take care of feeding the flock with the body and blood of Christ and to care for the flock by teaching the truths drawn from the mind and will of God as expressed through Jesus. This double task of Peter puts him in sharp contrast to those scribes and Pharisees of Jesus' time with whom Jesus had quarreled so often precisely about things which involved the good of God's people. Finally, it is from this story that popes, patriarchs, and other bishops have traditionally drawn their symbols: the staffs by which they show that they are pastors, shepherds of their flocks, responsible for feeding and tending the beloved people of Jesus.

Prediction of Peter's Death
~ JOHN 21:18–23 ~

The third element of Jesus' appearance at the shore of the Sea of Galilee is his prediction of the kind of death Peter would suffer; it also tried to clear up a misunderstanding among certain Christians who thought that John, the gospel writer, would never die—before the end of this world. Jesus had told Peter, after Peter had heard about his own dire end and had asked about the future of John, that what happens to John was no business of Peter—indeed, Jesus went on to ask, "what does it matter to you, even if I want him to stay until I return?" It seems that some Christians understood Jesus' question to imply that John was not actually going to die, but would live till Jesus' return as judge of this world. John went out of his way, in this appearance story, to say that Jesus' question was merely a question with no implication that John would not die. Peter was to concentrate on his own fate, that in Rome he too would be crucified.

Mount of the Beatitudes

"BLESSED ARE YOU . . ."
~ LUKE 6:20

On a hilltop less than two miles west of Capernaum is the lovely chapel dedicated to the most famous sermon given by Jesus in the Scriptures, the Sermon on the Mount. The chapel is modern, but a shrine was built in this area in the fourth century and another in the fifth century—each later destroyed—in honor of the discourse which has been called a blueprint for Christian holiness. The gardens of the present church or chapel are very inviting and the view offered from the south porch of the chapel overlooking the Sea of Galilee rewards the pilgrim and evokes the many events of Jesus' life in this area.

The chapel is dedicated explicitly to the Beatitudes with which the Sermon on the Mount begins. But the chapel should serve to recall all that Jesus said, for practically every sentence of his discourse has had its influence on the cultures which have accepted Christianity. This Sermon on the Mount has done much to make Matthew the primary Gospel for Christian teaching from the earliest times; this sermon, in its full length of three chapters, is found only in Matthew. A closer look at this sermon shows what Matthew had in mind in giving it to his readers as Jesus' first major teaching in the Matthean Gospel.

Many scholars suggest that the Sermon on the Mount was actually not one, uninterrupted sermon given by Jesus on one occasion, but that Matthew added to a core sermon various sayings of Jesus which he spoke to his disciples at different times and occasions. Looking at the Sermon in this way best explains three things: first, why no other Gospel has a sermon of the size and importance of what we have in three chapters of Matthew; second, why some sayings of Matthew's Sermon on the Mount are found, not in one place (as in Matthew), but scattered over Jesus' public life described by Mark and Luke; third, why for all their differences, Matthew and Luke essentially agree on a core of a sermon that Jesus gave his disciples while at a mountain.

Indeed, Luke has a sermon given by Jesus which in two aspects closely parallels what we read in the Sermon on the Mount in Matthew, although in Luke the sermon takes place at the foot of the mountain and was reduced from Matthew's three chapters to *just thirty verses* of Luke's chapter six. Concretely, the material which is so much alike in Matthew and Luke is made up of Beatitudes and certain teaching about the love and integrity which should characterize the actions and thinking of a follower of Jesus. The sermon as given in Matthew will be discussed here, with attention given to some of the differences in Luke where the sermon in Luke transects that given in Matthew. Let us, then, look to this magnificent discourse of Jesus, given to his disciples, as Matthew reports it, on "the mountain top."

The Sermon in Matthew
~ MATTHEW 5–7 ~

In a sermon of three chapters' length it may not be easy to recognize at first reading the topic sentence or essential theme which holds it all together. But here most scholars agree that the topic sentence, the idea around which the entire Sermon on the Mount revolves, is this: "For I tell you, if your virtue goes no deeper than that of the scribes and Pharisees, you will never get into the kingdom of Heaven" (Mt 5:20). A more positive way of putting this idea, though we lose the sense of "doing better than many of the Jewish leaders," is the later statement, "You must be perfect as your heavenly Father is perfect" (Mt 5:48). In the concrete circumstances of Jesus' audience this meant that "the person who keeps the least of the commandments from the Mosaic Law and from the Prophets and teaches them would be considered great in the kingdom of Heaven" (Mt 5:19). These three elements, then, characterize the follower of Jesus:

perfect as the Father is perfect, which is to say that one has to do better than the scribes and the Pharisees, that one keeps the law of Israel's tradition as that law is reinterpreted by Jesus. Let us see, then, just what that perfection was for Jesus' audience.

The Beatitudes

The first section of the Sermon on the Mount is dedicated to the Beatitudes. Beatitude is a Latin word *beatitudo* made into an English word; it means blessedness or happiness, and a person who has this quality of blessedness is called *blessed, happy—beatus*. A beatitude is a particular form of teaching; the Scriptures have over 250 beatitudes; eight are in the Sermon on the Mount as given in Matthew, whereas in Luke's sermon there are only four beatitudes. A beatitude is simply characterized: it is a saying which starts with the word *blessed*, then usually identifies the kind of person who is blessed, and often concludes with the reason why this kind of person can be considered blessed. Since Jesus taught orally rather than by writing, he constantly sought out forms of speech which were simple, but capable of carrying a deep teaching, and which could help people remember, even memorize what he taught. Thus this kind of saying is a good form to help people recall even many years later the essence of what Jesus thought important; indeed, the Sermon on the Mount is filled with many formulaic ways of conveying teaching and gives us direct contact with Jesus' methods. The strengths of such beatitudinal teaching are obvious: clarity, simplicity, memorability. But it must be admitted that such brief teaching gives no room for reasoning about the morality it teaches and thus makes it difficult to know precisely how Jesus might apply his teaching to specific situations.

By comparing the beatitudes given by Matthew with those given by Luke for the very same sermon, we conclude that Jesus probably addressed the Beatitudes directly to his immediate audience, hence, "blessed are *you* . . ." This means that Matthew changed the Beatitudes slightly to read, "blessed are *they* who . . ." By doing this, he extends Jesus' teaching beyond Jesus' initial hearers to all those who would read his Gospel. Various qualities are emphasized by Jesus and stressed in the Gospels of Matthew and Luke. In general, Luke recorded Jesus' effort to bring, by way of beatitudes, consolation and encouragement to the poor faithful of Israel, to those who are poor, hungry, and weeping and must suffer for their allegiance to Jesus; Matthew also wanted to assure such people of God's care for them and of his promises of love and encouragement for those who, whether rich or poor, emphasize the spiritual life and treat the material life, the "life of this world," as secondary to the demands of the "world to come." For instance, those "blessed poor in spirit" are no longer only "you here in front of Jesus who are physically poor, but faithful to God"; they are all those who, even though wealthy, remain detached from the things of this world and use these things so as to be rich in the things of heaven. They are the "poor in spirit," the spiritually poor or detached from this world.

The beatitudes of Matthew indicate the kinds of virtues or ways of living that characterize a follower of Jesus: humble and not proud or haughty, seeking justice as God defines it, being single-minded, that is, set on God, able to suffer persecution for Jesus' sake. In this way the Beatitudes are a lesson in what one should strive to be as a Christian. Implicit in this list, though, is a concern shown for those human beings who are simply poor, humiliated, sorrowing. God cannot tolerate the suffering of the human beings he has created; someday he will simply sweep up everything and restore everyone to the beauty and happiness he originally intended for us all before sin entered this world, with death. Jesus' beatitudes in part mean to sound a call to trust, to encourage those who suffer with the assurance that God intends one day to rectify all suffering. This sympathy of God for the suffering means he wants them saved; he will find a way to save them.

Christians are Light and Salt

Having described qualities of his followers by the Beatitudes, Jesus told them that they are the salt of the earth and the light of the world. To be the salt of the earth seems to mean that Christianity is what gives taste or meaning to an otherwise insipid or tasteless, i.e., meaningless, world. To be salt also means that, as salt preserves life, so the Christian preserves eternal life, for self and for others, and does not lead others to death. The term *light of the world* echoed Isaiah who once called Israel the light of the world in the sense that it would be through Israel that the true God and the true way to lead human life would be visible. Jesus, in the Gospel of John, identified himself as the "light of the world," thus indicating that those who sat in darkness and under the shadow of death would find light and see the way to life through him. Here in the Gospel of Matthew, Jesus' followers were told to be the way by which the rest of the world would be able to see the true God, to escape the darkness and death of this world, and to find the brilliant and life-giving God. Being the light of the world suggests that one live one's Christian life without excuse; to be what one is called to be needs no explanation, nor should one hide what one knows to be true living.

At this point in the sermon Jesus made explicit what he had implied. Jesus, a man of his times, was concerned for the welfare of his own contemporaries. He was eager to give what he considered a true understanding of God's will, an understanding different in many respects from what many of the religious leaders of Israel were teaching. To understand what God wanted—and to do it—are two immensely important concerns of the Israel of Jesus' time, for so much of all of the past history of Israel had been interpreted as events caused by Israel's obedience or disobedience to God. Happiness, in short, depended essentially on fulfilling God's will. Thus, it is of immense importance to know what God asks and not to teach falsely about it, or worse, not to obey it. Jesus defined his work, then, as teaching his contemporaries what was the true will of God.

Christianity and Judaism

To look at Judaism in its strict interpretation today and to compare it with Christianity is a good way to understand how differently Christianity, originally a group of Jews, developed out of Judaism. The key to this difference is the mind of Jesus: what he said—however like or unlike it might be to Israel's Law and Prophets—was now the starting point and criterion for all obligation on Christians. Often in the first century A.D. it seemed that Jesus' understanding of God's will would make him deny all that the Law and Prophets of Israel had said, but this is not true. It is truer to say that Jesus rethought the Old Law and Prophets, then kept what was still valid, but eliminated what was not necessary for holiness and readjusted still other elements of Israel's inheritance.

The criteria Jesus used to evaluate the old system were the fundamental laws of Israel: "Love God with all your heart and soul and strength," and "Love your neighbor as yourself." Each individual law or saying of Israel's tradition should be judged by these two laws; each individual law was kept, dropped, or adjusted insofar as it did or did not promote love of God and love of neighbor. Thus, Jesus never denied the laws forbidding idolatry, murder, stealing, and uncharitable speech and action. But Jesus did away with certain laws of worship and of special foods, because they did not really touch on the essence of proper worship of God or love of neighbor. Thus, Jesus adjusted the law about divorce, making clear that for his contemporaries there should be no divorce, though Israel had grown to understand that God would not consider divorce to be a cause of unholiness.

Jesus, then, saw his role as that of making Israel's Law more perfect; Jesus became, in effect, the new and surest way of knowing what God asks of human beings in order that they might stand worthily in his presence. This new way of understanding the mind of God has repercussions throughout the rest of the Sermon on the Mount. Let us look briefly at some of these effects, remembering always that Jesus was laboring here to show how his understanding of what God wants differed from the other contemporary teachings of Israel and how his teaching leads to the truest, fullest holiness.

Five Differences Between Jesus and the Tradition

Jesus gave five examples of how his understanding of Israel's laws was different from that of the authorities of his time. In none of these examples did Jesus give the philosophical or more broadly intellectual justification for his teaching; he simply supplanted the old laws by his new laws buttressed with one or two very brief arguments at most. The advantage of this approach is that it makes what Jesus says very clear, and the profundity of his teaching is also very clear. The disadvantage of this approach is that it does not discuss the many circumstances in which application of his precious insights is very difficult. But such a kind of teacher Jesus was; we are grateful for that, and try to understand his perceptions and live according to them in the many varied circumstances of our lives.

The first distinction Jesus drew for his audience (vv. 21–26) is that between killing, which Israelite law explicitly forbade ("Thou shalt not kill"), and bitter unkindnesses which are not directly forbidden by any Israelite law, but which, according to Jesus (and our own experience), were just as destructive as killing, and thus deserved the same punishments, as Jesus notes, assigned to killing. Jesus goes on here to observe two things. First, God is not pleased with a sacrifice from one against whom someone has a serious complaint; one should first resolve the complaint, then proceed to worship God in a pleasing way. Second, as in human affairs, so too in divine, a person should seek forgiveness for the evil one does to others before it is too late!

The second distinction Jesus drew (vv. 27–32) has to do with adultery. Here, while he agreed with the usual interpretation of "thou shalt not commit adultery," Jesus called adulterous two acts which his contemporaries did not judge to be adultery at all. First, though the Jewish law never approved of divorce per se, Jewish authority was long accustomed to divorce and was concerned only that the woman, who could never initiate the divorce or refuse to be divorced, be treated at least with minimal justice, once the divorce occurred. Jesus looked at divorce quite differently. He understood divorce to be adulterous; thus, not only was divorce wrong in itself—Matthew 19:1–9 argues this point most clearly—it was also wrong because it made the woman an adulteress. Second, the ancient law against adultery should be extended to include adultery committed in one's heart, even though one only lusts after a woman while never touching her physically. In this way, Jesus not only accepted the traditional understanding of what was prohibited as adulterous action, but included under this law lusting after a woman and divorce.

A word is in order about Jesus' words regarding "cutting off one's hand, plucking out one's eye." He is not actually encouraging such a violent act, but he is trying to emphasize by speaking metaphorically/figuratively the seriousness of the sin and the seriousness with which we avoid the means to committing sin.

The third distinction Jesus drew (vv. 33–37) has to do with an aspect of the law of fulfilling oaths; Jesus does not oppose taking an oath, but he finds all too common, especially among religious people, that element of oath-taking which involves swearing by God's name. Too often holy people were calling on God to confirm their own opinions. Jesus would prefer to keep the name of God holy and out of constant, petty usage to bolster an opinion; if we want to affirm something, we should do so without claiming that we have God to back it up. Just a "yes, yes" or a "no, no" will do, with no claim to have God on our side.

A fourth distinction Jesus drew (vv. 38–42) concerning the ancient law has to do with the Mosaic command: an eye for an eye and a tooth for a tooth. Originally, the intent of this Mosaic Law was very good; it limited punishment to what actually fitted a crime and thus forbade excessive punishment—"as many eyes as I can get for the one eye taken from me"—or the wrong quality of punishment—"I'll take a tongue for an eye." However, by Jesus' time this Mosaic legislation seems to have given rise to an attitude among many Jews which Jesus found odious. If I allow the law of retaliation to become my basic principle for dealing with people in my life, I will have to wait to see what a person does to me before I respond to that person. It means that I do not respond to the person instinctively with love, but respond only as that person has first acted towards me. Jesus proposes a number of examples, from non-retaliation to almsgiving, to show that my attitude toward my neighbor should be instinctively love, no matter what that neighbor's attitude to me might be. My relationships are not governed by giving to a neighbor who first gives to me; my relationships are governed by love of neighbor, a love which is real and actual before I know what the neighbor will do for or against me. Jesus teaches always and everywhere that love of neighbor, together with love of God, is what characterizes his disciples. In particular, then, we should note that the law of non-resistance and of "turning the other cheek" is not the primary law. The primary law is love of neighbor, and resistance (or non-resistance) is valid only to the degree that it promotes love of neighbor.

Jesus noted the traditional Israelite law, "you shall love your neighbor"; to it he added what had become the law in practice, though it appeared nowhere in the Old Testament, "you shall hate your enemy." The notion of "hating one's enemy" is a very limited one: it has to do with hating those who hate God. Thus, a sign of religious people was understood to be hatred for those who disobeyed God, who flaunted idols before him, who treated God's loved ones brutally and harshly. In a sense this matter has nothing personal in it; indeed, one's hatred grew or diminished to the degree that offense against God grew or diminished. This kind of hatred is a form of the old adage, "The enemy of my friend is enemy to me."

For Jesus, the distinction that separates the sin from the sinner must be maintained. True, the Old Testament way of story-telling often depicted God as angry and punishing his enemies, those who offended him. Yet here by word and example, Jesus taught that the love God has for a person, sinning or not, is to be the true and constant approach each human being should have towards every other human being. True, God punishes, but then again God gives rain and sun to those who dishonor him, thus helping his enemies to live better, happier lives.

Thus, whatever the circumstances of one human being in contact with another, love of neighbor in imitation of God's love for that neighbor should rule all actions done to that neighbor. Such things as self-defense, war, capital punishment, are ultimately governed by love which imitates God's love for the just and for the unjust. No other principle replaces love as the criterion for action.

Later Developments of Jesus' Teaching about Divorce

In all these differences between himself and the traditional interpretation of Mosaic morality, Jesus hoped to show that his way to pleasing God made the law more perfect and that it more accurately reflected God's will than the way his contemporaries—Sadducees, Pharisees, chief priests, Essenes, and others—taught and lived. Rooted as his sayings were in the circumstances of his moment in Israel, it is not surprising that his followers in later decades have had to adjust to some degree what he said, to cope with circumstances which Jesus never had to face. Thus, Jesus never approved of divorce—compare, for example the teaching in Mark (10:1–2) and Luke (16:12) and Paul (1 Cor 7:10–11). Yet, Matthew, and Paul in the First Letter to the Corinthians, face situations which they solved only by granting a (very restricted) approval of divorce.

For Paul, a converted spouse begins to suffer from his or her pagan spouse precisely because of the Christian religion of the one spouse. Paul was faced with this dilemma: let the pagan spouse pressure the newly converted Christian spouse so that the newly converted collapses and gives up the faith in order to save the marriage, or allow the two to divorce, in order to save the faith of the believer. Paul counselled the latter option, provided it be the pagan partner who urges the divorce.

In the Matthean Gospel it is not altogether clear what constituted reason for divorce, though it did have to do with some form or other of what can be called sexual sin. Some scholars, for example, think that the divorce was permitted by Matthew for the slightest infidelity a woman might be guilty of; others think that what Matthew has in mind is a most grievous offense against one's marriage vows. Other scholars think that Matthew is thinking of a partner who was guilty of a kind of idol worship involving intercourse with prescribed prostitutes (a not uncommon religious practice in pagan religions). Still other scholars think that Matthew has run across in his community some marriages which actually go against the law of the Book of Leviticus (c. 18), a law which forbids marriage between certain categories of people. For instance, this law of Leviticus forbids marriage between brother and sister, between first cousins, between mother and son. Perhaps for pagans such marriages would have been acceptable, but, on becoming Christians, spouses related in these ways violate God's Old Testament prohibitions. Thus, though Jesus is not on record as having permitted divorce, Matthew (like Paul above) thinks that he would have allowed for divorce if he had been confronted with certain circumstances, and Matthew (unlike Paul, who clearly distinguishes what Jesus taught from what Paul teaches) even puts permission for this divorce on Jesus' lips. Indeed, in later times, the task of fitting the teaching of Jesus to circumstances, while remaining faithful to the mind of Christ falls to the Church.

Three Practices

The Sermon on the Mount next takes up three practices which in Jesus' time were considered to characterize a person who was serious about seeking to stand worthily in God's presence: almsgiving, prayer, and fasting. Jesus did not create these three practices; they were part of the Jewish tradition he inherited. And he never forbade these practices, but he approved of them. Rather his intention was to correct wrong motives which seem to have inspired certain contemporaries to fast, pray, and give alms. In this part of the Sermon it is not a question of what act a person does, but of the *why* that moves him to the act.

Prayer

Within the discussion of prayer, Jesus offered a type of prayer which was most satisfying to God without it being the type of interminable prayer other authorities thought pleasing to God (see pp. 152-59). It was a simple prayer, divided into two parts and very faithful to the traditional prayer of Israel. First, one praises God and asks that God's kingdom come, that earth reflect the perfect harmony of heaven where God's will rules and brings about perfect peace. Then, one asks for one's most fundamental needs: food, forgiveness, freedom from the trials which would test to the breaking point one's fidelity to God. To these petitions is added the reminder that one can hardly expect forgiveness from God if one is unwilling to forgive others: there is little logic in such an expectation. With all of his persuasiveness Jesus was trying to bring to birth in his followers a willingness to forgive others; to him, it was this willingness which would prevent most of the actions done from bringing harm to one's neighbor. Thus, Jesus' teaching is the one which brings peace.

The "Our Father" is a prayer which contains the basic elements of many other prayers; it is not the only way to express oneself to the Father, but it does guide us to praise of God and it does point to the essential needs of life.

Jesus had given several statements in the Sermon on the Mount which outline the characteristics of those who want to be his followers. In many ways they are encouraged to be holy, as the Jewish traditions had encouraged them; prayerful, fasting, alms-giving, neighbor-loving, and possessed of all of those virtues described by the Beatitudes; in other ways, too, Jesus has described to his followers ways in which they should think differently from their contemporaries and should act differently from them. Jesus' concern is both to recommend the practices of prayer, fasting, and almsgiving, and to purify our motives in performing them. It was a long-standing tradition among his people that such pious acts would be rewarded in heaven; but how can they be, if one also wants as one's reward the praise of people on earth? If such praise is what is desired, Jesus indicates that praise, not heavenly reward, will be the only reward for these deeds. Hardly an encouraging thought!

Now Jesus turns to another major concern: riches.

Worry about Riches

Jesus offered three principal considerations about riches for those who wish to follow him. First, treasures are valuable to the degree that they are indestructible. It follows that we seek those treasures which would not fade or be taken away. This unending treasure of course can exist only in heaven, and so Jesus exhorts his followers not to commit themselves to things which would break their hearts when they lose them; wisdom says that one's heart would be happy if it has invested in treasures that last forever.

Second, human experience has taught that possessions and money can become effectively a god in one's life, a god which is more esteemed than the one, true God, and more sought after, more "listened to." A person does not readily recognize this fact always; yet, when we realize how money dictates our actions and how much we would sacrifice to have and preserve it and how much affection we have for it, then we begin to realize just what a god money has already come close to being in people's lives. Jesus' insight was simply built on this experience: we cannot serve two gods at once. Jesus' encouragement was to choose the true, the only God. True, service of this God may at times require that we lay aside the demand and service of money, but there is only one God and him we must serve above all else.

Given the revelation of God as our Father, we can only draw the conclusion that God will take care of us as a father would. Thus it follows that the kind of worry about life that assumes God does not care about us should be abandoned. Jesus was not saying that worry and concern and effort and labor to wipe away worry are bad; he was concerned about the conclusion people draw at times from life, namely that God does not care about us, that he cannot be trusted, and that therefore we should go elsewhere to find and secure our happiness. Amidst all life's trials, especially in the midst of his own, Jesus never doubted that God is a loving Father. If God does not answer our needs, the reason may not be apparent; but, for all that unclarity, we should not conclude that God does not care; we must solve our problems within the conviction that God is Father to us. That is the reality.

Let me rephrase this idea: God has made us to be concerned, to worry, if you will; that is the kind of being he has created when he created a human being. We must foresee, plan, be attentive, ready for this or that in life, whether for ourselves or others. But God has not made us to worry as though he is no longer functioning as a Father to us. That kind of worry, which implies that we must find someone or something else which will be a good god to us (e.g., money)—that kind of worry, i.e., the doubting that produces it—is what Jesus wants us to stop. God does exist for each of us, and is uninterruptedly our Father; to deny that is to deny the most important reality that is. Concerned we are then, about life, but always knowing that our Father is loving us and, as he knows best, intervening for us.

Judging One's Neighbor

The Sermon on the Mount concludes with further exhortation to love one's neighbor by not condemning, or being harsh in judging that neighbor. People have the tendency to ignore their own evil ways and to concentrate on the evils, often less significant than their own, of others. Fairness is a prized virtue in such circumstances; indeed, should we not be fair, if we expect to be treated fairly? Here in Jesus' words there is no statement that one's neighbor is without sin; he asks for mercy for the neighbor, and for fairness in knowing ourselves as we know our neighbors.

Jesus again called for trust in God as our Father; this time he is thinking specifically of prayer wherein we ask favors from God. We must truly ask, truly seek, truly knock; that is how we are urged to get what we want. If we do not ask, seek, knock, shall we conclude that God will take care of us anyway? It is clear from Jesus' knowledge of God that God wants us to ask, seek, knock. But, even then when our prayers are not answered, and we cannot explain why he does not answer, should we not trust that God is our Father and has not ignored us? Indeed, if we use the fatherhood of a person to explain why a child would surely be treated well, how can we doubt that God's child will be treated well? Surely, God is the best of fathers!

Disciples must be wary of false teachers, that is, those who teach differently from Jesus, and those who teach differently about Jesus than does his Church. Above all, Jesus' teaching provided the grounding for a life which leads to fullest happiness; to take another's teaching is to entrust one's life to another than Jesus—and this transfer of trust is like building on sand. Jesus' way, though a narrow road and often difficult because of what it might mean to love God and neighbor so thoroughly, is really the only way to full happiness. It is this suggestion that one has the sure way to a happy ending which makes the Sermon on the Mount finally so admirable.

The Sermon in Luke
~ LUKE 6:20–49 ~

Luke's rendition of the sermon—for Luke it is more properly called the "Sermon on the Plain"—concentrates on two facets of what we have seen in Matthew's longer sermon. First, Luke contrasts those poor, sad, and hungry with those who go their own way with wealth, joy, and plenty and ignore those who are in need. Concretely, this situation is unbearable for Jesus; it contradicts the very meaning of God's great commandment to love one's neighbor. Jesus' disciples could not live this contradictory kind of life. Second, Jesus goes on to work out further implications of love of neighbor, specifically, how this command relates to one's enemies. In brief, Luke looks for the same love and fairness and generosity that characterize the Sermon on the Mount in Matthew. Truly, the foundation of relationships, as far as Jesus is concerned, is only love. What a difference in the way human life might be lived if his sermon were really accepted and lived! It is a simple sermon but a narrow way. Yet it is the way to life, as many know by experience, by actually living Jesus' teaching.

The shrine to honor the Beatitudes is a holy place to remind us that Jesus' way of understanding what the Father is and what he asks of us gives contentment and peace. He died because of his teaching, because he claimed to represent God's mind better than all traditions and contemporary interpretations of those traditions. He could have backed off from his teaching and become silent about God's mind, but he did not, for he knew that he had to tell others, even at the risk of his life, what was for their deepest happiness.

Caesarea Philippi

"You are the Messiah,
the Son of the living God."
~ Matthew 16:16

At Caesarea Philippi there are a series of pools and a lovely grove which lie at the foot of a mountain, where a guide may point out Greek words inscribed in honor of Pan, the ancient Greek and Roman god of woodlands and pastures. Though his name originally came from a Greek word for *pastures*, an ancient pun linked up the name with the Greek word for *everything*, and he became the god of all nature. Caesar Augustus Octavian gave the ancient shrine and its surrounding town to Herod the Great. Herod's son Philip inherited the town and, to honor Caesar Augustus Octavian, who in 6 A.D. had made Philip tetrarch of this entire northern territory bounding Palestine, rebuilt the town into a more glorious one and named it after Caesar Augustus. Joining his own name to that of Caesar, Philip called the place Caesarea Philippi (the Caesar city of Philip). *Philippi* serves to distinguish this city from another Caesarea built on the Mediterranean coast of Palestine (see pp. 85-93).

Who is Jesus?
~ Matthew 16:13–20; Mark 8:27–30; Luke 9:18–22 ~

In or near Caesarea Philippi, Jesus asked his disciples who had been following him for quite a few months, "Who do people say I am?" The question seems to be one of curiosity, but it turns out to be a very profound question; indeed it really asks, "From all that the people have seen and heard in my public life, who do they think I am?" (And for the reader, who never met Jesus, the question is basically the same: "After reading the Gospel up to this point, who do you say I am?") The answers given in Matthew, Mark, and Luke (John does not have this question) are quite similar. Some think Jesus was the Prophet—by this they mean that Jesus is the one promised in Deuteronomy 18:15, 18: "Yahweh your God will raise up for you a prophet like me [Moses] from among your brothers." Jesus is this Prophet. Some think Jesus is John the Baptizer, in the sense at least that the spirit of John, who was beheaded at the command of Herod Antipas, was in Jesus. Others think of Jesus as the Elijah figure of the ninth century B.C. who worked astounding miracles and who the prophet Malachi, some centuries before Jesus, had promised would return to prepare the people of Israel for the great and terrible Judgment Day of the Lord (Mal 3:1). Still others think Jesus is a Jeremiah or one of the other prophets, for Jesus constantly exhorts the people to return to their God, even when Jesus, reminiscent of Jeremiah and others, is opposed by authorities.

Jesus never denied the aptness of these names by which people tried to express their perception of who he was and what he was attempting to do. Rather, he changed the question to "Who do you say I am?"; he speaks now to his Twelve. Peter answers this question, "You are the Messiah (of God)." In Mark and Luke Jesus does not accept or reject this title, a title which becomes the fundamental means by which we Christians identify ourselves today: *Messiah* means, in Greek, *Christ*, and so we are forever known as the Messiah followers or Christians. In Matthew Jesus implicitly accepts this title. Let us consider Jesus' attitude towards the title of Messiah more closely, and especially look at what he says to Peter in Matthew, after Peter answers Jesus' question by saying: "You are the Messiah, the son of the living God."

The Messianic Secret

As mentioned above regarding the Gospels of Mark and Luke, when Jesus heard Peter identify him as "Messiah," Jesus neither denied nor approved of the title, but he warned Peter and the others not to speak of this title to anyone. Mark is the source here for Luke and so we look to Mark as the text to understand. And we find that secrecy about Jesus' identity is a fundamental theme of Mark, not just a one-time subject occasioned by Jesus' questions at Caesarea Philippi. The point of what we call the "Messianic Secret" is that for Mark, the disciples were simply too inexperienced to know what they were saying when they said Jesus was "Messiah" (or applied any other title to him). They had seen him work fabulous miracles and heard his profound wisdom and witnessed his deep holiness, all of which suggested that he was the Messiah and not anything less. But they had not lived through the complete Jesus experience, which would involve both ignominious and powerless death and astounding resurrection. Mark was most precisely concerned with what the disciples would call Jesus when they see him hanging in pain and humiliation and failure on a cross until his life oozes out of him. Would they still call him Messiah, the only one who will fulfill all the hopes of our hearts? This crucified Jesus was hard to identify as Messiah, the one anointed by God to bring about the holiness and happiness of the people of God. First, where was God in this death? Second, why would Jesus be the beloved of God and still die like this? Third, how would the Messiah accomplish the task of saving for which he was sent, if his career, his life was so abruptly and easily ended by people who are proving themselves at Calvary more powerful than God? Until we have the answer to these questions, which lie at the heart of any attempt to make sense of Jesus, we should not speak too readily of him as Messiah.

In other words, Jesus did not want to be known as Messiah only because he worked miracles or taught well or appeared holy. Most essentially, he wanted to be known as Messiah, not only because of these things, but also because of his death; it was his death, even more than his miracles, which revealed the true saving task of Jesus, to die for our sins, and accomplished the happiness and fullest life for us all. Mark wrote his Gospel to protect this complete Jesus and to make sure that we do not follow Jesus only because he is a miracle worker. Just think of believers who are called upon to sacrifice their lives for Jesus; will they do it (or accept any of life's sufferings) if their leader is really only followed because of his miracles? If Jesus is not for me a miracle worker, then who is he and why do I follow him? Because of his teaching? But what if that becomes in its own way a cross, a martyrdom for me; will I follow him? Mark, and others too, want the reader to realize that the cross is part of the meaning of Jesus, a part with great meaning for understanding Jesus and for understanding what kind of leader I have committed myself to. In a word, as God asked the cross of Jesus, something no one expected of the Messiah, so God may ask me to follow Jesus with my own cross. That he has gone ahead of me, to die for me and to give me example and encourage me to get through suffering so as to reach unending life—that is the "full" Jesus I confess to be Messiah. Peter and his friends could know about this complete Jesus only at the end of the Gospel, not in its middle, at Mark 8:27–30. But know it the Christian must, or eventually lose understanding of Jesus and eventually loyalty to him.

Looked at from another direction, Christianity had to come up with a satisfactory explanation of the death of Jesus in order to keep on calling Jesus what his public life suggested, that is, Messiah. For Mark, Jesus' death was a death for others, a death by which the sins of others were wiped away so that they might have life with God forever. For Luke, Jesus' death was this, and, further, was a part of the divine plan: God knew what people would do to Jesus and thwarted the effects of death by raising Jesus from the dead—all according to his divine plan. Thus, in neither Gospel was the death of Jesus a proof in any way that God had abandoned Jesus; rather, the death itself was understood in such a way as to heighten the relationship between Father, who raised Jesus from the dead, and Son, who obeyed in fullest confidence and loyalty. But only after one has lived through the entire Jesus experience, and not just that part of it which had been shared in up to Jesus' questions at Caesarea Philippi, can one truly call Jesus "Messiah" with real understanding.

Peter's Confession in Matthew
~ MATTHEW 16:13–20 ~

Matthew's Gospel affirmed all that Matthew took from Mark's Gospel about Jesus the Messiah, but for Matthew, the episode at Caesarea Philippi meant something more. In Mark and Luke Peter's identification of Jesus is followed by an author's comment: "he [Jesus] cautioned them [the disciples] to say nothing to anybody about him." This comment is in Matthew, too, but it comes, not after Peter's identification of Jesus, but after a very important set of verses, a speech of Jesus, which appears only in Matthew. One often thinks that Matthew, after reading Mark here,

decided to reproduce Mark, but also add to Mark a speech of Jesus directed to Peter. What addition did Matthew make, once Peter had identified
Jesus as "the Messiah, the Son of the living God"?

Jesus' speech makes clear, first of all, that Peter's being able to identify Jesus as Messiah, Son of the living God, was a gift from God, that
Peter had not figured this out on his own; Peter was given a revelation
from God, his knowledge about Jesus did not come from "flesh and
blood," i.e., from human reasoning. Mark and Luke, however, do not suggest that Peter's statement is owed to God's revealing it to Peter.

Second, that Peter was the object of God's revelation meant to
Jesus that he could draw the conclusion that Peter, with his definition of
Jesus, should be the rock, the foundation of Jesus' church. God was signaling to Jesus, by his gift to Peter, that Peter was the suitable foundation
of the church of Jesus. And so Jesus made Peter the foundation of his
church. He gave Simon the name *Peter*, which means *rock*, whether in
Aramaic or Greek.

It is important to note two things about Jesus' act here. First, what
we should think of as the rock or foundation of Jesus' church is really
made up of two elements. On the one hand, the rock foundation of the
church is the belief that Jesus is the Messiah, the Son of the living God.
Whatever else the church may stand for, it is this belief about Jesus which
is its essential component. Should the church or Peter in any way deny
this belief about Jesus, the church of Jesus will crumble, for its foundation is lost. On the other hand, the rock of the church was identified not
solely as the profession of Jesus' being Messiah and Son of God, but was
identified as Peter, the man. One cannot say that only the belief in Jesus
is the foundation of the church; from the text it is clear that it is the man
Peter, while professing that Jesus is Messiah, Son of God, who is the foundation of Jesus' church.

Second, in further thinking about the above, note that, while the disciples are questioned by Jesus about what the people are saying about
him ("you" plural) and that they (plural) respond, it is only Peter who
answers the question about what the disciples say about Jesus. And it is
only to him that Jesus thinks the revelation of God has been given, and so
it is only Peter who is the rock of the church of Jesus. In this way, Peter
stands out from even his closest associates and is pictured as unique
among them.

Jesus' Church

What is meant by *church* in Jesus' words to Peter? Scholars agree that what we call *church* is best explained by looking to the Old Testament for its meaning. We do so because the Old Testament was really the primary dictionary for the speakers in the New Testament, and so we go there to find out the meaning of most of the words used in the New Testament.

In this case, the Old Testament is very instructive. It uses the Hebrew equivalent of our word *church* when it describes the Israelites who are *called out* of their tents to wait at the foot of Mount Sinai, to wait to hear the word of God and then to worship him. When the Israelites are *called out* to listen and to worship they are consistently described by a Hebrew word (meaning *to call out*) which is translated into the English word "church." When Moses brought the law down from Mount Sinai, after meeting with God, and presented it to the people who had been called out of their tents to gather to hear the law and then to worship the true God, at this historic moment the people, called out of their tents and gathered together, were "church." They had been called out to listen and to worship, for now they were formally, in God's plan, "God's People." And so, when Jesus wants to talk about the community which is his, which will become His People, he speaks of them as "called out" to hear his word and then to worship the true God.

This church is founded on the belief, expressed by Peter, that Jesus is the Messiah, the Son of the living God, and therefore his community or church is called out to listen to him and then to worship. This is the best description of the church of Jesus: listening to his word together, then worshiping together.

There is a certain tragic note here. Jesus speaks of "his church," thereby implying that "his church," his people, is distinct from those who do not base their togetherness on the belief that he is Messiah, Son of the living God.

A church founded on the belief that Jesus is Messiah, Son of the living God, is a church which the powers of evil cannot overcome, for they cannot overcome its founder. Jesus uses the image here of the "gates of hell," an image which is picturesque: it makes us see the armies of hell which pass through gates in the wall around hell to destroy the enemy, the church of Jesus. The powers of hell coming through hell's gates will not win over the church, nor will those powers be able to withstand the attacks of the church against the gates of hell.

Only one thing can overcome Jesus' church: the denial that he is the Messiah, the Son of the living God.

The Keys of the Kingdom

The notion of *rock* involves not only what is professed about Jesus, but also the person, Peter, who made this profession. To this person are given the keys to the kingdom of heaven. The idea expressed here is based on the Old Testament image of the special and only person assigned by the king to have all the keys which open and close all the doors of the palace. Obviously this imagery indicates that it is Peter who opens and shuts the doors of heaven. Presumably he is to do this opening for those who profess with him the belief that Jesus is the Messiah, the Son of the living God. To make this idea more clear, we look at Matthew 23:13. There Jesus excoriates the scribes and Pharisees because they "shut up the kingdom of heaven in men's faces, neither going in yourselves nor allowing others to go in who want to." These scribes and pharisees had the power to "open and to close" the kingdom to their fellow Jews. That is, these people had the power to understand the teaching of God which would allow them and others to enter or to be kept out of the kingdom of God. They failed to use this potential for themselves and for others, because they so often wrongly interpreted the will of God, by word and example. Peter, rock and keeper of the keys of Jesus' community, will teach correctly, so that people can rightly enter, or be kept from entering, the kingdom.

Jesus switches images now. "Opening and shutting" is replaced by the image of "binding and loosening." It was often the case that a religious Jew would go to a specialist in the Mosaic Law to learn what his obligation was in a particular situation: what would God, in the light of the Mosaic Law, say he should do in this or that circumstance? The specialist's task was to decide, on the basis of all the pertinent laws, whether or not a person was bound to a certain practice or loosed from it. The specialist in Jesus' community is to be Peter; whatever Peter binds, that is, indicates is God's will for life with God, and whatever he looses, that is, indicates is not God's will for life with him—that will be acceptable to heaven. God stands behind and ratifies Peter's binding and loosening, his teaching.

Such then was Jesus' immense gift to Peter, once Jesus had heard Peter say Jesus was Messiah, Son of the living God; when Jesus heard that, he knew God had blessed Peter above all others and he knew that he could found his community on Peter. On this profession and on this man the worshipping community of Jesus rests secure; on these two the Church depends for the true teaching of what is God's will for our life with God. No power will defeat this community that seeks God through belief that Jesus is the Messiah, the Son of the living God.

In this lovely, peaceful spot called Caesarea Philippi, on the north-eastern border of Galilee, Jesus pronounced words which have been of the utmost importance for the history of the world. These words were one more way of Jesus' extending to us means by which he could lead us to happiness—which, after all, was indeed his task as Messiah, Son of God.

Naim

"'Do not cry,' he said."

~ Matthew 7:13

About eight miles southeast of Nazareth and five miles southwest of Mount Tabor, the Mount of the Transfiguration, lies the village of
Naim. It is a Muslim village today and overlooks the mighty and fertile
Plain of Esdraelon which stretches from east to west across northern
Palestine. Naim has no Christian first-century A.D. archeological remains,
but a chapel was built by the Franciscans in 1880 over the remains of a
medieval Christian church and commemorates the astounding miracle
and wonderful generosity of Jesus to the poor widow of Naim who had
just lost her only son.

Luke's story says that Jesus met a funeral cortege near "the gate of
the city"; no one has found remains of a gate or its wall; many conjecture
that Luke had in mind a formal wooden or stone marker through which
the road passed just before it reached the outlying houses of the town.

Raising of a Widow's Son
~ Luke 7:11–17 ~

The story of what happened at the edge of Naim has much to offer Luke's
reader. Note that this miracle happened not because anyone requested it,
but simply because Jesus could not help responding to the pitiableness
of the situation. In a sense, he was like the Good Samaritan he himself

would later describe; he was moved by the sorrow and pain of another human being, in this case a woman who had lost husband and only son. Overpowering and exhilarating as was Jesus' act, one has to keep remembering that Jesus did not enter this phase of his life to work miracles. Yes, total relief from all pain and sorrow was an expected and signal characteristic of the kingdom of God everyone was waiting for, and to be in the presence and the love of God was to be assured of complete happiness; but to bring this about by working miracles was not the task of Jesus, and to expect it of him, his followers finally realized, was to misunderstand him and the plan of God.

If indeed there was to be a primary "miracle" that Jesus was to accomplish, it was not the curing of physical or mental illnesses, but the change of the human heart from sin to obedience. It is an odd kind of miracle, because it depends not only on the powers of God, and on his grace, but also on the free choice of the person inclined to choose sin. Many might think that a person will be happy if only God will change one's circumstances, make one healthier, richer, etc. But it is God's teaching, by sending Jesus to ask for a change of heart rather than to work miracles, that what will ultimately bring about one's happiness is the union with God which begins with a heart turned loyally in obedience to him. Eventually this union will end in one receiving life, the fullness of happiness. Indeed, Jesus' miracles are signs of what God can and wants to do for us in the most complete way, but first he asks for our hearts.

The Naim miracle is particularly poignant when we consider the social situation to which the miracle responded. Wonderful as was the raising of the young man from death, this particular miraculous word of Jesus was done on behalf of the woman. In her society, the woman depended for her well-being on the work of the men in the family. This woman had already lost her husband and now loses her only son; what is her future likely to be, even if charity is given to her? Yes, there were such charitable societies in her time, who would regularly care for people like indigent women; Acts of the Apostles, chapter 6, witnesses to this social phenomenon. But such support was meager and hardly an adequate replacement for what family members would provide for one another.

It was this situation, very precarious for the widow, which Jesus entered with his restoring word. Luke is very clear about what caused Jesus' rush of sympathy: "He was the only son of his mother, and she was a widow . . . and seeing her the Lord felt great pity and sympathy for her." Jesus could not abide the effects of death; he instinctively wanted to give life. But here he not only gives life to the young man (who, after all, will have to die again!), but he gives quality of life to the widow. It is this loving concern for others which moved people to follow Jesus and urges us, too, who admittedly cannot work miracles, to find our way to giving quality of lives to those in need.

Jesus and the Disciples of John the Baptizer
~ LUKE 7:18–28 ~

Though Luke emphasized the benefit the widow of Naim enjoyed from the restoration of life to her son, and though such a miracle as this was not the primary goal of Jesus' ministry, this resurrecting someone from the dead is something to think about. I mention this because the powers of Jesus for good, visible here in the resurrection of the young man, play a large part in the discussion which occurs now in Luke between John the Baptizer and Jesus. This discussion occurred immediately after the wonder at Naim and served as a way of interpreting all that Jesus had done for people up to this point in Luke's story.

John, while imprisoned according to Luke's presentation since Luke 3:20, sought through his own disciples to learn now if Jesus was really the one for whom John knew himself to be preparing. Jesus answered in terms of the Scriptures known to Jesus, John, and all Jews. He summarized the deeds he had just done and which Luke was good enough to narrate, but he used words in such a way as to remind John of what Isaiah had said God's servant would do: blind see, lame walk, unclean are cleansed, deaf hear, dead live; those who know no good news are given good news (Is 61:1–2). From these mighty reversals of human pain, of those terrible things which characterize this age and from which we cannot free ourselves—from all of this power used to give life, John was to grasp the identity of Jesus.

That Jesus had such power, and had it to such an extent as to raise a young man from the dead so as to help his widowed mother, meant that what was to happen in the next age was happening right here where Jesus was present: something reserved for the kingdom of God was occurring right where Jesus was. Who, then, was Jesus, and what, in particular, does his miraculous power, particularly his raising the young man at Naim, say about his identity?

Luke had already introduced his readers to the possible significance of Jesus. At the beginning of Jesus' public life (Lk 4:18), Jesus had used Isaiah's words to indicate what his life would be from then on. All that Isaiah foretold, quoted in chapter 4, is realized in the stories Luke tells, up to the visit of John's messengers to Jesus.

Through these Isaian words, set in chapters 4 and 7 of Luke's story, we are asked to grasp the identity of Jesus and the sense of his proclamation that "the kingdom of God is among you." There were still more words and deeds of Jesus to come which would justify the estimate of Peter that Jesus was the very Messiah of God (Lk 9:20). What Luke ultimately hoped, however, is that his reader would conclude from all Jesus' deeds and words that Jesus was what Luke described him as in his first chapter: "he will be called holy, Son of God" (Lk 1:35). It is to this title in all its profundity that Luke thinks all of Jesus' life, words, and deeds—including the raising of the young man of Naim from the dead—lead us.

Jesus and Elijah

Finally, Luke described the miracle of Naim so as to make one automatically think of the prophet Elijah, if one knows the Old Testament as well as did Luke's original audience. At one point in Elijah's preaching life, after being responsible for miraculously providing a widow with enough bread to see her through a prolonged drought and famine, Elijah was held responsible for the death of her son. Elijah prayed that the son be given back his life, and so it happened. "Taking the child, Elijah . . . gave him to his mother . . . 'Now I know that you are a man of God,' the woman replied, 'the word of the Lord comes truly from your mouth'" (1 Kgs 17:7–24).

Many interpreters think that there was enough indication in the Lucan way of telling the Naim story to say that Luke wants us to see the image of Elijah hovering behind that of Jesus and helping, in its own way, to make the identity of Jesus ever clearer. The people of Naim, like the woman in the Elijah story, confess Jesus to be a prophet, one who speaks for God. So great a figure had Elijah become by Jesus' day, however, that to think of him was to think of Israel's greatest prophetic figure: so great was he that he should be the one to return to prepare Israel to meet its God.

For Luke, so profound is the link between Jesus and God that what any Old Testament figure, Elijah included, contributes to clarifying this link is much appreciated. But no one Old Testament figure tells all there is to tell about Jesus; each figure has some traits which correspond to traits of Jesus, and thus are contact points in human experience which can help us appreciate just how full and intimate was Jesus' relationship with God.

Luke was not to be sold short, however, in his claim about Jesus. Jesus was not just another Elijah, was not limited to being Elijah returned. Just take the cases of the young men raised to life—one through Elijah, another through Jesus. It was clear that Elijah's prayer to God and his placing himself over the child was in marked contrast to Jesus' direct exercise of authority by word alone, without even a prayer to God: "Young man, I say to you 'Arise.'" Jesus has all the power and authority over death within himself; Elijah does not, and so must pray for it. And this kind of contrast makes all the difference!

Naim has much to say about its visitor, Jesus. One learns much about him here, both because of his sympathy for sufferers and his immense powers. Naim gives us an insight into the heart of the One who keeps calling for repentance; at times he will even step beyond unbelieving or disobedient hearts to console us with his power; and this action becomes another incentive to turn our hearts to love of him and live with him. In Zachary's song of joy on the occasion of the circumcision and naming of John, Luke had Zachary sing that God will visit his people who "sat in darkness and in the shadow of death" (see p. 107). At Naim, the people confirm that God has visited them: not death's shadow but death itself was made to yield to Jesus' word of life. May Jesus shine, too, in our darkness and sweep us from the shadow and touch of death. From his love can come only life for us.

Mount Tabor

"THIS IS MY SON; LISTEN TO HIM."
~ MARK 9:7

Rising from the Plain of Esdraelon south of the Galilean Hills to a height of eighteen-hundred feet is the majestic and most beautiful of Palestine's mountains, Mount Tabor. Since the top of Mount Tabor is the traditional site of the transfiguration of Jesus, we must go up the mountain, using the only means available now: a winding road with its many hairpin turns, built in 1954.

At the top of the mountain we meet an esplanade some 3,900 feet long and 1,300 feet wide, surrounded by the ruins of the fortress wall built about 700 years ago by Islamic forces in Palestine. We enter through this wall by what is known as the Wind Gate. The ruins remind us of the many battles fought here to gain possession of this holy site, battles between Christians and Moslems, particularly during the crusades when the Christians tried to recapture what Moslem armies had taken from the monks. Today the Greek Orthodox own the property on the left or north side of the road, the Roman Catholics, that on the right or south side of the road. Near the basilica we can see today a large monastery and a house for pilgrims; a tower built in 1955 after the fashion of a medieval tower is also nearby.

The beautiful Basilica of the Transfiguration was built between 1921 and 1924. The style chosen for the basilica is called Roman-Syrian, a style of the greatest splendor in the fifth and sixth centuries. As we enter, we can see two chapels—on the right, one dedicated to Elijah, and on the left, one dedicated to Moses. These two chapels are quite a bit older than the basilica; indeed, it was the intention of the architect of the basilica so to construct the entryway of the basilica as to unite the two old chapels with the new basilica.

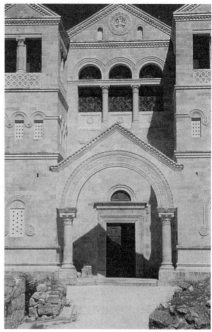

The basilica is divided into two levels. The lower level is marked by the splendid window of the peacock, the bird which is a traditional symbol or sign of the resurrection from the dead. Indeed, the peacock window marks the site of the ancient Byzantine church which stood here many, many centuries ago to celebrate the transfiguration of Jesus.

Mount Tabor: Church of the Transfiguration today

With a guide we can go further under the level of the peacock window to see ancient walls and a very old altar brought to light by excavations of this century. On this lower level there are mosaics of four "transfigurations" in the sense of revelations of Jesus: the Nativity, the Eucharist, the Passion, and the Resurrection.

The upper level contains a mosaic celebrating the wondrous transfiguration of Jesus, for which this entire basilica was built. There are also striking side chapels commemorating St. Francis of Assisi and the Blessed Sacrament. The alabaster windows of the basilica enhance the sense of mystery and glory that is associated with the transfiguration of Jesus.

Transfiguration
~ MATTHEW 17:1–9; MARK 9:2–10; LUKE 9:28–36 ~

Matthew, Mark, and Luke speak of a wondrous change in Jesus' appearance on a mountain. This mountain has long been identified in tradition as Mount Tabor. The change in appearance included a whiteness of garments and generally a gloriousness of Jesus' features which can only be likened to what divinity of Jesus must look like if it were to break through the humanity which hides it, or to the projected glory of the Son of God in his coming at the Last Day.

While Jesus' face "glowed like the sun," as Matthew says, Moses and Elijah appeared on either side of him; Luke says they conversed with Jesus about Jesus' departure or "exodus" from this earth. All scholars understand Moses and Elijah to stand for, to symbolize two great traditions which make up Judaism and prepare for the coming of Jesus: Moses represents the law, Elijah represents the prophets—and each has much to say in foretelling the coming of Jesus and the particular twist his life took at its end. Thus, the two traditions of Israel spoke with Jesus—seen for a moment in his glory—and discussed with him how these traditions prefigure the way in which he would pass his last days and enter heaven.

To Peter and his friends James and John, this meeting of Jesus with Moses and Elijah was awe-inspiring; the natural response of these three was fear and reverence. In keeping with his impulsive nature, Peter suggested a way to honor these three persons, a way which would keep them and this experience forever. But before Peter's words lost their force, he and his friends were covered by a cloud, out of which came the voice of God. This voice aimed to impress on Peter, James, and John the unity between God and Jesus: "This is My Son," the voice began and then went further, asking that Peter, James, and John "listen to him." With these words, the cloud passes and the three disciples find they are alone with Jesus, the Jesus of their normal and human acquaintance.

This event has two parts. First, God made visible, if only for a brief moment, the reality of Jesus' true gloriousness, which is revealed for the sake of the disciples, surely. Second, God pointed out once more, that Jesus is his Son; surely, this too was for the disciples' benefit. But God added here that, because of this relationship between him and Jesus, the disciples were to listen closely to Jesus, to obey him and believe him. To this call to listening were added the witnesses of Moses and Elijah; their presence, too, tried to tell the disciples something about what is for their good. But what was that something they tried to tell the disciples?

When we look to see where literally the Transfiguration takes place in the sequence given us in the three synoptic gospels, we cannot fail to note that the Transfiguration follows the startling words of Jesus that he would soon die in Jerusalem. Within the larger frame of stories, the transfiguration is one of the very few bright spots including miracles, to occur in the gospel structure, especially once Jesus turns his attention to the imminent pain and grief which await him in the Holy City, Jerusalem. Given this distinctive placement of the transfiguration right after the prophecy of death in Jerusalem, scholars come to the conclusion that the Transfiguration of Jesus is a way of revealing to the disciples the reality of Jesus which they will have to trust in mightily when he will soon be utterly without a trace of gloriousness. In short, the Transfiguration is meant as an encouragement in anticipation of a time when the disciples would have to call on any kind of strength or encouragement they could find to keep their sanity and wits at the crucifixion. Added to this touch of momentary glory is the voice of God and the witnesses of Moses and Elijah, that what Jesus foretold about himself must be believed and not rejected; the very Scriptures of Israel themselves had prophesied for centuries the fate of the One sent by God to bring Israel back to him. Indeed, though one would have preferred that Jesus not die and one is confused about why he had to die, the realization of the nature of his true gloriousness is a help, for we know from it the true identity of the person who is crucified, and we know further that God was on his side as his Father, and we are reminded that what is happening at the cross is nothing more nor less than what the Old Testament had foretold would happen to him. There is a large measure of consolation and encouragement in the words of God and in the revelation of the true divinity of Jesus, and in the fact that all that happened to Jesus was already long ago planned and foretold.

Connected with the prophecies of Jesus about his own fate at the hands of the Jerusalem authorities are Jesus' words about those times when being a Christian requires cross-carrying. Someday, Jesus says, his disciples will have to stand like Jesus before kings and magistrates; they will be asked to profess belief in Jesus at the cost of their lives. To these, too, Jesus offers the vision of himself glorified, in the hope that their brief glimpse of the Lord Transfigured, a glimpse into the reality which reveals his power and majesty, will encourage his disciples to profess their faith in him courageously. Similarly, Christians will be asked, if not for their lives, at least for death to their sinful selves—in itself a martyrdom, even if undertaken by one's own self. Here, too, in this form of death for Jesus, we are encouraged to think of the gloriousness of the Lord we serve and obey, to think deeply on the trustworthiness of the one who asks us to put our lesser, evil selves to death so that the greater, truer, better selves might live. It is to bring about life for our better selves, after all, that the Son of God became man and asked for our trusting obedience to his will.

Here, then, on Mount Tabor, we relive that experience of Peter, James, and John; in this reliving we hope to grow in trust that, despite the pain, the ignominy, and apparently absurd death we are asked to undergo out of obedience to Jesus, it is the divine Lord who wants what is best for us, what is life-giving for us: his words are truly the words of life itself.

Faith and Miracles
~ MATTHEW 17:14–20; MARK 9:13–28; LUKE 9:37–43 ~

When Jesus and his three disciples left the top of the mountain and gained the plain below it, they ran into an argument and an angry mob. A man had asked the disciples who did not accompany Jesus to the top of Mount Tabor, to cure his possessed son, but they were unable to effect the cure. And so Jesus was met with the consternation of this group of frustrated people and asked to do the curing. Jesus performed the cure, an exorcism, but not without again challenging everyone to faith, the kind of faith that would produce a miracle, with or without his presence.

Clearly, this story is pitched in the Gospels to the audiences among whom Jesus no longer walked. They must trust and show their unwavering faith in order that God work a miracle among them. Moreover, exorcisms can be worked at times only by those who persevere in prayer before God, and persevering prayer is a possibility only for the person who has strong faith.

Caesarea by the Sea

When the Roman general Pompey came into the area of the world we know today as Lebanon, Syria, and Palestine, he quickly took control of a small village on the shore of the Mediterranean Sea. This village was called Strato's Tower, because of a tower which rose over the town as both a watchtower and a beacon for sea travelers. After Pompey and his successor Julius Caesar died, Mark Antony gave the town to Cleopatra, who in turn lost it back to another Caesar, Augustus Octavian, after he defeated her and Mark Antony in 31 B.C. at the famous battle of Actium. In 30 B.C. Caesar Augustus gave the town to Herod the Great, who had been ruling this entire area of Palestine since 37 B.C.

Herod always had an inclination toward and great talent for building, and he turned his hand to make the small village of Strato's Tower into a magnificent port city, the best on the Palestinian coast. In honor of Caesar Augustus Octavian, Herod named the newly developed city Caesarea. To distinguish this Caesarea from the inland Caesarea Philippi, we call this city Caesarea by the Sea, in Latin *Caesarea maritima*.

It is easily understandable that Jerusalem, the religious center of Israel, held many Jews who were quite hostile to every exercise of pagan influence there, even though we see from archeological remains the impression pagans made on life in Jerusalem. The further one went northward from Jerusalem, the more likely one was to meet a blending between Jews and Gentiles. Thus whereas Jerusalem and its enivrons were devoted so energetically to creating a society dedicated to God of Israel and his law and worship, an area like Galilee produced faithful Israelites living very close to Gentiles. Given this situation, the Romans realized that it was best for them to live as a group away from Jerusalem and in an area which had grown more tolerant of Gentiles, in a city in which there were no strong traditional ties to ancient Judaism. So the Romans took advantage of Herod's newly built Caesarea and settled the administrators of Palestine and almost all of their army there. Thus, the normal living quarters of Pontius Pilate and other procurators was Caesarea; only at the great Jewish Festivals—Passover, Pentecost, Tabernacles—did the procurator and his legions come to Jerusalem. These legions then reinforced a small band of troops always billeted in the Holy City, in the Fortress Antonia located at the northwest corner of the Jerusalem Temple platform; the Romans thought it necessary to increase the number of military in Jerusalem at festival times, since the huge number of Jews coming to participate in religious rites could easily catch fire with the desire for freedom from Rome.

Caesarea by the Sea: a precious memento of Pontius Pilate

A Precious Memento of Pontius Pilate

Today we can only imagine from its ruins what was Caesarea's beauty and grandeur. One usually begins a visit to Caesarea by entering through walls which remind us of a castle surrounded by its moat. These walls were built by crusaders, who found a very dilapidated Caesarea dating from the times of the seventh-century A.D. Islamic invasions. Rather near this entry through the crusader walls was a replica of a stone discovered here with the name of Pilate inscribed on it, a clear indication that Pontius Pilate, governor of Judaea and Samaria on behalf of Rome from 26 to 36 A.D., resided here. The stone is unique, for it is the only record, outside of written documents, bearing Pilate's name.

Four areas of sites are important remains of Caesarea today. Within the crusader walls are the remains of the center of ancient Caesarea—they go right down and into the Mediterranean Sea. To the south of the city center is a still well-preserved theater; indeed it is used today for outdoor concerts. To the north of the city center is a famous Roman aqueduct, and to the east of it are the few reminders of a hippodrome or racetrack.

Caesarea remained the capital of Roman government in Israel until the Moslems overran it in the seventh century. At Caesarea, Eusebius of Caeserea wrote his famous history of the Church about 300; earlier the famous biblical interpreter Origen had set up his school of interpretation in Caesarea (231–233). But more important for our purposes are two significant biblical events which occurred in Caesarea by the Sea: the conversion of Cornelius and the defense of Paul before he was sent to trial in Rome.

The Conversion of Cornelius
~ ACTS 10:1–11:18 ~

The Acts of the Apostles is twenty-eight chapters long; its stories stretch from Jerusalem to Rome, from 30 to 63 A.D. Why is it that almost two chapters (7 percent) of this book are taken up with the story of the conversion of Cornelius, a gentile soldier stationed in Caesarea?

In reading chapter 10 of Acts, one is impressed with St. Luke's storytelling: two people—Peter and Cornelius, a Jew and a Gentile—are brought together by a series of powerful divine interventions, until Peter, finally understanding all that has happened, baptizes Cornelius. What is at stake here?

Cornelius, a pious Gentile who followed Jewish ways (worshipping the true God, fasting, giving alms, praying), is instructed simply to "invite Peter"; Cornelius, puzzled, follows the divine order. Peter, at prayer, is instructed that, though Moses said that eating certain animals would make a person unacceptable to God, God declares "all food clean"; Peter remains simply unclear about the full meaning of this new teaching.

Under the direction of the Spirit of God Peter meets Cornelius and realizes that God's new teaching was not only that "all foods are clean," but that all human beings are clean, acceptable in God's sight. For many historical and religious reasons, Jews had thought Gentiles to be unclean, to be people who would be a threat to Jewish faith; even if Gentiles practiced the Jewish religion, as did Cornelius, the Gentiles were still not to be associated with intimately, for their not being children of Abraham and of the Covenant was always considered a danger for pious Jews: even well-meaning Gentiles could lead Jews astray, and so a Jew should avoid close association with Gentiles, even pious ones.

Then God changes Peter's understanding of reality: God recognizes no distinction any more between the clean Jew and the unclean Gentile, and so Peter should not either. Peter performs an important act: he enters the house of Cornelius, an act which pious Jews should not do, for it showed precisely that sympathy for Gentiles which could well cause a Jew's religious destruction.

But not only is an old division between Jew and Gentile struck down; Peter is further led to speak the words of salvation to Cornelius the Gentile. In his speaking these words Peter says to Cornelius that he, Peter, now understands that anyone who reverences the true God and acts justly (like Cornelius) is pleasing to God; this is a step in understanding which goes beyond what Peter learned at the start of this story. At first, Peter came to understand that all persons on the earth are clean. Then he realizes that, among all clean human beings, those who reverence the true God and act justly are pleasing to God; it is no surprise now to Peter that God should want the words of salvation to be addressed to this reverent and pious Gentile.

Finally, as Peter reaches his final observations about Jesus, the Savior, Cornelius and his household begin to speak in tongues. This speaking in tongues can only be a gift from the Spirit of God, and it is a sign to Peter that Cornelius and his household have become believers in Jesus the Christ. Indeed, as Peter observes, how can Peter refuse the waters of Christian baptism to people who have been given the same gift which Peter and his friends received at Pentecost?

When, with chapter 11, Peter retells his Cornelius experience, he ends with the same kind of question: what else could Peter do but baptize people who believe, as do the disciples, in the Lord Jesus? God clearly had taken a powerful hand in bringing Cornelius to baptism; so no human being could mistake God's will in this or be an obstacle to God.

Peter had started out at the beginning of chapter 10 with a certain belief about who was clean (Jew) and who was unclean (Gentile), but he was corrected; then he gained a certain understanding of who was acceptable to God (one who reverenced him and acted justly); Peter finally realized that God wanted any Gentile who believed the preaching about Jesus to be baptized, just as he and his friends were. In this way, the original members of the Church, all Jewish, realized that God was calling the Gentiles into God's People and giving them the grace to believe in Jesus; in this way, Luke teaches that the baptizing of Gentiles was not something Peter and his Jewish friends planned, but was something which the early Church had to learn. This story is, in its own way, as much a story of conversion of Cornelius to Jesus as it is a story of Peter's conversion to the will of God for Gentile membership in the Church. It is clear from the rest of Acts that some Jewish Christians never did understand what Peter understood to be God's will; it is to insist on the rightness of Peter's new way that Luke spends so much time in Acts on the Cornelius story.

With chapter 11 Peter offered a defense or explanation to his community in Jerusalem for baptizing Cornelius, entering his house, and eating with him. Chapter 15 is another case in which complaints within the Christian world called leaders to solve problems to the satisfaction of the Church. The problem of chapter 15 of Acts is different from the problem Cornelius represents, i.e., what legitimated baptizing Gentiles and eating with them in their houses. In chapter 15 the problem was whether or not the Gentile (who had been baptized and dined with) needed also to be circumcised and made to keep the entire Mosaic Law, as Jews had been since ancient times.

The solution of this problem of circumcision and obedience to all the Mosaic Law involved three points. First, Paul and Barnabas baptized many Gentiles in chapters 13 and 14, in accord with God's will, and circumcised none of them. Second, James interpreted Sacred Old Testament Scripture to show that Gentiles need not be circumcised and made to obey the Mosaic Law in full. Third, Peter tells again, briefly, his experience with Cornelius: all he, Peter, could conclude from that experience was that faith in Jesus was the one thing required for salvation, that faith in Jesus cleanses from sin and makes one a child of God. God demanded no circumcision from Cornelius, only faith. Only acceptance of Jesus as one's Lord and teacher is required for salvation; all else, circumcision and carrying out all the Laws of Moses, is secondary for the Gentile and it is wrong to teach that these things are necessary.

One recognizes how important the lessons and decisions of chapters 10, 11, and 15 of Acts are in the history of the Christian Church. The story of Cornelius of Caesarea is of eternal and monumental significance for the Christian Church.

Paul's Defense in Caesarea
~ ACTS 23:23–26:32 ~

The Acts of the Apostles, chapter 21, tells us that St. Paul arrived in Jerusalem from his far-flung mission journey, only to learn that many Jewish Christians were upset with him. These Jewish Christians of Jerusalem had heard stories that Paul was not requiring Gentiles to be circumcised, to keep all the Mosaic Law, and to worship in the Temple at Jerusalem. Paul tried to correct the excesses of these stories by a pious visit to the Jerusalem Temple. There, however, he was surrounded by angry Jews who claimed (erroneously) that he was bringing a Gentile friend into areas of the Temple compound where Gentiles were forbidden to go. Roman soldiers, ever watchful from their barracks overlooking the Temple platform, intervened before the crowd could kill Paul for this

Caesarea by the Sea: Roman aqueduct

supposed sacrilege; from this moment, in chapter 21, until the end of Acts, Paul is a prisoner of Rome.

It became clear to Paul and others that he could get no fair trial in Jerusalem; the Romans were willing to take him away from Jerusalem under guard to Caesarea by the Sea and bring him to trial there, where the Roman Procurator usually resided. The Roman Procurator at this time (52–60) was Antonius Felix (Pontius Pilate had finished his rule in 36). While having saved Paul from the Jewish authorities in Jerusalem, Felix really meant Paul little good; he kept Paul in jail in hopes of a bribe from whatever source for two years, i.e., until he was replaced by another appointed Procurator, this one called Porcius Festus.

Festus, in his first days in office, noted among his prisoners that Paul had been jailed now for two years. Festus decided to win over his new friends and colleagues in Jerusalem by sending Paul back there for trial, but Paul refused to go and grasped at the one straw left him: since Paul was a Roman citizen, he had the right to ask for a trial before Caesar in Rome, and Paul now demanded that right. Festus could do nothing but agree to send Paul to Rome . . . but he had to have some clear charge against Paul, otherwise Festus would look like a fool for having sent Paul to Caesar without a sufficient reason.

So Festus set a date for Paul's trial, and picked a time when Festus had useful visitors, King Herod Agrippa II and his sister Bernice. This Agrippa, a great-grandson of Herod the Great, and ruler of certain territories on the northwest edge of Palestine, was particularly knowledgeable about things Jewish, and Festus thought that, since the whole matter of Jews against Paul was only a fight about the Jewish religion, Agrippa would be able to help Festus draw up a charge against Paul for the Emperor in Rome.

Paul's great speech before Festus and Agrippa II has three parts to it. First, Paul shows how his life was a model of Jewish devotion before his conversion to Christianity; indeed, left to himself Paul would have obliterated Christianity in the name of the Jewish tradition. One should conclude from this point that, if Paul did change his mind towards Christ, it was a choice forced on him by Someone Else. Second, Paul speaks of that holy moment on the road to Damascus, while he was on his way to arresting Jews who had become Christians. In this holy moment Paul was blinded by an immense light and was addressed by the Lord: why do you persecute Me? Chapter 9 was the first time that we heard this story about Paul meeting the Lord on the way to Damascus; there it was a part of the narrative of Luke. In chapter 22 we again heard this conversion story, but this time it is more than a narrative; it is part of a speech insisting that, if Paul associated with Gentiles in the Mediterranean Basin, it was God, not Paul, who chose this way of life for him. Now, for a third time, we hear again, but with profound imagery, what Jesus wanted from Paul on the road to Damascus.

Chapter 9 had told us readers that "he is the instrument I have chosen to bring my name to the Gentiles and their kings and to the people of Israel. I myself shall indicate to him how much he will have to suffer for my name." In chapter 22, we are told that "the God of our fathers long ago designated you to know his will, to look upon the Just One, and to hear the sound of his voice; before all people you are to be his witness to what you have seen and heard . . . be on your way; I mean to send you far from here, among the Gentiles." But in chapter 26 we read the most majestic and sweeping language: "I have delivered you . . . to open the eyes of those to whom I am sending you, to turn them from darkness to light and from the dominion of Satan to God; that through their faith in me they may obtain forgiveness of their sins and a portion among God's people."

The third and final part of Paul's speech here in Caesarea draws the conclusions from his meeting with the Lord: what could he do but obey the will of God; indeed, all he has done over these past years of missionary work is ask people to repent and to perform deeds befitting repentance—where is the harm in that? All he has done, in fact, is say just what the prophets and Moses had said: that the Messiah, raised from the dead, would proclaim light to Jews and Gentiles alike.

Luke, in a short space, has presented as strong a defense of Paul as he could; in fact, Luke's three descriptions of Paul's conversion show how protective Luke was of Paul and his reputation, and how convinced Luke was of Paul's great contribution to the spread of God's offer of salvation to all nations.

Chapter 26 describes the reaction of Festus and Agrippa II to Paul's speech; there really is no fault to be found with Paul and, if he had not earlier said he wanted to appear before Caesar, Festus should let him go free. Throughout Acts, it is clear that Rome found nothing harmful to the world in Christianity, as it had found nothing harmful to Israel in Jesus.

Chapter 26 is the last witness to this innocence; yet Paul will set sail shortly after his trial for Rome. But whatever the situation, joyful welcome or hateful opposition, the word of God must, and will, reach all people; God's love makes sure of that.

Sychar
(Jacob's Well in Samaria)

"WHOEVER DRINKS THE WATER I WILL GIVE
WILL NEVER BE THIRSTY AGAIN."
~ JOHN 4:14

Travellers today between Galilee and Judea often stop at a site called Jacob's Well, so called because it was thought that the well here was dug by Jacob, son of Isaac and grandson of Abraham. To reach this well, travellers pass through a gate and a lovely garden into a church, in the midst of which is the venerable well. Much of the church is modern, dating from the early part of the 1900s, and, in parts, from after World War I. The ancient water source beneath the church surely goes back to the time of Jacob. The present well is about one hundred feet deep, as we can sense from the time it takes a dropped object to hit the water. The water is fresh and good for drinking, thus precious and preferred; it is what is called living water, i.e., water which flows freely from the deep recesses of the earth and is distinguished from water gathered from rainfalls into cisterns which becomes brackish and stale after standing a long time.

In St. Jerome's time, about 404 A.D., there was already a church here, and before the church the site had been occupied by a baptistry. In Jesus' time a town called Sychar was near this freshwater well. One day about noon, Jesus stopped here to rest from the heat, and sent his disciples into the village for food. Alone and resting, Jesus sees a woman coming to draw water from the well; as she begins to draw water, Jesus asks her for a drink. This is the beginning of the famous encounter of Jesus and the Samaritan woman at the well, told in John 4.

The Samaritan People

It is clear that the Samaritan woman is not Jewish; no Samaritan is. How is it then that Samaritans live in the center of Palestine? The Old Testament tells us that the Sons of Jacob came into possession of the Promised Land under the leadership of Joshua, lieutenant of Moses. The Jewish People then occupied the land for centuries, down through the times of King Saul, King David, King Solomon. At the death of Solomon, the kingdom of Israel was divided into two uneven halves; the larger northern kingdom built its own capital and called it Samaria, while the southern kingdom kept its capital in old Jerusalem. In 722 B.C. the Assyrians, who were the great power at the time in the mid-east, conquered the Jewish northern kingdom. In accord with their harshness and shrewdness, the Assyrians sent elsewhere the Jews they had just conquered in the northern kingdom, and brought in here to live foreigners who were not Jewish and knew not the God of Israel. The Assyrians also extended the name of the city, Samaria, to the whole upper half of Palestine; Palestine was now divided into Samaria (north half) and Judah (south half, with Jerusalem as capital). It is from these imported peoples, pagans, that the woman at the well, and all Samaritans of Jesus' time, were believed to descend.

(The Samaritan people themselves today tell a different story. They, only 600 now in the world, of which there are 300 in Israel, are descendants of Jews who had remained faithful to Moses' teaching, even when all other Jews turned against the true God. To today's Samaritans, they are the faithful children of Abraham, and all other Jews are sinners.)

The southern kingdom of Judah went into its own exile in 587 B.C. When Cyrus the Persian in 538 B.C. allowed the southern Jews to return to Jerusalem and its surrounding land, the Samaritans tried to block the eventual effort at building Jerusalem's walls; this was an obvious attempt to keep Jerusalem, only recently destroyed and struggling to rebuild, from becoming a power again.

Once the Jews of the south began to settle more surely in Jerusalem, they rebuilt their Temple, dedicated in 515 B.C. Sporadic disagreements continued between Jerusalem and its neighbors to the north; Samaria, the capital of the north, was only 40 miles from Jerusalem. Fighting often broke out, culminating in the destruction of the Samaritan

Temple on Mount Gerizim about 100 years before Jesus' birth. History can recount the reasons for the unhealed scars of Samaritans and Jews; on any given day, in Jesus's time, one could sense the bitter antagonism between these two groups, even though Samaria was now no longer the upper half of Palestine, but just the middle third of Palestine (Galilee being the top third, Judea being the bottom third). Ironically, it was not Pilate's bloody treatment of Jesus that got him removed from his procuratorship over Samaria and Judea, but his bloody massacre of Samaritans (36 A.D.), years after his killing Jesus.

If we grasp the hatred that existed betweeen Jew and Samaritan, we have the essential key to understanding the extravagant teaching of Jesus about the Good Samaritan who cared for a Jew so thoroughly and at cost to himself, when a Jewish priest and a Jewish levite had preferred to leave the half-dead Jew to his grim fate (Luke 10:29–37). And we can better understand the astonishment found in the story of the ten lepers, cured of their leprosy; it was only one of them who returned to thank Jesus for the cure—and he was a Samaritan (Luke 17:11–19).

Jesus and the Woman at the Well
~ JOHN 4:4–24 ~

John the Gospel writer uses a dialogue format here. It is through a dialogue that the evangelist means to bring out the deepest meanings of Jesus of Nazareth. He also uses symbolism and subtle references to achieve his goal.

We remember how Jesus started off this dialogue: he asked for a drink of water from this woman. She immediately underlines how shocking it is that Jesus, a Jew, speak to her, a Samaritan; we can add that the shock is the greater since this pious person speaks to someone he, and everyone for miles around, knew to be a flagrant sinner, by Jewish and by Samaritan standards. Jesus immediately turns the discussion to symbolism: if she had asked Jesus for water, he would have given her living water. Of course, the woman understood Jesus to refer to fresh, spring water, the water of this well, for instance. But we know that Jesus was speaking of something else: if water is necessary for life, it is Jesus who can give the water that will make one live forever—by this he meant that he could give the woman the Holy Spirit of God, who is the source of life for all of us.

After this lesson about the identity of Jesus, the Gospel writer moves to another aspect. Jesus shows he has special knowledge which a stranger would not have: he knows that the woman has had five husbands, and that her present mate is no sixth. The woman, rightly, calls Jesus a prophet for having this knowledge.

Next, the woman is brought to think of Jesus as Messiah, when he speaks of a worship of God which will no longer be in Samaria (on Mount Gerizim) nor in Judaea (on Mount Zion, i.e., Jerusalem), but will be wherever are gathered those who profess the true God, who profess that Jesus is his Son, who are baptized with the Holy Spirit of God. Indeed, true and perfect worship of God would one day be led by the Messiah, everyone believed. If Jesus knows this much, might he be the Messiah to come? Jesus says, "I who speak to you am He."

Giver of the Spirit of God, prophet, Messiah—these titles begin to settle upon Jesus by virtue of Jesus' dialogue with the Samaritan woman. But scholars point to a further revelation about Jesus. When God was asked by Moses at the burning bush, "what name should I say is the name of the One who sends me to free Israel from Egypt?" God answers, "Say that my name is 'I am who am' or, for short, 'I am.'" Now, when Jesus answers the woman, "I, who speak to you, am he," scholars remind us that, "I am he" in Greek is written *(ego eimi)* so that one can read the words to say "I am he" or simply "I am." Because the evangelist uses these two words of Jesus elsewhere (e.g., John 8, 24 and 8, 58), scholars think we should read them here here: Jesus is saying that his name is "I am." As the first lines of the Gospel already said: In the beginning the word was God and the word became flesh; we call this word-made-flesh "Jesus" and he calls himself by God's own proper and personal name, "I am."

Jesus had said enough about himself to move the Samaritan woman to go into the village of Sychar to spread the news that a prophet, quite possibly the Messiah, was at the well. The townspeople believed her witness enough to come out to study the stranger, then to invite him to stay with them. Jesus acceded to their wishes and remained with them two days. The Gospel writer notes particularly that the townspeople told the woman that they needed her witness about Jesus no more; they could testify on their own, from their own experience, how great Jesus was. Thus, we are encouraged to move beyond what others tell us about Jesus to know him from our own experiences of him.

The notable visit of Jesus to a Samaritan town is something not really spoken of in other Gospels; rather they insist that Jesus concentrated on the towns of Israel. I am sure Jesus did spend most of his time with his own people, but from earliest church times (e.g., Philip in Acts 8) we read that Samaria was open to receiving Christian missionaries; in part, this was due no doubt to Jesus having first visited there and made a great impression on the people.

When the woman had gone into the village to tell the Samaritans there about this striking stranger at the well, Jesus' disciples return with the food Jesus had sent them into the village to find. They were astonished that Jesus had been speaking to a Samaritan woman—but then Jesus' sense of charity broke many barriers others had, even for religious reasons, erected; indeed, no human barrier has kept him from loving each one of us. They bring Jesus food, which becomes an opportunity for Jesus to express to his friends the deeper hunger he has—a hunger for all peoples to know and love his Father, to know he is in the Father and the Father is in him. So ripe was the harvest, so ready are people to accept true preaching about the real God, the God who alone can give them eternal life—if only, Jesus cries, there were people to bring the saving words of God to those ripe for such harvesting!

Other Samaritan Sites

Such then were the revealing events associated with the well traditionally noted as the well dug by the Patriarch Jacob when he pitched his tents with his family outside the town that existed then, Shechem. When Jacob's children returned from Egypt to the Promised Land, they brought with them the remains of Joseph, one of Jacob's sons, and buried them at Shechem; this was the Joseph who was so likened to Jesus: Joseph was betrayed by his brothers and made a slave, only to become the savior of his brothers and all Israel.

Eventually, the ninth-century B.C. town of Samaria succeeded Shechem as the most important city in the north of Palestine. One can still explore, near the Well of Jacob, the remains of ancient Samaria, where such famous people as Ahab and Jezebel lived and died, where the great prophets Elijah and Elisha performed their prophetic duties. Not far from ancient Samaria and Jacob's Well is the famous mountain, Gerizim, on which the Samaritans built their own altar to Yahweh. Too, it was on Gerizim that six tribes of Israel stood, and another six on the Mount Ebal opposite Gerizim, to sing the blessings and curses that belonged to the covenant of devotion and trust Yahweh and Israel made to each other upon Israel's entry into the Promised Land.

In time, the ancient town of Samaria, destroyed in the invasion of the Northern Kingdom of Israel by the Assyrians in 722 B.C., was resurrected from the dust and, much later, gloriously renovated by Herod the Great and given a new name, Sebaste, which is the Greek equivalent of Augustus; in this way, the ancient city was newly dedicated to the famous Roman emperor and protector of Herod the Great: Caesar Augustus, who ruled the Roman world, and Palestine, 31 B.C. to 14 A.D..

Finally, as noted earlier, this district of Samaria was preached to by Philip, a Jew become Christian who is mentioned in Acts 6. The church leaders, Peter and John, visited these Samaritan converts and showed their approval of this first effort to preach Jesus outside Jerusalem, and to a foreign people. Indeed, if it was Philip who did the preaching and baptizing, it was Peter and John who performed the rite of Confirmation upon the fledgling Samaritan church. A negative note was struck at this ceremonial moment, when a certain Simon, a Christian noted for his magic, wanted to buy from Peter and John the power to give the Spirit of God that comes at Confirmation. Peter harshly rejected any suggestion that the divine gifts can be sold and bought. From this experience comes the term Simony, the evil attempt to buy divine powers.

For many reasons, then, the area here at and near the Well of Jacob is famous, offering us much food for thought, especially about the Son of God, Jesus who gives the "living water," the Holy Spirit of God.

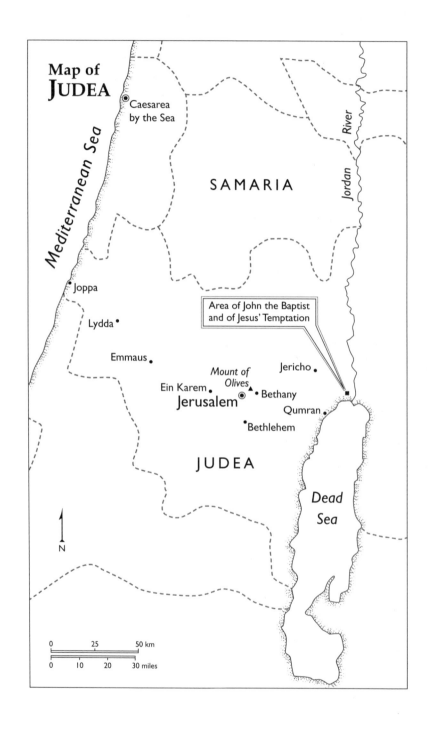

Map of
JUDEA

Caesarea
by the Sea

Mediterranean Sea

SAMARIA

Jordan River

• Joppa

Lydda •

Area of John the Baptist
and of Jesus' Temptation

Emmaus •

Mount of Olives

Jericho •

Ein Karem •

• Bethany

Jerusalem

Qumran •

• Bethlehem

JUDEA

Dead Sea

↑
N

0   25   50 km

0   10   20   30 miles

PART TWO

Judea

Ein Karem

"OF ALL WOMEN
YOU ARE THE MOST BLESSED."
~ LUKE 1:42

About four miles west of Jerusalem is the little town of Ein Karem. Ein Karem is famous because, according to tradition, here lived Elizabeth and Zachary, and their child John, someday to be called the Baptist, and here Mary visited Elizabeth. Here we find two church buildings associated with the events of Christian tradition: the Church of St. John the Baptist in the town and the Church of the Visitation on the outskirts of the town. The usual route from one church to the other takes the

Ein Karem: a view of the city

traveler by a spring of water called, since the 1300s, the Fountain of the Vineyard, which is the meaning of the town's name, *Ein (= Fountain of) Karem (= the Vineyard)*. Both churches, though rather updated with paintings of great worth, trace their roots to traditions that John and his parents lived in the areas on which the churches were built.

Two major gospel episodes are associated with this small village. The first we shall consider is the meeting of Mary and Elizabeth, called the Visitation of Elizabeth by Mary; the second is the psalm spoken by Zachary, John's father, at the time of the circumcising and naming of his child John.

Visitation by Mary
~ LUKE 1:39–56 ~

In Nazareth, Mary was visited by an angel who, to support the message he was delivering to her from God, told Mary that her relative—no clearer relationship can be defined—Elizabeth was to have a child; indeed, the ages of Elizabeth and Zachary were against child-bearing, and Zachary at first doubted that they could have a child, but with the help and will of God they did produce a son, and Elizabeth, at the time Gabriel told Mary of this impending birth, was already in the sixth month of her pregnancy. Mary, responding with what she knows will be appreciated help in the last three months of pregnancy, hurries from Nazareth to reach the "hill country of Judah" about eighty miles south of Nazareth. The Bible does not identify the town Mary hastens to, but tradition says it was Ein Karem.

Elizabeth is inspired by the Holy Spirit to say and understand things she would not have understood without the Spirit's help. Elizabeth speaks of "the mother of my Lord"; also, she knows that Mary deserves to be called blessed, that Mary believes that what God told her will surely happen. How does Elizabeth know these things, except that the Spirit guides her? Perhaps the most astonishing moment occurs when John leaps in Elizabeth's womb in recognition of the Jesus in Mary's womb. Elizabeth is guided to speak as a prophet would, to interpret the sign and express the inspirations that God provides for her.

Mary responds to the title given her by Elizabeth: "Mother of my Lord." This response is in the form of a psalm or hymn often known by the first word in its Latin translation, the *Magnificat*, which means (my soul) *makes much of* or *glorifies* [God]. The psalm is divisible into three parts. First, Mary acknowledges that God's gift of Jesus to her will make her famous for all time: everyone will praise her who, without this child, would have lived and died unknown, lowly, like most human beings. Now, glory will be hers, a gift from God; and we should realize that in the world of Mary and Jesus, glory was considered a very precious possession, often more valuable than wealth or beauty—one can appreciate this attitude when one reads in the ancient literature how feared and despised was any humiliation, or loss of glory.

Second, Mary's reflection on what God has done for her personally turns into a remembrance that God has often, many times intervened and raised from lowliness, and indeed, humiliation, the poor of Israel, the suffering, the lowly, the downtrodden, the people so often oppressed by the uncaring powerful and rich. Thus, Mary sees that what has happened to her is rather typical of God: he is always aware of and caring for the lowly, and Mary's case, she realizes, is the most recent example of this awareness and caring for God's people. Third, this reflection about God's continuous eagerness to give dignity to the lowly, especially to those downtrodden by injustice, brings to mind the ancient fact that God had long ago promised Mary's forefathers, indeed Abraham himself, that he will intervene in his people's history, to defend his chosen ones.

In watching how the psalm develops from Mary's particular glorification to the promise that God will glorify all his people, one realizes that Mary knows her child is not for herself alone. In a sense, she is Israel, the people chosen by God, who are lowly and liable to be forgotten, but now destined, as in the past, to enjoy the blessing of God, this time through Jesus. Mary's psalm is a hymn of encouragement: the lowliness of Israel (indeed enslaved to Rome) should not discourage one from trusting that God will remain faithful to his agreement to protect Israel. Israel should always remember, should never forget the many times God has intervened on its behalf, for those past interventions are constant proofs that God will intervene again, for he is faithful to his word. Mary's pregnancy is the latest, indeed we believe the most glorious, of God's loving interventions, an expression of God's love rooted in his promise to Abraham: "I will be your God."

Thus the psalm Mary sings is, in the plan of Luke's infancy stories about Jesus, a powerful expression of conviction that Jesus is the flowering of promises traceable all the way back to Abraham; Jesus is the completion of all God's promises of safety, of salvation. Jesus intervenes and saves human beings forever, giving them unending glory rather than extinction in death. The Virgin Mary will herself be praised for all ages for being the mother of Jesus, and for accepting God's will that she be just this, but, as she herself indicates, praised even more will be the God who constantly shows his intense desire to glorify mankind, no matter what the odds. Jesus is God's fullest response to our lowliness, God's mighty savior.

Ein Karem: mosaic in the Franciscan church

Psalm of Zachary
~ LUKE 1:57–79 ~

Some three months after the meeting of Mary and Elizabeth, and eight days after the birth of his son, Zachary is asked to give the name for his child. He writes, for he has been dumb since he disbelieved Gabriel's message in the Jerusalem Temple, that the child should be called "John." A strange name, in that no one of Zachary's family has ever been called that. But, as the reader of Luke already knows, God wanted this child named John, probably to signal publicly what the name means: "God is kind, loving." Zachary now obeys the divine will. At this favorable moment, Zachary can speak again, and his first words are those of praise of God.

Zachary begins with a typical Jewish prayer style: "Blessed be God." The first word *blessed* was early translated into Latin by the word *benedictus;* hence, Zachary's prayer of praise, a psalm and also, as Luke indicates, a prophecy, has classically been called the *Benedictus.*

The first part of the *Benedictus,* about 55 percent of the hymn, has to do with praising God for the coming of Jesus, who is the answer to the promises and hopes of Israel. The second part of the hymn, from verse 76, begins with a direct address to the small child John, but this part also ends with reference to the greater event, the coming of Jesus.

In the first part of the hymn, Zachary is at pains to bless God for his raising up, in the house or lineage of David, a Saving Power. Zachary remembers how God had promised for centuries such a Power through so many prophets, a Power to free Israel from its enemies. Going a step further, Zachary recalls that this wonderful Saving Power fulfills the covenant God had made with Abraham, who lived even before the prophets. For God had promised Israel that its very purpose for being, to serve God devoutly and through all its days be holy in his sight, would be achieved because God would send a savior who would free Israel from all the enemies who would try to prevent Israel from fulfilling this great goal. Jesus, then, is the one to free Israel so that it can be what it was intended to be: a people living properly, perfectly according to God's will. Thus we learn why God created Israel, and thereby we learn why God created all of those who share in the existence of God's People. Bless God, Zachary insists, for freeing us so that we can be what we know we should be; it is by knowing God, praising him, and living in union with him that human beings can be their best selves. Bless God for Jesus, for he is the one person who can free us so that we can live as we were made to.

Zachary now turns to his child, and thinks of the role this child is to play in the great plan of God now unfolding. Although he is not the savior, John does have the role of a prophet who prepares God's People to meet the coming God and worship him properly. John's preparing of Israel consists in helping Israelites to repent, to free themselves from the state which keeps them from their true purpose in life: the worship of God. God would surely respond to this repentance, all were confident; God would forgive sins and reestablish the harmony with the repentant which is the beginning of living one's life as one should. Did not John, though not the savior, contribute in some way to the sense of one's being freed from one's enemy? Zachary identifies here forgiveness of sins as an experience of salvation, an experience of being set free from bondage so that one could be fully human, that is a worshiper who could worship fully, holily. In helping a person to experience this worship, John was a prelude to the one who would offer the complete salvation, Jesus.

Zachary concludes his praise of God with imagery which again indicates the immenseness of what God is about to do. Zachary returns to consider Jesus, but leaves behind the earlier imagery of a military or royal Power who overcomes enemies in favor of a much more subtle, but just as penetrating and rewarding symbol. Zachary sees mankind living in darkness and under the shadow of death. For ages, these two images—darkness and the shadow of death—have dominated the imaginations and lives of many societies and cultures, to depict in image what reason itself cannot fully express, but thoroughly fears about the human condition. The natural shrinking before darkness and the shadow of death shows these to be powerful images of the bondage in which human beings are caught and from which they cannot ever hope to extricate themselves. The surest way to corruption, to bitterness, and to total unhappiness is to be a fool, to be ignorant; the worst enemy to all human hope and joy is death. How much, then, can we appreciate the final appearance of the light, which removes all darkness, and all shadows (or nearness) of death, as it leads us along the sure path to peace, to unending life, a path forever denied us until Jesus came.

Both the *Magnificat* of Mary and the *Benedictus* of Zachary are filled with the language and thought patterns of the Old Testament, signaling to us that Jesus is the fulfillment for these Israelites of all that was promised and hoped for among their ancestors. Jesus fulfills these hopes and promises, and it is Luke's contention, particularly in these Infancy stories about Jesus and John, that the followers of Jesus are those who enjoy the fulfillment of these promises and hopes. Now the Savior is here; the longing for freedom to be what one knows one should be, the eagerness to have completed the promise of freedom so that one can be a complete human being—this is what Mary and Zachary sing about in Ein Karem in their glorious psalms in praise of God's merciful salvation.

The Jordan River

"THERE IS THE LAMB OF GOD WHO TAKES
AWAY THE SINS OF THE WORLD."
~ JOHN 1:29

John the Baptist
~ LUKE 3:1–20; JOHN 1:19–36 ~

We are not certain just where John performed his baptisms, but we cannot be far off in looking to an area along the west bank of the Jordan River and just north of the Dead Sea. John the Gospel writer said that John the Baptist was active in "Bethany on the far side of the Jordan" (Jn 1:28), but no one has ever discovered where this Bethany was. Somewhere in this desert area, people of Jerusalem and the nearby countryside were the first to listen to John and to repent as he asked. Soon many other people flocked in ever larger numbers to John from farther distances to respond to his plea that they change their lives.

As Luke recounts it, Zachary, John's father, had been told by an angel that John was to go before the Lord, to prepare a people for him. He would prepare them under the inspiration of the Holy Spirit because, as the angel said, the Holy Spirit would be with John from his very conception. In a real sense John could be likened to Elijah, who was the greatest of Israel's prophets. Elijah, in the middle of the ninth century B.C., stood alone in Israel to uphold and insist upon Israel's obligation to worship the one and only God, Yahweh. Some nine hundred years later, "another Elijah," John, would again call Israel to recognize the rights of Yahweh to Israel's obedience. But John added a new dimension to this

The Jordan River

call to repentance: Israel must realize that the Lord is "at hand, is very near." The ax, John says, is right at the root of the tree, not far away in some shed; thus, as close as is the tree to falling when the ax is at its root, so close is God and his kingdom. John thus underlined both the *need* to repent and the need to do it *now*: the Lord is coming! It would fall to Christian thinkers of the first century A.D. to labor to keep alive the truth that the kingdom of God is near, that the Lord is close, while time seems to pass on without the kingdom's appearance.

The Kingdom and Its Messengers

When speaking of John the Baptist, one is always reminded of a prophecy spoken by the prophet Malachi. This prophet sang God's words: "I will send my messenger before me to prepare my way." God is coming and his messenger goes before him. Malachi, in eager anticipation of the renewal of Israel after its destruction and humiliation by Babylon (587 B.C.), looked forward to the coming of Yahweh himself, who would introduce a new state of things called God's Kingdom. In this new state, God would be king, and the result would be justice and protection and security and happiness; indeed, if only God would, like a king, take absolute control of life, would not the effect in his kingdom be perfect happiness?

To prepare Israel for God's coming, for this new state of things, for this kingdom, prophets like Malachi foresaw various figures who would get Israel ready. One of these figures, for example, was "the angel of the covenant between God and Israel," and another was called "my messenger." One we are interested in is identified as Elijah, described as the one who would come "before my day, the great and terrifying day." (Here one should recall the unique fact that Elijah never died, but was taken up to heaven in the fiery chariot; why, Israel asked itself over the centuries, was Elijah kept alive, if not so that he might return once again to prepare God's people for him?)

The Israelites of Jesus' time longed to be under the rule of God, and not under the rule of Satan, or any human power like Rome. Their scholars had alerted them to the possibility that this divine kingdom would come soon. Israelites were in Jesus' time inclined to look for this kingdom, and many expected some human being who would be God's agent in establishing God's Kingdom. The prophecy of Malachi noted above, joined with many, many others, made the first-century Israelites particularly sensitive to anyone like John who claimed that the kingdom was near, that one should prepare oneself to enter worthily into this kingdom, that one should prepare oneself to go out to meet the Lord worthily. John, with his message to repent and with his baptism, was at this time a major figure who asked just this kind of preparation, for "the Lord was near." Indeed, as people tried to read the times, many thought Jesus, too, was this kind of prophet or preparer for God, for his message was essentially that everyone must repent and change one's moral life, "for God was coming." Not many saw Jesus as more than another John or Moses or Elijah; those who did, those whom we follow, learned that Jesus was the Messiah, that is, not only one who prepares for God, but the one who establishes the kingdom of God and rules over it. Thus, a prophet like Malachi promises that the kingdom is near and speaks of someone, like John, whom God will send to prepare the people to enter it. John the Baptist, in his turn, is the one who, like Elijah, prepares people both for entry into the kingdom and for a kindly reception of Jesus, who, beyond any prophet, is the Messiah, the Son of God, he who will present us with the longed-for kingdom of God.

The Message of John

What exactly did John preach? Certainly, as noted already, he called people to repentance, to change of life, and various sources in the New Testament attest to this. But what should one say is repentance? Let us take Luke's presentation as a good answer to this question. In Luke 3, John was interrupted in his speech by three groups of people, all asking what should we do if we repent? To the ordinary person, John answered simply, "If you have two tunics and your neighbor has none, share—and the same goes for food." To a second group, tax collectors, who had a just reputation for cheating and injustice, the answer is, "Exact no more than is your due." Finally, to a third group, the military police, who had a great deal of power in patrolling the Temple area, John said, "Do not intimidate people, do not extort, but be content with your salary." Though we cannot go beyond what the Scriptures allow us to guess at what else John might have said, we are struck with the fact that in each case given us what is appropriate to repentance, to change of life, is acts of justice and of charity. It is true that Luke's general tendency is to emphasize the justice and charity that John, and then Jesus, preached. But it is particularly striking that John here is cited as asking nothing but charity and fairness, if one really wants to prepare oneself to meet one's God.

One wonders where John learned to define "change of heart" in terms of justice and love and charity and fairness. Luke says of John that as a boy he left home to live in the desert. This must mean that he moved from Ein Karem to be brought up in one of the numerous religious communities that existed in the Dead Sea area and along the Jordan River. The now famous Qumran community just west of and almost parallel to the north end of the Dead Sea was a group that, while it differed with Jews of Jerusalem to the point of moving out to the desert, still studied avidly its Jewish Scriptures in the hope that it might understand well the will of God. We know from its documents that the Qumran community thought itself the last Jewish community before the coming of God, and that it expected at least one Messiah to bring into existence God's kingdom. These same documents, which cherish the Old Testament, knew very well the ancient cry of the prophets for justice and love, that one should love one's neighbor as oneself. From such a group young John may have learned what he eventually preached so effectively along the Jordan River.

But John's greatest contribution to the Christian tradition was not his seconding the powerful teaching of Jesus; it was rather his witness to the meaning of Jesus. John turned people's attention from himself to Jesus: John was only the best man, Jesus the groom; John must decrease, Jesus must increase; John considers himself to be less than a slave to Jesus, for John says that he is not worthy to even loosen the strap of Jesus' sandals—a task of a slave. John presented his whole mission as a preparation for the coming of Jesus, not simply as a preparation for the coming of God. John was not the Light, but only gave witness to the Light.

John and Jesus

To understand the New Testament's presentation of John, it helps to reformulate traditional thinking of John's time. John was not followed immediately by the coming of God's kingdom. Rather, John was followed immediately by Jesus, who, in turn, would bring about the kingdom of God. What eventually distinguished Jesus from John was the reality, slowly understood by the disciples of Jesus, that in certain ways Jesus himself was the kingdom of God and not just the preparer of that kingdom. For what characterizes the kingdom where God is king, if not perfect obedience and harmony with God and love of neighbor, if not the divine power for good and the truth? And is not all of this found in the most profound degree in Jesus? Indeed, the forgiveness of sins won by Jesus for all and his own entrance into the new age and his giving the Spirit of God—these, too, are signs that he not only calls us to prepare for God's coming, but that he already lives life with God in God's kingdom and has created some of the characteristics of that kingdom. Thus, Jesus was finally understood not just to talk about the kingdom, but to have entered it, and, indeed, to be the kingdom, at least as it might exist in one person and be a source for others of that happiness which was always thought to be a sign of the kingdom of God.

It is to the Gospel of John that we owe the information that some of Jesus' first disciples were disciples of John the Baptist. These religiously minded men soon found others who were, like them, looking for the fulfillment of the prophecies, who were looking for the Messiah. In a very concrete way, John did indeed go before Jesus and prepare his way, when he pointed to Jesus and said, "There goes the Lamb of God." When John's disciples took this hint, John lost disciples that day, but to what a greater person!

That there were still disciples of John as late as the 50s A.D. (as Acts witnesses), over 20 years after John's death, shows that not all John's followers became disciples of Jesus; indeed, no Gospel ever says that John himself became a follower of Jesus. But these facts support, rather than detract, from witness to Jesus. John's independence from Jesus, yet his preaching that "one is to come after me who is greater than I, the one who will baptize with the Holy Spirit, and not just with water, as I do," suggests an honesty that this most trusted and famous religious figure of Israel could be counted on as a truthful and uncompromised witness to the real presence of God's Messiah. Jesus counted John as one of the five primary witnesses to him, even if John never followed him (the other four are the Father, the deeds of Jesus, the Old Testament Scriptures, and Moses). Jesus' own confirmation of the ordinary Jew's esteem for John shows the integrity and value of John's person and of his witness.

Not only, then, as one who encourages us to prepare to meet God is John deservedly famous, but, even more so, as the one who lessens his own greatness to shed all light on the one who is the embodiment of all hopes, Jesus of Nazareth.

John and Herod Antipas
~ MATTHEW 14:3–12; MARK 6:14–29; LUKE 3:19–20; 9:7–9 ~

Along the eastern shore of the Dead Sea lies a range of mountains which contain a fortress called Machaerus, one of the forts developed by Herod the Great to protect the eastern side of his territory and the traffic all along the Dead Sea area. According to Josephus, a first-century A.D. Jewish historian, John the Baptist was first imprisoned, then beheaded in Machaerus. What brought about this tragic death?

About 28 A.D. Herod Antipas, who was ruling Galilee as an inheritance from his father Herod the Great, met a lady member of the large Herodian clan in Rome. This was Herodias, and she and Antipas fell madly in love. Unfortunately, they both were already married, and Herodias had a daughter; but each divorced to have the other—in Galilee.

This marital state was highly criticized by Galileans, and John the Baptist publicly excoriated the couple for flaunting the Mosaic Law. One evening, at a state dinner, Salome, the daughter of Herodias by her first marriage, danced, and so entranced the audience that Antipas, in front of everyone, "promised her anything." Upon the urging from her mother, Salome asked for the head of John the Baptist, and Antipas, though greatly embarrassed, gave in and ordered the beheading.

John was a simple person, dressed in the poorest garments and ate the poorest of foods. All of this behavior was a witness, not so much to the value of poverty, but to devotion to the only thing that mattered in his life: obedience to the will of God. His message spoke of absolute devotion to God's will, in the spirit of the ancient prophets before him, and the way he lived mirrored this total dedication to God alone. Other Jews might not have the integrity of John or his courage, but everyone admired and honored him because everyone knew he lived and died for God's truth. That this kind of person would encourage faith in Jesus and call himself not worthy to be Jesus' slave—this testimony was extremely impressive and credible for all John's contemporaries.

The Two Baptisms

The Gospels make clear the nobility of John and the support John gave to faith in Jesus. Also, the Gospels indicate the great difference between the baptisms each offered. John's baptism hoped for forgiveness of sins by God, once a person confessed his sins and proposed to change his life, to live according to the will of God. Entering the water of the Jordan was understood to be symbolic of the cleansing from sin one was asking for from God, and of the new life one pledged.

The baptism Jesus promised included the forgiveness of sins, but even more. Most important, one received the Holy Spirit of God who would dwell in the baptized person. St. Paul teaches that to be baptized by Jesus is to die to the old sinful way of life, to rise morally determined to live in accord with the teaching of Jesus and the enlightenment and strength of the Holy Spirit. And the baptized becomes a member of a people he did not belong to before, a people founded on belief that Jesus is the Messiah, the Son of God. Finally, it is this baptism which blunts and eventually removes the effects of Original Sin.

It is John who gave witness to these different baptisms by his brief sentence: "I baptize with water, but he will baptize with the Holy Spirit." Yet, for all the difference between their baptisms and their life-styles, Jesus praised John as "more than a prophet," as one of the greatest human beings. The Jordan desert still rings with his piercing cry and his passionate integrity of life: Repent, the kingdom of God is at hand; prepare for Jesus, God's Lamb.

Jericho

"HURRY, I MUST STAY AT
YOUR HOUSE THIS DAY."
~ LUKE 19:5

W hen the Israelites finished their forty years of wandering in the desert and entered the Promised Land under Joshua, the second city they met and conquered was Jericho. As Joshua 6:1–6 tells us, the Israelites captured the city of Jericho when, at the direction of God, they blew their horns and the walls of Jericho came tumbling down to let them in. Today, we see three Jerichos before us. There is the present-day Jericho, pretty and rich in agricultural fruits and vegetables. Then, quite near modern Jericho is the famous hill which covers over at least 15 layers of cities and towns going back to 7000 B.C.; it was excavations begun in 1867 which eventually led to discovering all these levels of human life here. Finally, to the south of this archeological site are the remains of the Jericho built by Herod the Great, in which he died miserably from a painful disease.

In the New Testament, two events in particular are associated with Jericho, a cure and an encounter with Zachaeus. These events would have taken place near the archeological hill site, for modern Jericho did not exist in Jesus' time and Herod's Jericho was only for Herod and his friends; Jesus would have walked by Herod's Jericho, but that is all. That Jesus would have traveled through Jericho might surprise a person, until one realizes that the best and safest way to reach Jerusalem from Galilee in Jesus' time was to follow the valley of the Jordan River from north to south, until one reached Jericho. Only at that point would the traveler turn due westward and begin the ascent to Jerusalem.

Cure of the Blind Man
~ MATTHEW 20:29–34; MARK 10:46–52; LUKE 18:35–43 ~

While passing through Jericho, Jesus, from out of the praises shouted at him by crowds, heard the cry: "Jesus, Son of David, have mercy on me!" Jesus, the Son of David (= Messiah), responding to this call, gave a man his sight. This miracle gives us the opportunity to reflect on several things pertinent to Jesus' miracle working.

First, there is no record in the Gospels that Jesus ever denied anyone a miracle. Certainly he hesitated to work a miracle for the Syro-Phoenician woman—a Gentile from the area we know today as Lebanon-Syria. But this hesitation was only due to the fact that Jesus knew he had not yet been sent to exercise his powers on behalf of other than Jewish people; even so, in anticipation of later miracles on behalf of many Gentiles, Jesus, moved by the plight of the woman, does do what she asks. No, Jesus did not shy away from helping people through his great powers; indeed, he spent many hours healing, and so often he cured people without even being asked. Curing people's ills was not Jesus' main task in life, but part of his fame was rooted in his extreme sympathy with the sick and his willingness to heal them.

Second, given this visible show of immense power, which can only be called God-like, it is difficult for the Gospels to explain why people kept asking Jesus for a sign to prove that he was authentically from God. For John, the miracles of Jesus are clear signs by which we are to understand who Jesus really is and how intimately related he is to God; indeed, the miracles are signs of nothing less than the divine Father-Son relationship. Why these signs or miracles could not be read properly is for the Gospels an unsolved mystery. One can argue that miracle working does not make one the Son of God, the Messiah, because there were many claims of other people having powers of healing in the Mediterranean Basin at this time and no one called any of those healers "Son of God." However, while there may have been healers elsewhere, no record shows anyone to have the powers Jesus had: complete control over nature, over the demon world, over all types of illness, over death itself; he was an inexhaustible well of power and could perform the most difficult miracles with only a word and from afar. Most of all, his power was God-like because it was exercised for any of God's creatures; there was no "criterion" for deciding whom Jesus would love with his power and whom he would not. No wonder-worker of the ancient world could compare with Jesus. About people who were unable or unwilling to see the reality miracles revealed, the Gospels use such terms as "people of this world," "blind," "from below," "not taught by my Father," "children of the father of lies," "soil in which the seed cannot grow." Perhaps these terms are too negative for us today, but the reality they represent is still there. It will always be something of a mystery to the believer, as it was to the earliest Christians, just why some see the truth the miracles reveal and others do not.

Third, for all the episodes concerned with miracle working (e.g., Mark's Gospel recounts over twenty miracles for individuals) and despite Jesus' unflagging willingness to work the miracles, it is clear that Christianity through the centuries is not a religion which depends on constant or even occasional miracles. On the contrary, Christianity, compared to other suggested ways of finding life's ultimate happiness, is hardly one that promises its members physical and psychological, sociological and political health, peace and well-being. Christianity is, in essence, a religion concerned to promote a thorough love of God and of the neighbor: the completion of one's longings for physical, mental, and spiritual perfection is usually expected to occur in the next world. Certainly, Christianity does not deny the possibility of miracles, and it does urge everyone to pray for miracles; but unless one designates conversion and repentance as miracles, miracles have a secondary place in Christianity.

The surest sign of the secondary role of miracles in Christian life is the death of Jesus. If anyone deserved a miracle, a saving from suffering, it was Jesus, the Son. Indeed, as the words of his enemies indicate, "If God is his father, surely he will save him." And who better could have saved Jesus than Jesus, "He saved others, he can surely save himself." God should have saved Jesus whom he loved the most, yet he did not. Obviously, then, there was something more essential in the death of Jesus than just escape from suffering. Christianity is concerned with love of God, with obedience, and with trust in God's wisdom, whether this wisdom asks for suffering or joy. It is this obedience, this trust, this love that

God wanted from Jesus at the time of his suffering, and not Jesus' good health. Jesus understood this, and loved the Father—and refused to work a miracle for himself. Miracles, then, support belief in Jesus, because they do reveal that he is Son of God, but they never are more important than love, obedience, trust, faithfulness—whether for Jesus or for his follower. In these things one finds the essence of Christianity, of discipleship. An occasional miracle, but a daily and unrelenting devotion—the difference in "frequency" indicates what is essential and what is secondary in Jesus' life, and in the Christianity which models itself after him.

Many scholars believe that Mark wrote his Gospel out of a certain wariness about miracles. Though recounting so many wonders, Mark's Gospel ultimately describes Jesus as dying so painfully, ignominiously, like a fool, powerless. To embrace Jesus because of his power, Mark insists, is to run the risk of misunderstanding Jesus completely and thus being unable to find Jesus as leader when the disciple must suffer, even give his life for his faith in Jesus. The fundamental lesson of Christianity is to be found, not in miracle working, but in the cross, where the seed dies so that beautiful things, living things might blossom. It is not the healing of my circumstances that is the central issue; it is the turning of my heart to God, to love of God and neighbor, which defines the life of Jesus and of his followers in this age. The emphasis, then, is on growth in love, not on the avoidance of pain.

But once one realizes what it is that God wants of a human life, one can not only realize the secondary nature of miracles, but also estimate more perfectly their value. It is true that St. Paul could write his letters without any mention of Jesus' miracle working (or of his infancy, or of most of his moral teaching); Paul could center his writings simply on the death and resurrection of Jesus and find there guidance for what it means to be a follower of Jesus.

Yet, the Gospels go further than Paul; they *do* recount the public life of Jesus and his miracles. Jesus' miracles serve as part of God's plan. They are assurances of the presence and love of God in Jesus. Through these miracles one becomes aware that the fullest purpose of God is to restore every human being to the most complete perfection on every level. That most people must wait for this completion until after death does not deny the reality of God's intention. The miracle which occasionally bursts through the laws of this age and overcomes the corruption which is our lot shouts out the eventual destiny of everyone who belongs to Jesus. Miracles serve as a solid reason for our hope.

The people of Jesus' time failed to grasp the relationship between the call of Jesus to everyone for immediate repentance and the miracles of Jesus, intentionally done only sporadically, which certify his divinity and promise the fullest perfection after death. Indeed, the miracle is often interpreted in the New Testament as the visible healing which tells of the deeper spiritual healing God wants to work in us, if we will only let him. If the New Testament can say that the kingdom of God is present now, and not only when it is at its fullest after the end of this world, it can make this assertion because the miracle, like repentance, is a sign that God, the life-giver, has taken charge, is king at this moment, in this place, and has defeated evil. Because God had such thorough control of Jesus' life, we can say that Jesus embodied the kingdom of God and shared this kingdom through his call to repentance, his teaching, and his miracles.

In sum, one must balance miracle working with the call to a change to love of God and neighbor, which call was Jesus' main purpose during his public life. Jesus refused to work a miracle to take away his own suffering, when he knew that love of God was more important than his safety and better served by his suffering than by his escape from it. One does not forget the fact that Lazarus, like the young man whom Jesus raised from the dead outside Naim, had to die again; one miracle did not save him ultimately from death. Thus, Jesus never changed "the rules" of the condition we live in to the extent that death no longer waits for us. What he did do was ask us to love God and neighbor, and by this means to live beyond our deaths. In his work, the miracles are extremely helpful and consoling, for they show us who it is who is powerful enough to bring us to rise from the dead, and who it is whose love is such that we have every hope that he will bring us to the most complete life, forever. Jesus' miracles should help us to believe his message of repentance, to trust that his call—which can cost us pain (for love of God and neighbor can do that)—is for our good, just as the miracles are. The preaching and the curing all come from the same love which wants only our good. It is this divine love in which lies all of our trust, all of our hope for final and complete happiness.

Zachaeus

In Jericho one day, as crowds swarmed about Jesus, a very short man had trouble seeing Jesus because everyone was taller than he. But this short man was enterprising; he found a tree to climb, a sycamore. (The sycamore, the oak, and the carob are the three wild trees indigenous to Israel.) Jesus noticed Zachaeus up in the sycamore, said that he had been looking for him, and offered to come to his house—if Zachaeus wanted him. Jesus was quite aware of the kind of man Zachaeus was. Zachaeus was a tax collector for the Romans; as such he was considered a cheat and totally untrustworthy, and he himself suggested that he had grossly overcharged people in collecting their taxes. That Jesus said he wanted to dine with Zachaeus meant that he has been looking for him, as for all sinners, in the hope that all would repent. Jesus' willingness to dine with Zachaeus was a call on Zachaeus to accept all that Jesus stands for. Indeed, Zachaeus offered the invitation and showed that he did understand, when he promised to return four times (the amount the Old Testament says is just) the value of what he had stolen.

Jesus, then, sought repentance from Zachaeus. Many of the crowd only thought of Jesus' breaking the law which said that a just person should not eat with an unjust person. Jesus tried to correct their imperfect grasp of the situation: This is a son of Abraham; he deserves being cared for by the Son of Man who comes to seek out the lost and bring salvation to all. That Zachaeus changed his life upon meeting Jesus is Jesus' greatest kind of miracle, and a sure sign of Jesus' divinity, and the most solid reason for all hope that God's love will bring all of us salvation.

Bethlehem

"FROM YOU WILL COME A LEADER WHO WILL
SHEPHERD MY PEOPLE ISRAEL."

~ MATTHEW 2:6

Birth of Jesus

~ LUKE 2:1–21 ~

The Gospels of Mark and John do not speak at all of Jesus' birth in Bethlehem, a name meaning *Temple of (= beth)* [the god of] *bread (=lehem)*, and a town about seven miles south of Jerusalem; it is the Gospels of Luke and Matthew that inform us that Jesus was born in Bethlehem. Matthew does not explain why the Holy Family was in Bethlehem at the time Jesus was born; it falls to Luke to give the clearest explanation.

Caesar Augustus ordered a census to be taken; Luke says this was a census of the entire empire of Rome. To participate in the census, one should really go back to where one's family originates; for Joseph this meant leaving his home for some days and going back to Bethlehem, for Joseph was a descendant of King David (who died about 950 B.C.) and his family roots were there. Luke tells us, without saying why, that Mary, Joseph's wife, traveled with him to Bethlehem for the census. She was pregnant.

Thus we can explain in purely human and historical terms why Joseph and Mary are in Bethlehem when she is about to deliver her child. Yet another world of influence is to be considered here, Luke indicates. This is the world of God and of his plans for the salvation of the world.

According to the Old Testament, God wants the world saved by a person who comes from "the line of David." If David was *anointed* king of Israel, then the savior of Israel would be called *The Anointed*, which means *Messiah* (in Hebrew and its derivative, Aramaic) and *Christ* (in Greek). Jesus, it will be argued by the New Testament, was not only the physical descendant of David, but he was even born in David's town—thus, one sees how, even because of physical descendancy and place of birth, Jesus qualifies to be considered the Promised Anointed One, the Messiah, Son of David. And thus, while Joseph found himself in Bethlehem out of obedience to Caesar's command, the plan of God, which overarches all human devising, was fulfilled in having Jesus born of the line of David, in David's town. (The Old Testament tells us that Bethlehem was David's town, for he was born there.)

Strangely enough, neither Matthew nor Luke spends time telling the details of Jesus' birth or of the moments which led up to it. Luke does tell us that Joseph and Mary could not be received in the usual overnight kind of stopping place because of the crowds seeking room, but ended up in some place that had a manger. He also tells us that the child was wrapped in swaddling cloths and laid in this manger at night. But that is all the detail we can gather from Luke. Matthew tells us only that Jesus was born; this fact he places between the stories of Joseph's first noting Mary as pregnant and of the Magi's visit, thought by scholars to have occurred over a year after Jesus' birth.

The New Testament, then, gives little detail about the moments surrounding Jesus' birth. Why might this be so? To answer this question we must ask about the purposes of the Gospels, particularly about Matthew and Luke, since they do bring up the matter of the birth of Jesus. Specifically, how might the purposes for which these Gospels were written determine whether or not they tell about the details of the birth?

In the scientific study of the Gospels, most scholars believe that Mark's was the first Gospel and that it was read by Luke and Matthew. These writers decided to write their own Gospels, but did so in such a way that what they wrote are expansions of Mark; many verses of Mark, as well as his general geographical and temporal outlines, were taken over by Matthew and/or Luke. From this evidence we can conclude that both Matthew and Luke decided that their Gospels would benefit by an addition to what they inherited from Mark: they would add infancy stories about Jesus.

When we look to Mark, we find his to be an organization of stories which did not originally belong to one another and which had their own histories of development from the first telling of them to Mark's recording of them. Mark clearly thinks that the person of interest in his Gospel is the adult Jesus, the period from Jesus' baptism by John to the resurrection of Jesus, and so organizes his stories to reveal the meaning of the adult Jesus.

It was the adult Jesus—preacher, teacher, and wonder-worker, opposed, betrayed, tried and killed, and raised up on the third day—who forms the center of the Marcan Gospel; Mark's concern is the words and deeds of this adult who proclaims the good news to all people.

From this point of view, the stories of Jesus' childhood are not at the center of the gospel story; rather, they serve as an introduction to that center, to the adult Jesus. The Infancy stories intend to convey to the reader the meaning of Jesus before the adult Jesus steps onto the stage as central actor. These introductions are precious. They give the reader something that the contemporaries of Jesus—Peter, the Twelve, the crowds, the Pharisees and Sadducees, Pilate—never had. These groups of people had to grope and struggle to figure out who Jesus was, and often individuals had only a few hours, or even minutes, to draw a conclusion about him. When the adult life of Jesus, which was the real matter over which Jesus was judged and killed, is introduced by infancy stories, the reader is in a much greater position to understand his entire adult life correctly. This is all the more true since the writers Matthew and Luke are using hindsight, and so have the benefit of the entire Jesus experience to guide them in presenting Jesus, infant and adult. Thus, the reader knows more about Jesus before he ever begins his public life than many of Jesus' contemporaries ever grasped about him. The Infancy stories of Luke and Matthew serve a wonderful purpose for us readers. It is in these stories Matthew and Luke chose for this part of the Gospel that we see clearly who Jesus is. Let us consider the purposes of the Gospels for a moment.

Throughout the Gospels the question is present and often is expressed: from where will the Messiah come? At times, and in some Jewish circles, the Messiah was to have no known origin, and this underlines his mysteriousness. He is from God; to say he is from some particular place on earth would be to undermine the supernaturality of the Messiah who was "from above."

Most Jews of Jesus' time, however, understood that the Messiah would come from David's line; it seems that they even expected him to come from David's city. When Herod the Great, prodded by the Magi, asks his own wise men, "Where is to be born the King of the Jews?" the answer is: Bethlehem. The Jewish expectation that the Messiah is from David, from Bethlehem is clear; that Matthew and Luke give this precise information about Jesus serves their purpose to show that he does, in every sense, qualify to be the Messiah of Israel. That Jesus can be said to be from Bethlehem, from David is proof that he should be accepted as Israel's Messiah.

This effort to identify Jesus' Davidic origins also explains the genealogy which begins the Gospel of Matthew. A primary purpose of the genealogy is to show how Jesus is physically related to David (and to Abraham) and thus qualifies to be considered the Son of David, Messiah of Israel. But there is more to giving the genealogy of Jesus than just offering a sure physiological link to David. Notice how Matthew singles out Abraham and David before he gives the actual list of generations from Abraham to Jesus. Matthew singles out Abraham because he thinks his Gospel will show that Jesus is the fulfillment of the promise to Abraham that through his offspring will all the world be blessed. Similarly, Matthew singles out David because of the promise made to David, that his offspring would rule over Israel forever. Thus, while establishing that Jesus genealogically merits to be called Son of David, and Son of Abraham, too, Matthew also makes his first claims that Jesus is the fulfillment of what God promised the great forefathers of Israel: Jesus is the One through whom, as God promised Abraham, all nations would be blessed, and Jesus is the One who, as God promised David, would be Israel's king (or Messiah) forever.

While Luke does not pursue so vigorously Jesus' sonship from Abraham, he is equal to Matthew in his emphatic affirmation that Jesus is that Son of David who will rule over Israel forever. The Gospel's first description of Jesus at the annunciation to Mary is in these terms. Peter's Pentecost speech, which opens the witnessing to Jesus in the Acts of the Apostles, also insists that Jesus is the one promised to David to sit on

David's throne. Both Matthew and Luke, then, present the infant Jesus as the completion of Old Testament hopes and promises.

Both Matthew and Luke insist that Mary was a virgin when she conceived Jesus, and was so when she bore him. This factor makes Jesus' relationship to David a bit more precarious than what one might expect from the prophecies about the Son of David. Joseph, in other words, was only Jesus' legal father, not his natural father. Yet, legal paternity was thought sufficient to make the claim valid: Jesus is Son of David and thus qualifies to be the fulfillment of the promise made to David about his son.

Both Matthew and Luke were intent on revealing through their Gospels the deepest identity of Jesus. The infancy of Jesus was a period which served this purpose admirably, and we have seen how Matthew and Luke have linked the infant Jesus to the promises and hopes of the Old Testament. To answer our original question, then: we can say that Matthew and Luke chose to narrate those details about the infancy of Jesus which would best reveal who Jesus really is. Thus, precise and plentiful details about his birth are not automatically what Matthew and Luke want; rather what they want and choose, are elements of Jesus' infancy that open up his identity to the reader. We now might be interested to hear more of the actual historical details of the birth of Jesus, but the evangelists searched rather for stories which they found to be means of revealing to us who Jesus really is—in accord with their purposes for writing their Gospels.

Visit of the Magi
~ MATTHEW 2:1–12 ~

Son of David was understood to mean "King of Israel." It is with his eye on this title that Matthew presents, as an event associated with Bethlehem, the visit to Jesus of the Magi. Not all scholars agree that Magi actually came to see Jesus; even those who do think that these Magi really did visit Jesus find details of the story hard to explain, especially the nature of the heavenly body that appeared to the Magi. Let us study the story for a moment to understand how it might have happened, and especially to understand what it teaches.

Magus—plural *magi*—is a term drawn from the ancient area we know today as Syria and Iran. The term designates a "wise man." The greatest wise men were usually taken into the courts of kings. It was to these wise men that kings (and lesser folk) turned for guidance about life, particularly about the future. Kings always wanted to control through knowledge the future, so that they could better protect and develop their kingdoms; success in wars, crops, health could be improved if one only knew what the future holds in store. There is not much difference between our own desires to control all aspects of the future and the desires of these ancients to know the most elusive of all human time, the future. The wise man was to provide, through daily study, the knowledge which would let the king plan well for the stability and peace and prosperity of his people.

The world of the magi was filled, it was thought, with all kinds of knowledge, if only one could uncover it. In this time there was a particularly strong relationship between the heavens and earth (the flat earth, and only that part of it known to the wise men); if one could only read the heavens, one could, it was thought, learn much about the earth. So the court wise men kept eternal vigil in looking for revelations about earth in the heavens.

We have good reason to think that, at the time of Jesus, the heavens were divided into sections (a zodiac arrangement) which corresponded to sections of earth. Too, certain planets and stars represented powers and gods; Mars, for instance, stood for war. Thus, if Mars were prominent

On the way to Bethlehem: a camel caravan

in an unusual way in a certain part of the heavens, one might say that war was imminent in the section of the earth that corresponded to this part of the heavens. With this kind of thinking in mind, we turn to our Magi story.

A famous astronomer, Johannes Keppler, discovered that in 1604 A.D. there was a very strange relationship among the three planets Jupiter, Saturn, and Mars. Indeed, so unusual was this geographical relationship that it occurred only every 805 years, i.e., that it occurred in 799 A.D.—and in 6 B.C., the time most scholars think was just about the year of Jesus' birth. Thus, around the time of the birth of Jesus Jupiter, Saturn, and Mars were in an arrangement never known to humans before. This phenomenon would have struck magi as a definite sign from the heavens that something of immense importance was being revealed about earth.

The three planets had such meanings in this time that it became clear that the revelation from heaven concerned a king to be born in a western area (west of where the magi lived), in the area ascribed to Israel; this king would be powerful in war, for Jupiter signified *king*, Mars *warrior*. The zodiacal reference shows that the appearance of these three planets occurred in the Pisces section of the heavens, a section which corresponded to Israel on earth; associated with this part of the heavens was a notion of "the last days of earth." All of this data yielded the following conclusion: there was to be born in Israel, among the western peoples, a warrior king in the last days of our earth. It was only proper that the magi reported this revelation to their king. And it was only prudent that the king send an embassy, not unlikely some wise men, to create and assure good relations with the new king, for now and for the foreseeable future. Thus, wise men would have been sent with precious gifts to win over for their king the friendship of the newborn king of the Jews.

So far, what we know of astronomy in biblical times fits with Matthew's story, except that Matthew does not talk of a triple-planet phenomenon, but of a star, and indeed of a star which appears, disappears, then appears again. Is there any reason for speaking of a star instead of the three planets?

We think Matthew substituted a star for the planets, one heavenly body for another, because he thought that, while remaining true to the heavenly nature of the phenomenon, he could draw out the meaning of the heavenly revelation better by use of a star. Why? Matthew consistently turned to the Jewish Scriptures to help make sense of his story about Jesus. One such piece of Scripture was a statement we find in the Book of Numbers (24:17), that God would raise up a leader for Israel, and this leader is described as a *star*. Scholars suggest that the star of Matthew's magi story is used to reinforce the revelation that a leader for Israel, as Numbers had prophesied, was being given in the heavens. This star, then, links Old Testament prophecy with the revelation of nature: all conspired to reveal to the magi the existence of Jesus, King of Israel.

The magi learned of, and in their own way, announced the birth of the King of the Jews. In search of the child, the star led them as far as Israel, and so they go to the capital to learn precisely where the child can be found. Here, Herod the Great (who was to die in about two years) and "all Jerusalem" grew fearful; after all, Herod did think he was, as Rome called him, the King of the Jews. We noted before that Herod's own court wise men had found the prophecy that said the King would come from Bethlehem, and so Herod sends the wise men on their way to this small town (just about six miles south of Jerusalem) in the hopes that through their naïveté Herod might find a way to kill the child.

The star appears again, to stop over the exact house (no longer the place where Jesus was born) in which the child is resting; the revelation is complete, and the magi present their respects and gifts to win over the newborn king. Are the magi three in number? The gifts are three, so many people over centuries concluded that there must have been three magi. Are the magi kings? We explained how these wise men can be carrying gifts fit for a king without being kings themselves. And these gifts are truly precious.

Gold needs no explanation. Frankincense is a special kind of aroma, called "Frank" because it was highly valued by the people called Franks. (Today the French people live in the territory of the earlier Franks.) The importance of perfumes or aromas in the ancient world can be gathered from the fact that bathing was not a frequent exercise for most people and was compensated for by perfumes. At a temple where there were animal sacrifices one could also find an altar of incense, which was an attempt to reduce the smells of the sacrifice, both for the people and for the gods worshipped. Myrrh was an ointment used for various purposes, particularly together with wrapping cloths for burial of a body; myrrh helped preserve a body for a short time.

The gifts brought by the magi, then, were valuable and indicated the worth of the recipient. So did the prostrations performed to the child Jesus by the magi. Matthew's Gospel here is ironic, for it contrast strongly the reaction to Jesus of "Jerusalem," headed by Herod the Great, with that of Gentiles. How is it that "Israel" seeks to kill its King, while the Gentiles adore him? But this brief encounter between Herod and the child is only meant as a prelude to the greater encounter in which Jesus will be put to death by his own and thus offer himself to the Gentiles: "Go to all nations. . . ."

Grotto of the Nativity

When one thinks of Bethlehem and the New Testament, one's thoughts turn to the contemplation of the building and grotto or cave of the Nativity of Jesus. It was the call to register for the Roman census that brought so many visitors to Bethlehem that Joseph could find no room in the usual overnight resting place of travelers. It was not a unique experience that Mary and Joseph would spend a night out of necessity in a cave which had the depth to protect a family and its animals from cold and thieves. Nor was it unique that a child be born outdoors, or perhaps in a cave. For all that, it is deeply sobering to read of such an experience for a young couple and their child. If there be any justification behind the statement that Jesus, Son of God, could have chosen whatever society and whatever level of society he wanted to enter for his incarnation, we can only stand in wonder at the choice he made for himself, and for his mother and father. This was the Messiah, the Lord, the Savior of the world, the King. We can only conclude that, if the choice was intentional, it was a choice that was made for our benefit, and for our instruction. The adult Jesus would speak of love of the Father and trust in him to such a degree that all else that belongs to the Father and was made by him pales in importance; all creation is good, as God said, but God is very good—never to be equaled by or substituted for by creation. Jesus spoke in this way and he lived in this way, a constant corrective to human tendencies to put trust ultimately in the things God made rather than in God himself. Jesus' choice of poverty was meant to highlight for us the importance of God; he began this lesson in this grotto in Bethlehem.

Ironically, it was this puzzling preference for poverty that made Jesus accessible to the poor and thus to all mankind. His deeds of power would impress people, as would his wisdom; but his poverty showed him to want to share the life of the poorest and made him appealing to them, for they knew someone who felt life as they did and whose desire to help them was true and strong. If Jesus was to share human life, he seems to say, he would share it in such a way as to be intelligible to all, to be sensitive to all. But above all he would so live life that no one would have any doubts about what makes him tick: from his earliest moments, he wants only to love God and love his neighbor. Jesus never showed dislike for the things his Father made, nor did he teach us to dislike them, but he let his love burn fully, and it was this love which pushed aside all else that he might have had, so that he could have, shorn of all else, the richest union he could imagine: union with his Father, uninterrupted by possessions and the desire for them. The grotto so silent, the little child so silent, begin the message of Jesus' heart: love God totally and love neighbor as you would like to be loved.

Slaughter of the Innocents
~ MATTHEW 2:16–18 ~

Herod the Great directed the Magi to Bethlehem; he ordered them to report back to him the exact location of Jesus so that he could kill Jesus. God frustrated Herod, however, for the Magi, under God's guidance, returned home without seeing Herod again. Incensed and determined to do away with this child whom he saw to be such a threat, Herod ordered his troops to descend upon Bethlehem and kill all male babies two years old and younger because Jesus must by now be nearer to two years old. Through a dream Joseph learned of Herod's intention and was commanded to take his wife and child southward, along the Mediterranean Sea into Egypt; thus God saved his Son from the Bethlehem massacre.

Many are the questions about this story, and the questions have no thoroughly satisfying answer; not the least important question is: if such a massacre of children took place, why is there no record or mention of it anywhere else in the literature we have of the first century except in Matthew? On the other hand, this massacre must have been one of the last bloody acts Herod the Great ordered, before he went off to die in 4 B.C. in his private town outside Jericho.

Whatever the answers to all questions asked about this Bethlehem episode, the purpose of the story Matthew tells seems clear. The story lets the deadly anger of "Jerusalem" towards Jesus play itself out, while the identity of Jesus is revealed by the care which God takes to preserve him. This anger prepares the reader for the more successful anger of Jerusalem authorities when Jesus will be put to death. At the same time, the story is set against an Old Testament citation about Rachel, to show that even such a bizarre event as this slaughter revealed how Jesus brought new meaning and completion to the Old Testament.

That the life of Jesus could, in so many ways, be brought into line with so much of the Old Testament was a very important element in establishing the credibility of Jesus. If Jesus had not fitted at all the expectations of the Old Testament, the argument could be made that the Sacred Scriptures of God have nothing to do with Jesus—and so why should he be believed to come from God? But if he does complete the Old Testament, this is a strong argument that those who believe in the Old Testament should now believe in the one who completes and perfects it.

The particular Old Testament text fulfilled in the story about the slaughter of the Bethlehem children concerns Rachel, who "weeps for her children." This Rachel is one of the two freeborn wives of Jacob; from her and from the other freeborn wife and from two slaves were born the twelve sons of Jacob. Since these twelve sons are the fathers of the Twelve Tribes of Israel, one can understand why Rachel can be called Israel's mother.

In giving birth to her last son Benjamin, Rachel died. She was buried where she gave birth, just east of Jerusalem. Many centuries later, when Israelites were being force-marched out of Jerusalem eastward towards conquering Babylon, Jeremiah in a poetic style imagined that Rachel could see from her tomb the sad procession of captives, of her children, forced into grim slavery in Babylon. As they passed her tomb, "she wept" (Jer 31:15).

As often happens in the history of religious sites, another area later was identified as the tomb of Rachel; this tomb was just south of Jerusalem, on the road between Jerusalem and Bethlehem. Matthew saw the propriety of applying Jeremiah's words to Rachel who would watch from her grave the slaughter of her children of Bethlehem. Thus, an ancient tradition having to do with Rachel's burial was used by a prophet in the sixth century B.C. to describe the poignancy of the Babylonian exile—and then used again by a writer of the first century A.D. to describe yet another suffering of Israel. In seeing the aptness of this quotation for an event of Jesus' childhood, Matthew stresses that, though the quotation was fitting for the suffering undergone in sixth century B.C. Israel, the prophet's words come to their fullest significance as they are seen to rightly fit the painful circumstance occurring in the life of Jesus. It was not that Jeremiah foresaw the Jesus event in his own words, but he said the words which would have their full meaning realized once the Jesus event had come to pass. God often talked of things through his prophets, sayings which were fully understood only in the light of the events which could make them fully understood.

Connecting this Bethlehem story to Rachel gives new, fuller meaning to the Jeremiah citation, and Jeremiah's words, understood anew, place the life of Jesus in the God-directed history of Israel. In this way the Old Testament is more intelligible and Jesus is more credible—and more clearly revealed in all of this is the God who stands behind the motherhood of Rachel, her weeping over the Babylonian exile, her weeping over the slaughter of innocent children in Bethlehem, and the saving of Jesus.

Basilica of the Nativity

It is time to turn our attention to the Basilica of the Nativity, beneath which is the cave wherein, tradition says, Jesus was born and laid in a manger. To enter the basilica we must bend very low, for the doorway is not high; the reason for the lowness of the door was to keep out of the basilica animals like horses and camels, though we may, with Chesterton, see the aptness of lowering oneself to enter the place where God made himself lowly and welcomed the lowly. This small door was made about 1500; above it we can still see, before bending down to go through it, the outline of the pointed arch of the entrance built by the crusaders about 1100, and above that a cornice of the entrance built by the Byzantine emperor, Justinian, about 535.

Having passed through the low door, we enter the vestibule of the basilica and move directly across to the ancient door (1277) which, when

Bethlehem: Basilica of the Nativity

opened, allows us into the main body of the basilica. The basilica in which we stand is a tired, old building, the scene of many, often violent changes. It is essentially the same basilica built by the Emperor Justinian, who intended to restore to its former glory the original basilica built here by the Emperor Constantine about 330. In rebuilding the basilica nearly destroyed by Samaritans in 529, Justinian installed a new floor about thirty inches above Constantine's floor; today, at certain easily-reached spots, one can raise a square of the Justinian floor to see the underlying floor of Constantine. Another change by Justinian is visible after we walk the complete length of the basilica and stop at the end of the last set of pillars. Originally, Constantine had built an octagon at the end of the rows of pillars; this octagon, with a high altar in the middle of it, stood directly above the cave in which Jesus was born. Justinian did away with the octagon shape and extended the sides of the church so that the length of the main aisle of the basilica now intersected with the new width of the church to form a cross; now directly beneath the central point of the intersection is the holy cave of Jesus' birth.

On the way up the main aisle of the basilica, we pass mosaics and frescoes decorating the walls above the pillars of the main aisle of the church. As we walk up the central aisle, high up on our left are the ruins of the twelfth century mosaic busts of Jesus' ancestors, and long inscriptions which highlight the decrees of the ecumenical councils of Constantinople in 381 and 680. On the upper wall on our right as we walk up the main aisle from the entrance we can see mosaic fragments depicting the famous and ancient churches of Antioch and Sardica, as well as portraits of Jesus' ancestors and frescoes commemorating certain provincial councils of the Church.

As we stand at the intersection of the main aisle and the cross aisle, it is apparent that many Christian religious groups worship at the altars scattered about the sanctuary. Indeed, just as the outside of the entire basilica is hemmed in on three sides by the convents of Franciscans, Greeks, and Armenians, so we can expect that these groups have certain rights to space in the sanctuary. Depending on the decisions made for a particular day, we must look for the altars and side chapels for the entrance through which we pass to descend to the complex of caves below, one of which is the holy site of Jesus' birth. By and large, most of the caves have been starkly, but respectfully, restored and marked as to their significance. Of particular interest is the cave of St. Jerome, the patron of all biblical scholars, who came to Palestine in 382, at the age of forty-six, and settled here to study and translate the Scriptures. From this cave Jerome had his "polite disagreements" with such greats as St. Augustine.

The sacred cave of Jesus' birth has undergone many changes. The Roman Emperor Hadrian, who ruled 117–138, tried to take an area here sacred to the Christians and dedicate it to the god Adonis; the sacred cave itself was turned into a place of liturgical weeping for this Greek god. The first physical change has to do with smoothing walls and ceiling to make what was once a rough cave a respectable place of veneration. The second change was the establishment of altars to distinguish the place of birth, which has a star imbedded in its marble flooring, from the place of the manger. Later, a third altar was added in honor of the visit of the Magi. If we look directly at the altar over the star, we need only then look over our right shoulders to see the altar of the manger. To honor these spots marble slabbing was used, which further removes us from the sense of being in a rough cave.

One further notes the fifty-three lamps lit to honor the site of Jesus' birth, clearly an addition of later ages and tastes. Nineteen of these lamps belong to the Roman Catholic Church. One cannot ignore the blackened walls; the blackness is in part due to the ever-burning fifty-three lamps, but in greater part due to a fire which broke out and scorched these walls and ceiling in the nineteenth century. Thus, although white marble covers the floor and walls, we are strongly impressed by dark and dirt. And we may be strongly attracted to the leathery asbestos wall coverings which were precious in their day (1874) when they were sent by the president of the French Republic.

Finally, we become aware that there is no natural outlet from the cave, thus no entryway visible by which the Holy Family entered and exited the cave. One must use one's imagination to lift from the cave the entire basilica above and to open the cave at the end opposite to the altar of Jesus' birth. From here we can see the stars and look over the valley where the angel spoke to the shepherds. In this fashion we may begin to get a sense of how Palestinians, today as well as in ancient times, used caves for housing, whether permanent or transitory. It was not impossible that what Joseph found for his pregnant wife was a house of a poor family who divided its dwelling so as to stable their animals in the deepest part of the cave, away from the cold. It was possibly in such an inner room of the cave that Joseph and Mary settled for the night's emergency.

Whatever the precise circumstances of Jesus' birth, the most powerful of lords, the one to whom all the world's lords do homage, was laid to rest on straw in a stone cave near the small town of Bethlehem, far from the palace of kings. Why should he choose to be one of us? Why so poor among us? Such was the mystery of Bethlehem, and the assurance, too, of this cave, that his love for us, embracing even those not loved by us or by anybody else, was of inestimable greatness.

Shepherds' Field
~ LUKE 2:8–20 ~

Just east of Bethlehem, on the road from Manger Square through Beit Sahour, are the fields which evoke the memory of the angels' visit to the shepherds on the night of Christ's birth nearby. With the help of the people of Canada, a chapel was erected here in 1954 to the memory of the shepherds and their vision; this chapel, in the shape of a nomad's tent, is one of many designs and restorations in the Holy Land by architect Antonio Barluzzi; Noni's lovely frescoes adorn the interior. Most visitors go to this chapel to spend some time in thinking about the event that happened in these fields. But it is not surprising to learn that throughout these fields are traces of towers, monasteries, chapels, dating back to the fifth century, which served earlier Christians contemplating the visit of the angels to the shepherds.

Given interpreters' penchant for seeing symbolism and analogy, type, and fulfillment between the Old and New Testaments, today's reader of the Gospels can expect to be reminded in this Bethlehem incident how the shepherds fit into a larger picture and expectation. Indeed, it seems to many that the shepherds stand for those faithful Israelites who for centuries waited with patient hope, "in darkness and in the shadow of death," as Luke puts it, for a divine light to shine and set them free (Lk 1:79; Is 9:1). They are particularly poor, corresponding to the poverty of the Holy Family now passing an anxious night in the cave nearby. To these poor the messenger of God spoke words that prophets and kings longed to hear, but never heard. To those faithful, deprived for so long of the good news, was now given the proclamation. The shepherds thus combine two qualities which particularly please God: they watch faithfully in poverty while longing for and trusting in the coming of God.

Matthew obviously chose a different kind of person, a magus, as the first recipient in his Gospel of the good news that "a king is born in Israel." Yet, he was not really far from Luke's preference. For the wise men, though probably court figures bringing royal gifts to Jesus, are not kings and they are not otherwise rich, for they are pagans. That is, they represent the poverty, not of wealth, but of the Gentile who did not know the true God and so lived perpetually in the darkness of folly and estrangement from the only Source of goodness, truth, and beauty. This Gentile might be materially well-off, but to know his darkness of soul and the corruption of his life lived apart from God and without hope of anything beyond death—this is to know a truly poor person.

One cannot deny that God loves deeply every human person, but some kinds of poverty move his fatherly instincts in particular haste. A parent understands this response. It was the shepherds in Luke's story who moved God to announce the good news to them first. To them came a messenger of God and the glory or brilliant light of the Lord; no cause for fear, but reason for the greatest joy, for it was very good news the angel brought. Luke everywhere, especially about Jesus' resurrection, emphasizes what one sees and hears as helps for belief. Thus here the angel gave two signs: the words he spoke and the sight of a child wrapped in swaddling clothes and lying in a manger. It was important, then, that Luke include in his following verses that the shepherds did in fact see the "child lying [wrapped] in the manger." This discovery led them to give credence to the claims of the angel, led them to make the effort to understand what these words mean. In this way Luke shows how Christian faith profits from concrete words and deeds, from hearing God's word and seeing his deeds.

What the angel announced was nothing less than the longed-for news so worthy of an Angel of the Lord, who in the Old Testament brought mankind the best of news. The message, a message of joy for all the people, was simple: a savior was born who was nothing less than Christ Lord, a descendant of David the shepherd and king. How Jesus is savior to each individual is known only in the depths of each one's heart and soul. Luke's effort here was to bring out elements of that saving which are to be experienced by all of us.

This savior is Messiah. He is, therefore, the one who would bring about the shift of entire ages; from this age we move with him to the age to come. With him we move from pain and unhappiness and grief and trial and deprivation and death; God promised to do this, then indicated that he would anoint "one of us," born a child of David, to introduce this change of the ages—and through and in this anointed one, the Messiah, God would act for us. Little did the Old Testament writers think that this Anointed One is actually the divine Son of the divine Father, inexplicably become man, now named Jesus, born in a Bethlehem cave!

For St. Paul, Jesus was anointed, i.e., designated ultimately to bring about the change of ages by his death, which ended death, and his resurrection, which begins life without end with God. Luke, who was aware of this Pauline understanding of Jesus, adds that Jesus is heir of the throne of David. This image is understood to mean that Jesus is that person who receives authority over others in order to bring all the benefits of the kingdom of God to individuals who cannot provide these for themselves. In this sense of "king," Jesus is really a servant, for his purpose in life is to mediate to all people the good things of God, as a servant would do. Thus, when Jesus saves, he saves with kingly power over Satan, but only so that he, like a servant, can serve to us the goods of God's kingdom. Thus Jesus performs the greatest services: he frees us from the slavery to this age and distributes to us the many gifts which characterize the age to come.

Jesus, the angel also said, is Lord. This, too, was a title of dignity, of royalty, for it was David's Lord who was to sit at God's right hand in glory—something Jesus did after his ascension, the logical conclusion of his resurrection from the dead. But "Lord" also means to say that we who have given ourselves over to many lords in our lives—as human beings have desperately done through all centuries—can now identify the Lord designated by God himself to whom we can commit ourselves for the benefit of life which we thought other lords would give us if we served them faithfully. Even more, the most dominant lord of our lives, Death, can now be rendered powerless once we throw in our lot with the Lord Jesus. Indeed, we would die, we would suffer the little deaths which lead to the final separation of soul from body; but the foreverness of Death was now removed by our Lord who was greater than the tyrant whom we cannot overthrow ourselves. Again, Jesus, whose name signifies one who "saves," serves us in his lordly power, as he removes from us so many tyrannies and false lords, so that we may enjoy the life and power and love of the one true Lord.

It was indeed a happy message which the Angel of the Lord brought to the shepherds. It was reasonable that Luke follow the angelic message with a host of angels in chorus singing a song which proclaims that God, pictured as living in the "highest" heaven, is given glory by all his creatures in acknowledgment of the great act he has done in the birth of Jesus, a song which also announces that God, who so generously has offered Jesus to mankind, thus gave mankind the peace which union with Jesus should bring about. Glory to God and peace—two effects most befitting the good news and reality of the birth of Jesus.

The shepherds must follow the direction of the angel, for the good news was too good to miss. The results of their doing what the angel bade them do were three. First, they pondered over the words of the angel as they gazed upon the child—how would this child be savior, Messiah, Lord, source of great joy for them? To their ponderings were added those of Mary who, in addition to all else that has been told her and has happened to her, must make sense of the story of this band of shepherd strangers. Second, Jesus was the good news and the fulfillment of the hopes of the shepherds, but also of all Jerusalem. How could they not become messengers to others about the good news given them? The shepherds understood that Jesus answered the deepest longings in a person for life and love, and so were glad to tell others who want life and love about Jesus. Third, the shepherds glorified, praised God for what they saw he had begun in this little child. They recognized God in this birth and praised him for what he had done.

The shepherds were invited to see that Jesus was the gift of God and was the flowering of God's love for them, for all Jerusalem. We shall have to see if the adult Jesus' contemporaries interpreted him in this way. But we realize that the Infancy stories of Jesus are, on the level of story-telling, an introduction to the adult drama which will soon unfold. The reader, through hearing the story of the shepherds, knows so much more than do Jesus' contemporaries. May the Bethlehem stories, like all the others, give strength and support to faith—and glory to God and peace to us all.

Bethany

"YOU ARE THE CHRIST,
THE SON OF GOD, THE ONE
WHO WAS TO COME INTO THE WORLD."
~ JOHN 11:27

T he mountain directly to the east of Jerusalem is the Mount of Olives. If one stands in Jerusalem and looks to the Mount of Olives, one will not see Bethany; Bethany is just over the top of the mountain, on its eastern side, and thus is hidden from Jerusalem's view—nor can one see Jerusalem from Bethany. Bethany is famous in the Gospels for being the village of the sisters Mary and Martha and their brother, Lazarus. Even today we can visit a tomb traditionally considered to be that of Lazarus;

Bethany: ruins of the house of Lazarus behind two trees

near this cave-like tomb is a modern church commemorating not only the raising of Lazarus to life, but other stories of the Gospels which speak of Martha and Mary. Jesus passed many nights in Bethany, presumably always as a guest of Martha, Mary, and Lazarus; particularly was he appreciative of their hospitality at Passover time, when finding lodging in Jerusalem was so difficult since so many came to the Feast. Jesus would teach all day in the Temple area, then retire for the evening over the top of the Mount of Olives to Bethany. The Gospels tell us that, on his way one day from Bethany to Jerusalem, Jesus cursed a fig tree for not providing fruit—a symbol for the imminent punishment from God upon those who will reject Jesus. Israel was often symbolized in the Old Testament as a tree or vine cultivated and trimmed by God with the hope that it would provide God with the fruits he desired. And, on the slope of the Mount of Olives Jesus urged his disciples to have faith like his own, that "can move mountains."

Mary of Bethany
~ LUKE 10:38–42; JOHN 11:1–44; 12:1–8 ~

There seems to be some confusion in the traditions the Gospel writers inherited about Mary, sister of Martha and Lazarus. According to the Fourth Gospel (Jn 12:1–8), at a dinner in Bethany sponsored by Lazarus and his sisters before Passover, Mary anointed Jesus with ointment, pure nard (a perfume derived from the oil of a plant found in India). Her act was interpreted by Jesus as a preparation for his death, foreshadowing the imminent anointing of his dead body for burial. Mark, for his part, tells of a woman anointing Jesus before the Last Supper (Mk 14:3–9), but does not say the woman is Mary, nor does he say that the anointing took place in the house of Lazarus and his sisters, but rather that it took place in the house of a certain Simon the leper. Matthew follows Mark's lead in this matter (Mt 26:6–13). Luke, however, is conspicuous for not mentioning any anointing at all just before Passover, even though in other respects his account here is like that in Mark. Rather Luke tells another story of a foot washing that occurred rather early in his gospel narrative (Lk 7:36–50); he says this foot washing occurred in the house of Simon the Pharisee (and not the leper) and was performed by an unnamed woman who was clearly a repentant sinner, something never used to describe Mary, sister of Martha and Lazarus.

In regard to Luke, many scholars think that his next verses (Lk 8:1–2) help to identify this woman as Mary, called Magdalene (i.e., from the town of Magdala), from whom seven spirits had been driven out; many scholars, too, suspect that the story of washing in Luke 7 is really talking about the same anointing event which Mark describes as happening in the house of Simon the leper, just before Passover, and is really talking, too, about the same anointing event described by John as happening in Bethany in the house of Lazarus and his sisters, just before Passover.

So appears the evidence which leads scholars to various hypotheses about the anointing of Jesus. Since it remains dubious that Jesus would have been anointed twice, in different houses, at different dinners, just before his Passover dinner, it is not easy to decide for sure which Gospel story (John, Mark/Matthew) has the details accurately and which comes from misunderstanding or intentional use of symbols. It is not easy to say that Luke's washing of Jesus' feet is a rewriting of Mark's anointing story, with Luke adding and deleting in accord with his own purposes. Nor is it easily assumed that the sinful woman of Luke's story is Mary Magdalene for, though Mary was possessed by seven demons, possession itself was not cause for saying she was a sinner. Ultimately we are left with the traditions of Luke, of Mark followed by Matthew, of John, with only guesses about how they might relate among themselves. One can only conclude that Bethany does not easily give up its identity as the place where Jesus was prophetically anointed for his death.

Bethany is also known in the New Testament as the place where Jesus said his famous words to Martha about Mary: "Let your sister be; she has chosen the better part and no one should take it from her" (Lk 10:38–42). Martha, we recall, had urged Jesus to nudge Mary to help her with the preparation of a dinner for Jesus, their visitor. Mary had chosen to listen to the Lord as he taught. Martha and Mary are now so arranged in the story as to highlight the one truth: above all else, it is listening attentively to the word of the Lord that is most important in life. This truth reaffirms what appears in many other explicit and implicit statements of the New Testament about the supreme worth of attending to the Lord's word above all else. Indeed, as Jesus had said earlier: "The one who listens to my word is my mother and brother and sister" (Lk 8:19–21). Jesus' first temptation ended by his reminding Satan: "A person does not live by bread alone, but by every word that comes from the mouth of God." And how often we hear Jesus cry out in desperation: "Let those who have ears, hear!" Throughout Luke's entire work, Gospel and Acts, Luke calls his reader to treasure Jesus' teaching, for he is the Son who alone knows the Father and can reveal his mind to us. It is this teaching of the Lord which the eyewitnesses, then the witnesses, to the Lord spread throughout the Mediterranean world in the first century.

For John, Jesus is that Word through whom God created the world. Genesis tells us of this Word, that every creative act of God happened because "God spoke and it came to be." Thus, the Word was part of the creating process and, as our words do for us, God's Word reflected everything God thought, as he chose what he wanted to create and then spoke it. Jesus, then, is the Word become human that brings us to know the mind of God. Thus, Jesus' teaching about life is the Creator's teaching—a most precious gift to us, indeed.

Raising of Lazarus
~ JOHN 11:1–44 ~

Perhaps Bethany is most famous as the place, noted by John's Gospel, where Jesus raised Lazarus, his dear friend, from the grave. The miracle itself is stupendous; indeed, it is the last, in John's Gospel, of Jesus' works or signs about himself, and so the greatest, the culmination of the seven signs in John. It is after this sign that John's story leaves the world of signs and takes us into the profoundly mysterious world of Jesus' death and resurrection. The Lazarus story, apart from Jesus' revelation of his power, anticipates the death, burial, and rising from the dead of God's Son, and means to say that, as Jesus restores human life to Lazarus (who will die again), he will give us who believe in him life everlasting, with no more death.

Signs are very crucial elements to John's conception of Gospel writing. The purpose for which John wrote is clearly stated in the verses that originally ended the Gospel: "There were many other signs that Jesus worked and his disciples saw. . . . These are recorded so that you may continue to believe that Jesus is the Christ (or Messiah) and Son of God, and that believing you may have life through his name" (Jn 20:30–31). Thus, faith and life are served and confirmed by the signs.

In particular, we can see how central was the sign of the raising of Lazarus: it is a question of nothing less than giving life, overcoming death; the raising of Lazarus confirms faith that Jesus is the one who can do this, that through him we will, like Lazarus, be raised from death—only we will be raised by Jesus to live in unending and perfect life.

It is important to be clear about "life" as used in John's story. One always begins discussions of this matter with creation. The effect of God's creating love was life; life always and only comes from love, as human experience knows. The life God gave at cre-ation was a share in his own, but

Bethany: the tomb of Lazarus

this life was, because of a broken friendship with God, given a termina-tion. This termination was Death, preceded by all the little deaths that prepare for it. Because life is our essential quality, the deprivation of it ends in bitter and total corruption, and we have nothing to say about it. With the coming of Jesus, the Word who was God's instrument in creat-ing life, we have the opportunity to be one again with the Source of life. But when Jesus gives us life, it is not life as Lazarus, when raised from the dead, knew it; Lazarus was only brought back to the life dominated by sin and death. Lazarus would die again and, conceiveably in worse circum-stances than those at his first dying. That life Jesus restored to Lazarus is not the life Jesus intends to give us. When he said so often: "and I will raise them up on the last day," the life he gives will know no end. This is no resuscitation or return to life in this world characterized by corruption and dissolution. This will be life as it should be, unencumbered by any tiniest element of death, undimmed and in fullest strength. Sometimes in this life we sense, even if for only a fleeting moment, what perfect life, unlimited by any imperfection, might be; that is our personal sign to teach us what Jesus will give us forever. To believe in Jesus, John insists, is the beginning of this eternal life, even if we are still "alive" in this corrupting age; in time we will be freed from all evil's effects and will live life with God in its fullest. Lazarus coming back to life is meant to be a firm assurance of the power that Jesus has to give us perfect life, and of the love that will move him to give this life to us.

Jesus is the creating Word of God, who not only was in the beginning and was with God, but is God. Thus it is clear why Jesus, the divine Word become human, can say so authoritatively: "Your brother will rise again." Equally, it is clear why Jesus called himself "the Resurrection and the Life"; it is he alone who can and will provide us with the fullest life, the life without any more death. And one can understand from John's account why Martha could so openly and in such powerful perception confess: "I believe . . . you are the Christ, the Son of God."

In regard to this last point, one can wonder how Martha so swiftly achieved the profound appreciation she had of Jesus; such pyschological maturation in the space of a few moments is questionable here and elsewhere in John's Gospel. But at stake here is not psychological development, which may, for most of us, take a long time. Rather, John tries to show the logical (not the psychological) conclusion he hopes his reader will draw from the miracle, the sign that Jesus works. In this short amount of space, John hopes to give his reader, who never knew Jesus personally, the sense of Jesus' true meaning and the hope that flows from it.

The raising of Lazarus is a wonderfully told story about a wondrous miracle. As a miracle story it brings home to the reader how deeply into the depths of corruption Lazarus had gone—yet not so far that Jesus could not bring him back. But there is more to the story than the miracle. There is the objection that, if Jesus really loved his friend, he would have saved him from death. In fact, Lazarus was saved, in the sense that death was not allowed to continue its hold on him. But in a greater sense, Jesus, too, was saved from death, in that he was saved from continued death—and so, the story of Lazarus teaches, will we be saved from death, not by avoiding it but by overcoming it, by the gift of unending life. Jesus also assures his friends that Lazarus died "so that good could come from it." Jesus' words assure us that he can draw good from all of our physical and psychological evils, even death itself.

The story also retains in several ways a precious remembrance of Jesus' actual responses to the human suffering and sorrow of his very dear friends. In a Gospel which is so set on showing that Jesus is divine, one with the Father, we are grateful for the moments that show Jesus' humanness. Finally, the story is good drama, as it leads the reader through a variety of empathies until the story ends with the glorious words: "Free him and let him go."

The Lazarus story clearly can be read to go beyond the raising of Lazarus from the dead. Immediately after the miracle at Bethany, some who heard of it decided to "eliminate" Jesus. Also, it would be wise to get rid of Lazarus, whose very existence now urged faith in Jesus as Messiah, Son of God, for now Jesus was seen as the source of life. Particularly worrisome to many was the possibility that, with this powerful act over death itself, Jesus might be the rallying point for a rebellion against Rome; the Roman-appointed High Priest and others concluded that it would be better that one man die, than that the whole nation foolishly bring down upon itself the wrath of Rome—a punishing wrath which sadly Israel experienced only forty years or so after the death of Jesus.

Bethany, amidst its few remains, was the physical site of the sign most clearly asking for belief that Jesus is the one source of life, perfect and everlasting, that he is Messiah and Son of God.

The Mount of Olives

The Ascension
~ LUKE 24:50–53; ACTS 1:9–11 ~

To enter the area of the Ascension of Jesus to heaven is to pass, first
through a wall and then to pass through the door of a small building into
a single room which is famous for a rough piece of rock in an otherwise
smooth flooring. An old tradition says that Jesus left this world from this
rock, and claims are made that we can even yet see the imprint of one of
his feet on this rock. The present building dates from the eleventh or
twelfth century and has over the centuries been used as a mosque. As
with other sites, to get a true idea of the Ascension area one must imaginatively remove this building and the wall which surrounds it, so as to
stand in open air. The Muslim authorities, who control this site, gra-
ciously allow Orthodox and Latin Christians to celebrate liturgies here
on their Ascension days.

   The mountain on which the rock of the Ascension is founded is
known in the New Testament as the Mount of Olives (sometimes later
called Mount Olivet), for on its lower western flank flourished rich
groves of many olive trees.

   Imaginatively, the Jewish Scriptures portray God, the great Lord, as
One who would come from the east, like the sun reaching out over the
Jewish world each dawn (Ez 43:1–2). When this God comes to judge

The Mount of Olives: Church of the Ascension

Israel and to purify his city Jerusalem, the many hills on his way would be leveled and the many valleys would be filled up, all to make his royal passage fittingly a smooth and easy one. The Mount of Olives, in particular, would be divided in half from east to west, so that between the newly created northern and southern parts God could approach his city with stately ease. That Jesus would "return as you have seen him go up," in the words of the angels to the disciples, suggests that it is Jesus who will perform this role of judge of Israel at the end of time.

The Mount of Olives is famous for several sites. Just over the top of the mountain, towards the east and out of sight of Jerusalem, is the gospel town of Bethany, home of Martha, Mary, and Lazarus. About halfway down the mountain on its western side facing Jerusalem is a chapel which commemorates Jesus' weeping over Jerusalem. Farther down the same slope, near the bottom of the mountain and across from Jerusalem, is the garden area where Jesus agonized over his imminent suffering and where he was captured. Also on this western slope we can visit a church dedicated to the memory of the great prayer, the Our Father.

In Jesus' time, the Mount of Olives was known for its roads which lead from Jericho near the Jordan River to the mountain's top and continued on to lead one into Jerusalem. The man who enjoyed the kindness of the Good Samaritan was on one of these roads to Jericho. Such then is the significance of this mountain, so near the holy city of Jerusalem, a mountain which oversaw the growth of the city of David into a major capital under Solomon.

But what of the event which has crowned this mountain's top? What is to be understood of the Ascension of Jesus? According to the thinking of Jesus' time, ascension represented a mode of entering the presence of God, a manner of leaving this world for everlasting life with God. Thus, though ascension is the term used for this moment of Jesus' life, we must really concentrate on the result of that movement into God's presence. For Jesus, this entrance was a return; moreover, it was a taking of a position at the right hand of the Father, the position of God's Favorite and his Beloved Son, the position indicated as that belonging to David's Lord, as the famous words of the psalm had said, "The Lord [Yahweh] said to my Lord: 'Sit at my right hand; I will put your enemies under your feet as your footstool'" (Ps 110:1). In essence, then, the metaphorical language of moving upward from this earth to God's dwelling in the heavens conveyed the conviction that Jesus has not only risen from the dead, but also reached the terminus or final goal of his resurrection and ascension: the sitting at the right hand of his Father.

Luke's two renditions of Jesus' return to the Father—at the end of the Gospel and at the beginning of his Acts of the Apostles—differ in their details. So different are they in regard to the time of the Ascension that one is not quite sure how to justify both accounts as accurate reports of what actually happened: the Gospel gives the impression that Jesus ascended within twenty-four hours of his resurrection, which is the impression given elsewhere in the New Testament, whereas the Acts indicates that Jesus ascended to the Father forty days after his resurrection—and indeed it is this ascension date which Roman Catholics use to determine their annual Feast of the Ascension. We must assume that Luke, the author of both stories, would more than likely not contradict himself in this matter of timing. We conclude that in giving different times to these ascensions Luke meant to communicate two different ideas. The ascension of the Gospel is meant to show the natural and logical conclusion to Jesus' resurrection; indeed, the Resurrection and Ascension are simply one continuous movement into the presence of God forever. The Ascension in Acts is meant rather to identify the last time Jesus appeared to his disciples; this definitive departure occurred only after Jesus had taught his disciples what still remained for him to teach them. Thus, on the one hand Jesus immediately went to his Father from his grave; on the other hand he definitively left his disciples after a period of teaching them final matters. But there is more to learn from these two stories of the Ascension.

What characterizes the Gospel Ascension is the joy and glory emanating from the narration. This is a wonderful moment, the culmination of Jesus' life on earth, the visible sign of Jesus' innocence before the world, and his chosennes before God. The disciples rejoice in this ending to the events of the life of Jesus, especially of his humiliating death. Jesus will be revealed as Lord through this ascension. Luke notes how Jesus, in leaving, blesses his disciples, the fitting climax to his life with them.

The Ascension in Acts conveys a different feeling. Here the disciples seem confused and hesitant; they realize that, with the passing of the one they knew to be Messiah, the chances that the kingdom might be restored to Israel were slim indeed. Thus, the aspects of joy and glory are missing from this description of ascension. The angels of God must encourage these disciples, must assure them that "he will return as you have seen him go up."

The key to understanding the Ascension is to give full meaning to the positions of these stories within their respective books. The first ascension closes a book, the second opens a book; this placement of stories is crucial to their understanding.

It is clear enough that the first ascension closes Jesus' life on earth; as such it is meant to be a story's joyful conclusion. The second ascension, while representing the definitive departure of Jesus from his disciples, is really the opening onto a period which, from the perspective of the disciples, was very unclear, uncertain, and threatening. Only knowledge given by the Pentecostal Spirit will calm the disciples and give them courage and wisdom, and they do not as yet have these gifts, nor any experience of the Spirit. Luke intentionally has shown the disciples still dependent on Jesus' teaching for clarity, shows them now diffident by his description of them as simply gazing up after Jesus, as though they could only remain rooted to the mountain with no knowledge of what to do next. Unsure of the future, the disciples return to Jerusalem, simply to wait in the Upper Room for God's next word to them. In its own way, this ascension story makes clear that, if great things are about to happen through the disciples, they will happen only when God intervenes and sends his Spirit; Christianity will not be the result of human planning, but of divine initiative, power, and direction.

The memory of Ascension, then, is meant to show the glorious outcome of Jesus' life, especially his triumph over humiliation and false accusation, for God's Favorite is returning to his Father to take up his place at God's right hand. The memory of Ascension also opens up the age of the apostles, people dependent for guidance and power and wisdom on the frequent intervention of God, Jesus and the Holy Spirit.

This place, then, commemorates a departure—and an assurance that those left in "this world" will enjoy the comfort and protection, the guidance and encouragement and inspiration of the Lord who resides in "the world to come," until he returns finally to take us all with him to eternal happiness. We rejoice in his glory, long for his return, and count on his presence in so many situations over which we have no control unless he is with us.

Pater Noster Church (Our Father Church)
~ MATTHEW 6:7–15; LUKE 11:1–4 ~

Near the top of the Mount of Olives is a compound whose center is the Our Father Church. This church is a complete restoration, done about 1874, of an earlier church built by the crusaders about 1160. The crusaders named their church Pater Noster Church.

Not far from the crusader church is what must be the site of the church Constantine had erected in honor of the events of the Mount of Olives, particularly the Ascension of Jesus. Since the Greek word for olives is *elaia*, we are not surprised to hear this Constantinian church called the Eleona. This Eleona forms the trinity of churches Constantine built on the advice of his mother, Helena: the Eleona, the Basilica of the Holy Sepulcher in Jerusalem, and the Church of the Nativity of Jesus in Bethlehem.

The present Our Father Church offers to the visitor a series of over sixty different plaques, in as many languages, of the Our Father.

The Gospels suggest that Jesus taught the Lord's Prayer twice. One version occurs in Matthew as part of his Sermon on the Mount in Galilee; the other version occurs in Luke, while Jesus is on his way from Galilee to Jerusalem. It was probably the Lucan geographical data which moved the crusaders to build their church of the Our Father on the Mount of Olives. The account just before Luke's Our Father story tells of a visit from Jesus to Martha and Mary; though the village of this visit is not named, John's Gospel indicates that Martha and Mary had their house in Bethany, which is on the eastern slope of the Mount of Olives. So, it was logical to conclude that Jesus spoke the Our Father somewhere on the Mount of Olives since he spoke it just after, the crusaders thought, his visit to Bethany. That the Our Father was given on the Mount of Olives is doubtful, since it is clear in Luke that the Our Father he offers occurs long before Jesus reaches Jerusalem; Luke himself says, two chapters after the Our Father story, that "Jesus was going through towns and villages, teaching, making his way to Jerusalem" (Lk 13:22). However one explains his having met Martha and Mary so early in this journey to Jerusalem, it seems more likely that Matthew is accurate when he puts the teaching of the Our Father in Galilee. Luke, for his own reasons, preferred to give it while Jesus was in the early stages of his journey to Jerusalem.

The wording of the Our Father appears differently in Matthew and Luke. Luke reports fewer petitions than does Matthew. Moreover, the circumstance which, in Matthew, prompted Jesus to teach the Our Father is different from that which, according to Luke, prompted Jesus to teach this prayer. In Matthew, Jesus criticizes longish prayer, lest it give the impression that simple length of prayer reveals that the one praying is holier than one who prays briefly. Prayer is valuable according to its content, not according to its length; good content does not mean much length. Luke, on the other hand, shows Jesus offering the Our Father as a response to a request from his disciples that he teach them to pray as John the Baptist taught his own disciples to pray.

A visual comparison will show the differences in the two versions of the Our Father, but we can see that they are substantially and essentially much alike; one can understand why most scholars think that the two versions really come from a prayer Jesus offered to his hearers one time. Our attention is more on the substantial agreement between the two versions, for herein lies Jesus' own suggestion of our approach to God.

Matthew	Luke
Our Father in heaven,	Our Father,
may your name be held holy,	may your name be held holy,
let your kingdom come,	let your kingdom come.
your will be done on earth	
as it is in heaven.	
Give us today our daily bread,	Give us each day our daily bread,
and forgive us our debts,	and forgive us our sins,
as we have forgiven those	for we ourselves forgive each one
who are in debt to us.	who is in debt to us.
And do not put us to the test,	And do not put us to the test.
but save us from the Evil One.	

The fundamental relationship between God and human beings is, according to Jesus' prayer, that of parent and children. Every religion has, through name giving and title giving, favorite expressions for God; these names and titles reveal the views religious people have of the divine saving power and loving care exercised for themselves and for their world. From this point of view, the Christian is asked to consider the all-powerful and only God under the title of parent. Jesus asks the Christian to apply to God all the positive meaning human beings attach to this figure. The Christian thus imitates Jesus who rarely spoke of God as anyone but Father, and never addressed God directly by any other name. Finally the dominance of the view of God as Jesus' Father forces Christians to recognize fellow and sister disciples of Jesus as brothers and sisters of one another.

In speaking of God as Father, Jesus made an inestimable contribution to each person's self-understanding and value before the eyes of the world; he opened up to us the secret by which we can understand a dominant motive for God's unending relationship with us—he approaches us in the best sense of what we know a parent to be. It is a constant source of wonderment that the Being we know as the one and true God is revealed to us by Jesus as Father and that God wants to be known this way; for thousands of years human beings more easily have understood God as Power, Authority, Lord, awesome Master, and Judge, than they have accepted him as Father, in the living out of their lives with their God. Yet this is the title Jesus knew is best to address God; he lived with God as his Father, and urged his disciples to do so as well.

Jesus is typically Jewish when, with the mention of God, he prays that God's name be held holy by all creation, in all times and places. Isaiah had long ago painted the picture of the heavenly beings unendingly calling "Holy, Holy, Holy" before the throne of God, and the tradition of Israel is replete with the call to be attentive to the holiness of God, to reverence him as holy, the source of all holiness. It is not surprising, then, that Jesus' first words should be the wish or prayer that God's name be held holy. It may be surprising to us, however, that prayer for God's name to be held holy comes before prayer for our own needs.

The entire New Testament is a witness to the basic frame of thought within which the appearance of Jesus took place: he comes to bring the kingdom of God into existence, the kingdom longed for and expected from early Jewish times. By this image of kingdom, Israel summed up its hope that the goodness and happiness and peace it knew under David and Solomon would once again be granted to Israel—if possible in even greater lavishness than ever before. After suffering severe disasters since enjoying the benefits of David and Solomon, what was left of Israel looked forward for its restoration to that position of Chosen One where it would know the dazzling effects of God's love when it would no longer be impeded by Satanic and human folly. Jesus, then, encourages his followers to pray to God for that kind of existence, still out of our grasp and ultimately ours only if God grants it, wherein God, the source of all happiness, controls human lives like a king, and wards off every grief from our lives.

Typical of Matthew is the addition of a petition which carries out the Jewish flavor of Jesus' prayer. That is, Matthew here develops beyond Luke what the Jewish Scriptures considered to be the primary requisite for establishing God's kingdom: the kingdom will exist and function only if it is governed by God's will. May that will, then, be done, for it is key to the establishment of human happiness. Heaven is a model, for it is clearly governed by the will of God and enjoys a perfection which even the pagans admired and chronicled; may that will which brings harmony, peace, and contentment to heaven rule the earth.

Not that Luke did not know the importance of following the will of God; on the contrary, he emphasized it, but in his own way, i.e., obedience to the teaching of Jesus. Jesus had always obeyed the will of God, as the bitter lessons preserved in the Old Testament encouraged all Jews to do. Jesus often evaluated his devotion and love for God by his obedience to God; he could only hope that the confidence he had in the effects of obedience would be shared in by his followers.

Adam had shown Israel the results of disobedience, a disobedience for which we continue to pay, not only by dying, but by a weakness which makes us prone to continue the separation from God which Adam had begun. Jesus appeared as the second Adam and fixed on the obedience which could repair what Adam had done; ultimately Jesus lived up to his preaching to others as he accepted his Father's will for himself and died so painfully out of obedience. In absolute trust that God's will is good for us, Jesus asks us to pray that God's will be done. If another will than God's has dominated the earth, or just a part of it, what has history taught us of such dominance? If that will is better for us than God's, let it be done. What does history say?

One of the most incisive teachings of Jesus has to do with the connections between our worldly needs and trust in God's love for us. Sometimes considered a naïve exaggeration, Jesus encourages us to trust that God will care for us as he does for birds and lilies; this teaching has become a monumental challenge to all Christians. What Jesus seems to be concerned with, when he asks us not to be preoccupied with gathering food and clothing, is not our legitimate efforts at survival and improvement, but with the apparent ignorance about the truth that, if you seek the kingdom of God first of all, the other things will be given you. Against the conventional wisdom that puts success solely in the hands of human beings, is the affirmation of Jesus that God is our Father, and if he is so, he will act like a father and provide for his children. One can always cite calamities which suggest that we should trust elsewhere than just in God, for he has not saved us from calamity. But Jesus is just as adamant that God is Father, and as such will provide for his children. The subtle call to someone or something other than God, for instance money, for salvation is idol-worship, and the expectation that this person or thing will free me from death is foolishness. It is against this looking elsewhere than to God as Father that Jesus so strenuously preached.

Jesus says "seek first the kingdom of God and all will be given to you." This sequence is the logical conclusion drawn from God's choice to be our Father. The history of Judaism and Christianity has long had to contend with this conclusion in a world where, in fact, God's intervention and provision for his children is not as constant or as dramatic as we might wish. Yet this absence of God in one's time of need has never been accepted as an indication that God's love for us has flagged. The insistence in Judaism and Christianity is that God is only good, that there is no evil intent in God, that he is not the source of evil. The story of Adam and Eve is meant to teach in part that, if there is an evil that can bring us death, that evil does not come from God, but from human choice and a force tempting us to evil. Over centuries, Christian thinkers have made a distinction which has become part of our thinking: God, while all-good, can cause physical evil, but never moral evil; at best, he can only permit us to make our own choices for moral evil. That is, God can cause physical suffering for our moral good, but he can never cause us to sin, only permit us to have our own way. While the problem of evil in a world dominated by an all-good God is difficult to comprehend, especially when one is truly "up against it," Jesus' words are insistent: God is your Father; trust in him.

Remembering always that we are speaking to our Father, Jesus encourages us to ask him for our daily food. It would be naïve to suppose that we work less hard, because God will provide. But the logic of the relationship between parent and child urges us to look to the Father for his contribution, whatever it may be, to our daily food needs. I remain aware that God my Father is a constant source of my total well-being. Jesus draws the conclusion that, should the Father seem uncooperative for a time, one should not look to another god, but have trust.

A second concern, after the mention of food, is a request for forgiveness of sins, that God forget our debts to him, as Matthew's version puts it. Such a request occupied the minds of many of Jesus' contemporaries, was one of the essential prayers rising daily to God from the Temple in Jerusalem, and so was part of Jesus' earliest memories and prayers. Forgiveness on God's part was considered the absolutely necessary condition for a renewed covenant with him which would bring us all the covenant blessings a Father has in store for his children. Forgiveness, too, was the free choice of the all-holy God, for which we creatures can only beg.

Both Gospel versions of the Our Father place our request for forgiveness next to the assurance to God that we forgive those who have offended us. While we do not here review all that Jesus teaches about forgiveness of an enemy, we are aware of his insistence on this forgiveness. We understand the principle underlying Jesus' joining together a request for forgiveness and the assurance of having forgiven others: how can one expect forgiveness when one will not forgive? Jesus' parable about the servant who was forgiven an immense debt by his master, only to go out and punish a fellow servant for not paying back an insignificant debt is an extremely powerful expression of Jesus' thinking. Forgiveness of others is ultimately a concrete example of Jesus' general exhortation: you know how you want to be loved—then love others that way. Even purely human wisdom knows that an unloving person cannot expect love.

Forgiveness of both good and evil people, Jesus says, is characteristic of God; he lets the life-giving sun and rain fall certainly on his friends, and just as certainly on his enemies. After saying this, Jesus then repeats in command form, "Be perfect as your heavenly Father is perfect," what Genesis had so long ago said of us: "God made them in his own image and likeness"; we were created to be like God, we were created to love and forgive—like God.

In Jesus' religious world, there existed many prophecies that the change from "this age" to the "age to come" would involve, unhappily, an exercise of power by Satan that would be nothing less than frighteningly traumatic. Satan, realizing that this was his last opportunity to control God's world, would wage a struggle worthy of his nature and of the stakes for which he fights. Since in Jewish thinking Satan could do no direct harm to God, his best plan was to destroy all that God loved and called good. Every human being can expect to be a target of Satan, but particularly those who are dedicated to the God Satan hates. To be protected from the eventual testing of faith that Satan will cause in these extreme circumstances is the final request of this prayer. What mere human being by himself can hope to withstand the cleverness, the guile, the intrigue of Satan, who boldly boasted even to Jesus: "All these kingdoms and their glories are mine"? It is the common understanding of his time that Jesus' petition reflects here; whatever we may think today of the likelihood of a "final battle" between God and Satan, our experience confirms Jesus' prayer: only with God's constant help can we hope to win the battle of daily temptation to travel Satan's way, rather than the way of Jesus. St. Paul is a welcome companion here: he is confident that ultimately nothing will separate us from God's loving us; this means that God will come to our rescue, that he will never allow us to be finally drowned in the temptations which so often seem beyond our strength to resist.

The Our Father sums up the key elements of a vibrant relationship between a parent and children. The Our Father is a prayer for "us," not for "me" alone. We are all seen as children together, and together we pray that the blessings coming come from a Father's heart be blessings on "us," not just on "me" alone. The single petitions of the Our Father are not unique to Jesus; they are all part of his Jewish tradition and there are many Jewish prayers which reflect the individual elements of the Our Father. But it is Jesus alone who has put these elements together and in their sequence, and it is Jesus alone who is so insistent that God be thought of as Father, that we think of ourselves and all human beings as nothing less than children of God.

Dominus Flevit Chapel
~ LUKE 19:41–44 ~

Near midway down the western slope of the Mount of Olives, within the ruins of a cemetery in which are burial materials going back to the first century A.D., is a lovely chapel, built in the twentieth century, with a grand view of Jerusalem, particularly of the area where stood the Temple of Jerusalem, where now stands the shining Moslem Dome of the Rock. This chapel stands close to the ancient route usually followed by travelers coming from Jericho and the Dead Sea area to Jerusalem.

The Mount of Olives: ancient olive trees

There is no claim that this chapel marks the exact spot where Jesus wept over Jerusalem, but it stands as an invitation to consider this powerful moment in Jesus' life. Jesus had insisted on his journey from Galilee to the Feast of Passover in Jerusalem that he must reach the Holy City. He is pictured in the Gospels as aware that his many efforts to lead his people to repentance and forgiveness would quite likely end in his death in Jerusalem. If he persisted in going there, Jerusalem would likely react to him as it had reacted to so many Jewish prophets. Yet, Jesus went, out of obedience to his Father, and with sorrow in his heart, even to weeping, for the refusal of so many Jews to return to their God.

This chapel *(Dominus Flevit = The Lord Wept)* represents a stage in the final approach of Jesus to Jerusalem; he had only now to continue his descent, cross the Kedron Valley and make the short climb to Jerusalem. According to the first three Gospels, this coming to Jerusalem will be Jesus' first—and last.

At a certain moment in this descent down the Mount of Olives, the crowds began to think of Jesus as their Messiah coming to take possession of God's Temple and city. Luke says they thought of him as Jerusalem's King because of "all the miracles they had seen" (Lk 19:37). Often enough it was the miracles which made people follow Jesus; how little prepared were these people for the moments of suffering and death when Jesus worked no miracle for himself—nor did God. Jesus had warned his followers of what would happen once he had entered into the stronghold of those who plotted against him, but his disciples "did not understand him when he said this; it was hidden from them so that they should not see the meaning of it, and they were afraid to ask him about what he had said" (Lk 9:45).

In contrast to this welcome was the attitude of some Pharisees in the crowd; they could only respond: "Master, silence your disciples." Such had been their reaction throughout Jesus' public life, and through the life of John the Baptist, too; these Pharisees could accept neither man, despite the notable differences between Jesus and John.

Mark, like Luke, also narrates a fervent welcome of Jesus as he approached Jerusalem and describes him as the one they thought to be their Messiah. Immediately following the sullen remarks of the Pharisees, however, Mark tells the story of Jesus' cursing of a fig tree (often a symbol of Israel in the Old Testament), for its lack of fruit; this curse was a symbol of God's reaction to these Pharisees' not believing in Jesus. Luke, having read Mark, did not include in his account the cursing story, but preferred to express a different form of the divine displeasure at Jesus' rejection: the forecast of the destruction of Jerusalem.

Jesus wept for Jerusalem, the site of God's dwelling, where his Name and his Glory dwelt. All the world had been conceived as circling around the holiest place, the center of the world, the Holy of Holies, the private quarters of earth's King and Israel's covenant partner. Jesus wept for the imminent destruction of city and Temple: one stone would not be allowed to stand on another. One cannot fail to hear in Jesus' words the many pleas for repentance and return directed at Jerusalem by Isaiah, Jeremiah, and still other prophets. Nor can we fail to recall the Old Testament's way of interpreting tragedies such as the destruction of Jerusalem: these things occur as punishment for turning from God. Thus, Jerusalem would be destroyed, not simply because the Roman army was stronger than the Jewish rebels. Such causes were seen by most Jews as secondary, for they operated only with permission from God. Jesus pointed to the radical cause for the destruction of Jerusalem: ". . . because you did not recognize your opportunity when God offered it!" (Lk 19:44).

Many had been the calls to return to God; Jesus' was only the latest. The Jews who did respond—especially noteworthy was the response to the preaching fifty days after Jesus' ascension (Acts 2:41–47)—these Jews, eventually with Gentiles, formed the repentant people who would follow the Messiah indicated by God's word in the Old Testament and would enjoy the fulfillment of the Old Testament's promises.

Jesus wept for Jerusalem, for his own people. Jerusalem was the city *par excellence* of Jesus' forefathers, the center of pilgrimage three times a year for all Israelite adult males, the Sion hymned in psalms, the symbol of God's union with Israel. Given his history, Jesus' weeping at what he knew would come to pass is not surprising. Sobering to Christians and to Jews are the words of John's first chapter: "he came to his own, and his own received him not" (Jn 1:11).

The destruction of Jerusalem was an immense tragedy. Yet the Scriptures did not perceive such pain and suffering as the worst effect of breaking the relationship between God and his people. No, the worst effect Israel feared was that God would simply allow sinners to continue to choose to live alienated from God. There is no greater punishment than this, for the simple withdrawal away from God, in free choice, is to set in motion and give sway to all the forces which will destroy ourselves completely. Human beings left alone without God—this is the greatest tragedy, as the Old Testament sees it, for in this condition are set free all the potentialities for suffering that we could possibly inflict on ourselves and others.

Jesus' prediction of the destruction of Jerusalem occurred not only on the western slope of the Mount of Olives as he wept over Jerusalem. During his few remaining preaching days while in the very area of the Jerusalem Temple, Jesus again predicted the state of "one stone not resting on another." This particular prediction before the Temple's main door was given to his disciples. Thus, it is not so much a promise of punishment as an encouragement to his disciples that knowing the future, they might have the insight to understand it and the strength to bear it. Indeed, this prediction of Jerusalem's destruction becomes part of the full reality Jesus sees leading up to the very end of this age and its replacement by the wonderful age to come. The disciple is urged, through all future calamities, to remain faithful, to watch, and, when the Son of Man comes to end this world and begin the new, to "raise up your heads, for your redemption is at hand." God purges the world of its evil, as he does cleanse us, too, of ours. What Jesus sees in all of this is the goal, the reign of God in which there will be for us only happiness.

The Lord's weeping, ultimately, is a weeping over the inability of human beings to respond to the one person who can free them for total happiness, over human preference for "living in darkness and the shadow of death"—a phrase drawn from Jesus' own tradition some seven hundred years old. To the doomed city Jesus now descends.

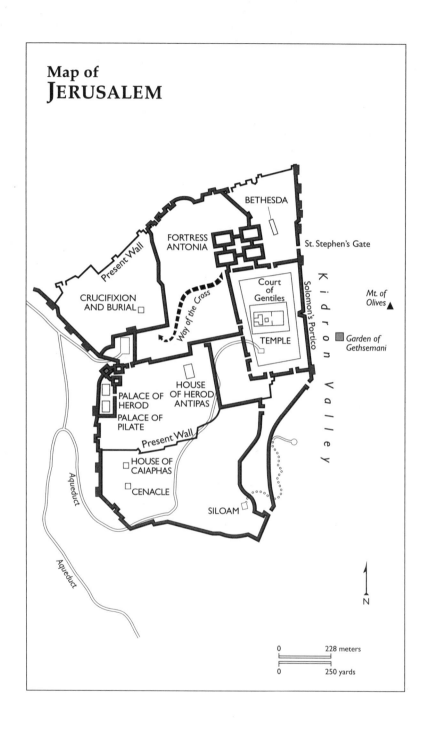

Map of
JERUSALEM

BETHESDA

FORTRESS
ANTONIA

Present Wall

St. Stephen's Gate

CRUCIFIXION
AND BURIAL

Way of the Cross

Court
of
Gentiles

Solomon's Portico

Kidron Valley

Mt. of
Olives ▲

Garden of
Gethsemani

TEMPLE

PALACE OF
HEROD

HOUSE
OF HEROD
ANTIPAS

PALACE OF
PILATE

Present Wall

HOUSE OF
CAIAPHAS

Aqueduct

CENACLE

SILOAM

Aqueduct

N

| 0 | 228 meters |
| 0 | 250 yards |

PART THREE

Jerusalem

Gethsemani

> "LET YOUR WILL BE DONE, NOT MINE."
> ~ MARK 14:26

Almost at the bottom of the western slope of the Mount of Olives, in the Kidron Valley, is a most holy site, the place of Jesus' agony in the garden and of his arrest. The site itself, long venerated by Christians, is marked today by a noteworthy church which includes in its

Gethsemani: garden scene mosaic on Church of All Nations

garden ancient olive trees reminiscent of the olive grove in which Jesus, as Luke notes, prayed through the night after teaching in the Temple area by day (Lk 21:37). So old do today's olive trees appear that we might suspect them to be the trees which mutely watched the terrible events of that night nearly two thousand years ago; an olive tree does not live so long, but it is possible that ancestors of these did witness the pain of that night.

The church marking this holy site, called the Basilica of the Agony or, more recently, the Church of All Nations, was begun in 1919 and consecrated in 1924. The basilica is readily visible and stands overlooking the Kidron Valley, looking directly at the eastern wall of Jerusalem. Very easy to pick out are the three great arches in the front of the basilica which separate the four statues on high, statues of the evangelists and their symbols. Matthew is symbolized by a young man; his Gospel begins with the family tree of a young man. Mark is marked by a lion; his Gospel begins with a mention of a voice, later identified as a lion, crying in the desert. Luke is symbolized by an ox; his Gospel begins in the Temple, where sacrifices were carried on—and the ox is the animal *par excellence* of sacrifice. John is characterized by the eagle; like an eagle, the Gospel of John and particularly its prologue, soars to the heights and penetrates the mystery of the Son of God.

Above the arches and the evangelists is a great triangular mosaic, whose theme is Jesus in glory offering his sufferings and those of the world to the Father. Thus the basilica invites us to reflect on what the evangelists reported about the tragic events beginning with betrayal in this garden area, the series of tragic events which ended in nothing short of Jesus sitting at the right hand of his Father in glory. The whole inner church promotes this movement from sorrow to glory, for upon entering it, we enter from the garden of sorrow into the place of sorrow, an interior which is meant to stir up in the visitor the grief of that terrible night. Only then do we exit into the light of day that symbolizes the glory of the Lord.

Within the basilica we must let our eyes become accustomed to the dimness. There is only faint light centered on the large rock, surrounded by a metal crown of thorns. This rock traditionally has been considered the rock on which Jesus knelt for time of prayer, apart from his disciples, just before he was arrested.

Many nations donated money for this impressive interior, the entire building, and its preservation. These benefactors are remembered on the ceiling of the basilica by representations symbolizing each nation. As we stand about the middle of the basilica facing the altar and look up to the right third of the ceiling, we can discern the symbols of the United States of America. Notable also in this church construction are the windows of alabaster, the small cupolas which remind us of Byzantine artistry, the mosaics of the cupolas executed by Italian artists, and the lovely mosaic floor on which we stand.

The mosaic floor deserves a particular comment. It is an exact representation of the mosaic floor of the church built when Theodosius was emperor of Constantinople (379–393), and called "elegant" in a document by a pilgrim in the fourth century. And beneath the covers of the floor is the mosaic flooring of the original Theodosian basilica, a precious archaeological remnant. We are, by virtue of this original flooring, in touch with a long tradition of veneration at this spot. And we can add that between the times of the present church and the church of Theodosius there was also a small church in the time of the crusaders dedicated to St. Savior. Here, then, Christians have come for many centuries to share in the sorrowful event of that night almost two thousand years ago; the vestiges of these ancient Christians allow us to share our moment with them.

Grotto of the Agony

Before considering the significance of this revered gospel site, a word should be said about the grotto which can be found once we exit from the Garden of Gethsemani and begin to follow the road towards the Grotto of the Virgin, not many yards from the Garden of Gethsemani. This grotto, between the Grotto of the Virgin and Gethsemani, is called the Grotto of the Agony, but is actually the place of the betrayal and arrest of Jesus, the place where Jesus went with his disciples to meet the betrayer and his accomplices. This area, then, contains three places connected with the sorrowful events of that night: the olive grove called Gethsemani where the disciples waited for Jesus, Jesus' own place of prayer (now within the church building), and the Grotto of the Agony where Jesus met his betrayer Judas. We have indications that worship services were conducted as far back as the fourth century in the grotto and at the site of Jesus' prayer and agony.

The Gospel stories about what happened at the Gethsemani area can be divided into two parts: what happened to Jesus before his arrest and the arrest itself with its attendant circumstances. Only John does not report Jesus' agony in this garden area; it is Mark, followed by Matthew and Luke, who asks the Christian to consider carefully the fear Jesus suffered at the realization of what his Father was about to ask from him. Yet, even John conveys some of this agony in the one verse he gives to its reality at a slightly earlier point in his Gospel: "Now is my soul terrified—and what should I say? 'Father, save me from this hour?'" (Jn 12:27).

The Agony in the Garden
~ MATTHEW 26:36–46; MARK 14:32–42; LUKE 22:39–46 ~

In the stories of Matthew, Mark, and Luke, two elements are the backbone of the narratives: the call to the disciples to pray lest they enter into a temptation they cannot resist and the prayer of Jesus to his Father. Indeed, the three Gospels follow the same sequence, first reporting the suffering of Jesus, then concluding with calls to attentiveness, watchfulness, prayer. These reports are concerned as much with the exhortation to prayer as with the moments of Jesus' private agony. In this way, the reader of a later generation is asked to be attentive, to watch, to pray when it is obvious that suffering with the Lord is to be the disciple's lot. While Luke goes furthest in detailing the physical effects of Jesus' mental anguish, all three agree that the suffering here is unparalleled in the previous parts of Jesus' life. Here we have an insight into the human reality of Jesus. His was a struggle between survival and obedience and his whole being was convulsed by it; his was not a purely intellectual struggle for comprehension, but a torture which brought him to ask to be set free from what was to come. The reader has at least a few moments' glimpse of what it took to wrench Jesus to obedience.

There are many elements to appreciate in these Gospel reports. The nearness of the reader to the terrible moment of his Lord is one. Another is the bitter contrast between one person struggling for his life and the weariness and inattentiveness of his closest friends; they are so physically close and so psychologically distant. A third value is the awareness of the seriousness of the sin for which Jesus must suffer. For, if Jesus has freed us from sins by his death, we can already sense, in his terror in the garden, how thoroughly evil must be the acts which please sinners.

In short, Jesus' suffering is the central aspect of these Gethsemani reports, and the reader finds encouragement when faced in his own loneliness with the choice to obey or not. But the story of Jesus' struggle goes hand in hand with the weakness of and warnings to the disciples. The disciple must learn to watch, to pray, especially to avoid yielding to temptation, especially to embrace the will of the good God.

We should not overlook the fact that the entire expression of Jesus' soul-rending prayer is set within his understanding that God is his Father. Even in suffering, Jesus and his disciple must know that the one who controls the world is Father, despite the apparent contradiction of a father's love and the call to die. Jesus called the decision of God in his regard the decision of his Father. If the problem of suffering is to be solved at all, it must be solved within the understanding of a parent asking obedience of a child, and not in the abandonment of that understanding.

Capture of Jesus
~ Matthew 26:47–56; Mark 14:43–52; Luke 22:47–53 ~

The second part of the Gethsemani story has to do with the capture of Jesus. All four Gospels narrate the basic elements of that event: Judas, one of the Twelve and now the betrayer, knows where to find Jesus, and he does find him; Judas betrays Jesus; the disciples try to prevent the capture by recourse to weapons and Jesus rejects that intervention; Jesus marvels that his capture is done in darkness and stealth, when he could as easily have been picked up in daylight right in the Temple area where he has been teaching openly, daily; Jesus is bound and led away.

Clearly, the evangelists present the conspiratorial and secretive manner of the authorities as a sign that Jesus really is a victim of injustice; indeed, if the ordinary people, who listened so pleasurably to Jesus, knew of what was happening, they would violently oppose his arrest. Thus, into this sad and violent story is built an apologetic or defense of Jesus' innocence; this innocence influences all of the Gospel writing, but especially the moment of greatest tension when it is injustice that puts Jesus, the innocent one, to death.

Matthew adds to these basic elements of the capture story the words of Jesus by which is explained Jesus' desire that his disciples not defend him; first, people who fight by the sword die by it, and Jesus did not want that to happen to his disciples here; second, given that God is Jesus' Father, surely the Father would defend his Son if he thought it right—but Scripture has already indicated what was the will of the Father for his Son, and Jesus wanted that Scripture fulfilled, that will obeyed. Jesus' whole life was guided by his awareness that he fulfilled the Scripture; those prophecies, even the ones foretelling his pain and death, are to be cherished, for in fulfilling them Jesus, the Son of God, is made perfect.

"The Shepherd will be struck and his sheep will be scattered": another Old Testament citation that helps interpret what is happening in this vicious garden scene. Mark and Matthew continue to interpret the events of Jesus' life by the Scriptures and continue to show that Jesus' life is the completion of the Scriptures.

Mark is unique in telling his reader that, among those who fled the scene of capture, was a young man, unnamed. Many interpreters have suggested that this young witness is Mark himself.

Luke, too, has something to offer in this story which is not accentuated by the others. Luke concludes his story by noting the words of Jesus: "This is your hour; now evil exercises its power" (Lk 22:53). Many interpreters see this sentence as the completion of what was suggested at the conclusion of Satan's temptations in the desert, just before Jesus began his public life: "and having finished tempting him, the devil left him till another, opportune moment" (Lk 4:13). Thus, the temptations are a prelude to the time when the Satanic power will have its full, destructive way with Jesus. The capture of Jesus is what the reader has waited for, ever since the reader learned that Satan was simply biding his time until he could get his hands on Jesus; Jesus overcame the temptations, but Satan knew there was another time when he would destroy Jesus.

Jesus Identifies Himself
~ JOHN 18:1–12 ~

With John's Gospel we have an approach to the capture scene which is notably different from that of the first three Gospels. Here no agony is reported; Jesus knows all that is going to happen, as his captors approach. John reports that when Jesus identifies himself to those cautiously crowding toward him, they fall back to the ground, motionless until Jesus bids them to speak to him. What does this unexpected description mean to say?

Jesus asks his captors: "Whom do you seek?" Hearing them answer "Jesus of Nazareth," Jesus responds with two words (in the Greek text): *ego eimi*. This can simply mean: "I am he"; as such it would mean to say that "if you are looking for Jesus of Nazareth, well, I am he." But these Greek words can also mean: "I am." This, for everyone who knew the Old Testament, was the name God gave to Moses, when Moses asked God at the burning bush: "Who should I say is sending me to free Israel from the Egyptian Pharaoh?" God first said: "Tell them I-am-who-am sends you," but then God gave Moses the shorter form of this name: "I am." The sacred name Yahweh is the Hebrew way of saying "I am who am" in Hebrew characters. Thus, when John records Jesus' response "I am," most scholars think he means to say that Jesus identifies himself as "I am," the God of the Old Testament; obviously, from other things Jesus says in the Gospel, it is clear that there is a difference between God and Jesus, yet the claim stands: Jesus calls himself "I am." And indeed, from the first lines of his Gospel John insists that, however one explains it, the Word that was with God and was God became a human being and dwelt among us. Why would John tell us Jesus is "I am" at the beginning of the Passion story?

This detail of the capture story seems to be an affirmation of what had already been stated in an earlier part of John; it is connected with Jesus' statement there, that "no one takes my life from me; I lay it down and I raise it up again." What Jesus means to say is that, despite appearances, there is no one who has control over him, not even Satan. If Jesus is captured and put to death, it is because he gives permission to mere human beings to do so. Jesus is above all the powers that control human destinies; to be so situated means to be divine. John, then, begins the suffering and death of Jesus with the clear profession of faith: the one who suffers at the hand of others and is led to the slaughter is divine, and the reader must remember this key to interpreting the person on the cross. Indeed, John presses the reader further by this faith statement: if the divine person dies on the cross of his own free will, what is his motivation? And there we see finally what John wants to reveal in the Passion of Jesus, God's love which brings God to submit himself to powers infinitely less than his, so that whoever looks on him with faith might be saved.

A final note: a first rush to defend Jesus results in the severing of the ear of the high priest's servant. Luke, ever the writer to stress the merciful compassion of Jesus, makes sure he reports that Jesus miraculously repaired his captor's ear. Love of enemy is never far from the pen of Luke.

Such then are thoughts which recall the significance of Gethsemani for the Gospels—moments of grief and terror, injustice, inattentiveness and abandonment, divine revelation. We stand in awe of our physical nearness to them in our presence here today.

The Pool of Siloam (Siloe)

The Pool of Siloam is about fifty-two feet long, about fifteen feet wide, and three feet deep. In the fifth century there stood here a sizable church with three aisles; the church was in honor of the miracle Jesus worked through this pool. The ancient church enclosed with four porticoes the pool where the sick of Jesus' time, especially the lepers, washed in hope of freeing themselves from their sicknesses. The church was destroyed in the seventh century and no one attempted to build any other church or shrine. Thus, the pool stands as a mute witness now of the first century, when Jesus used these waters to cure a man born blind.

The Tunnel of Hezekiah

The pool is snuggled against a hillside which curves around the east side of the pool. If we were to dig a tunnel into that hillside, working our way eastward through the hillside, we would reach fresh water flowing up from the Spring of Gihon on the other side of the hill. Such a tunnel was actually dug about 700 B.C. at the command of Hezekiah, king of Jerusalem.

Hezekiah, unable to encompass the Spring of Gihon within the eastern walls of the Jerusalem of his time, had a tunnel built so that water could flow from the spring through the hill into a pool which lay within the Jerusalem walls. This pool was called the Pool of Siloam. The

Assyrian enemy never figured out why Jerusalem under siege, did not surrender because of thirst.

The digging of the tunnel, 583 yards, was a remarkable feat of engineering: two groups of workmen with pickaxes, shovels and carefully calculated directions started out, one from the Gihon side of the hill and the other from the Siloam pool side of the hill. A plaque, placed in the tunnel, commemorated the amazing achievement of these men; the plaque now is stored in the Classical Museum of Istanbul.

Ever since Hezekiah's time, water has flowed through this tunnel to fill the Pool of Siloam. Occasionally, one can walk through the ancient tunnel connecting the Pool of Siloam with what is now called the Fountain of the Virgin, the pool where the waters of Gihon can collect.

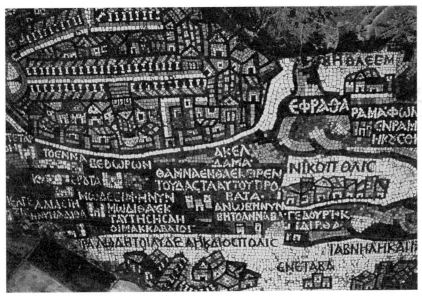

Jerusalem area of fifth-century mosaic Madaba map

Feast of Sukkoth

The Pool of Siloam had an important liturgical function to play in Jesus' time. At the time of the Feast of Sukkoth (or Tabernacles, or Tents), occurring annually within the September-October period, water was brought from this pool to the Temple of Jerusalem with great trumpet blasts; there it was poured together with wine into a tube beside the Temple altar which allowed water and wine to flow, ultimately, into the Kidron Valley. This liturgical ritual was partly a thanksgiving for the recently harvested summer crop, which depended on water received in the springtime and kept in wells for summer irrigation, and partly a petitioning of God that he would provide water for the growth of the newly planted seeds to be harvested the next spring, from March to May. It was during the Feast of Sukkoth that Jesus identified himself as the source of that water (= the Holy Spirit) which will quench all thirst (Jn 7:37).

Cure of the Man Born Blind
~ JOHN 9 ~

For Christians the most famous event associated with this Pool of Siloam is the cure of the man born blind. The cure itself is as simply told as it is marvelous. So marvelous was it that the blind man, once cured, could say that no one had experienced such a miracle as this since the beginning of time (Jn 9:32). But there are more verses to the story than just the description of the miracle. What is it all about?

The context surrounding the miracle is very significant. Jesus had just argued, for the length of two chapters, with "Jews" as they are designated at this point of the Gospel; indeed, great pessimism had set in at the end of chapter 6 where we read that many who had followed Jesus now began to leave him, and chapter 5 itself contains seeds of exasperation as Jesus tried to defend his curing a man on the Sabbath at the Pool of Bethesda. Chapter 9, then, continues the developing antagonism, for the cure through the waters of Siloam was also a cure worked on the Sabbath. We are also aware of the symbolism woven into this story: blindness and sight, qualities which each side of the debate—Jewish Christians and Jewish non-Christians—either claimed for itself or ascribed to its opponent. It is not surprising, given this climate, that the Pharisees end in condemning themselves, they who see quite well and need no help like blind people. Moreover, the following story, about the good and bad shepherds, is a fitting conclusion to the lengthy attack on Jewish leaders mounted through the preceding chapters of John's Gospel. In short, chapter 9 is not only the account of a miracle, but it fits into a lengthy description of the acrimonious feelings which were not only a part of Jesus' experience, but also a part of the Gospel writer's time, 95 A.D.

The interchange between the cured man and the Pharisees is very instructive—and is certainly meant to be, for much more time is devoted to it than to the account of the miracle itself. So many excellent defensive arguments are made here by the blind man, particularly his appeal to the fundamental fact: I was blind; he told me to wash, and I see. Against this realism there can be no other conclusion than that Jesus is from God. The healed man can only conclude that Jesus is a prophet; later he is offered the opportunity to believe in Jesus as Son of Man. The Pharisees are prevented from belief in Jesus on two counts; first, Jesus worked this miracle on the Sabbath, and this, for the Pharisees, was an act defying the Law of God to keep holy the Sabbath by not working; second, the Pharisees do not know "where this man Jesus is from." That is, they know he is from Nazareth, but for them, this fact argues that he is not from God. As Nathaniel had said many chapters previously, "Can anything good come from Nazareth?"—indeed most prophecies indicated that the Messiah of God would come from Bethlehem, and the general public did not associate Jesus with Bethlehem.

Two elements of the Pharisees' courtroom-like interrogation (and it is intentionally presented like that) should be noted. First, the man's parents sense they will be expelled from their synagogue if they are judged to be defending in any way the proposition that Jesus is the Messiah (Jn 9:22). For many scholars, what is described as the parents' fear in Jesus' generation of an excommunication was in reality the fear that Jewish Christians had at the time of the writing of the Gospel. The Pharisees of 85 A.D. had indeed moved to exclude from synagogues Jews who believed in Jesus—from services which Christian Jews until then normally attended. Many Jewish Christians saw no contradiction in professing Jesus as Messiah of Israel and worshipping the true God in the Temple and hearing his Sacred Scriptures in the synagogue. The Pharisees, however, in an attempt to resurrect Israel after the Roman destruction in 67–73, gathered the people around the true God, but they excluded recognition of Jesus as Messiah; had he not been crucified just over 50 years ago as a false Messiah? Thus, the Pharisees demanded separation of Jews from their dear ones in synagogue worship (the Temple in Jerusalem had been destroyed), and fashioned a prayer to curse anyone who misled Israel.

This sociological backdrop for the Gospel (a most likely backdrop as far as science can tell) accounts for the acerbic tone of the Gospel and the heightened anger at nonbelieving Israel, especially the Pharisees.

John's Gospel is essentially a vigorous reply in defense of Christian Jews against Pharisaic leadership of 90–95; it argues, chapter after chapter, often with impatient and challenging language, that Jesus was indeed the Messiah, and more—the Son of God—and that through him will we have eternal life (Jn 20:31). The teaching of opponents of Jesus is false and is caused by ignorance or willful blindness; can God have mercy on such opponents against him? Will God ultimately withdraw his offer of Jesus to the Chosen People? The conflict continues page by page, and at every page John tries to pierce to the meaning of events so that they reveal the truth about Jesus and the false interpretation of those opposing Christianity in John's time. True as it is that this whole bitter argument could be handled by letter writing, John plays it out through retelling and interpreting a series of past events, letting the frustrations and anger of his time become part of the time of Jesus.

Second, the Pharisees ultimately throw up their hands and send the cured man away; he is after all a sinner and thus merits no trust or credence. Such is a likely argument from the opponents' side to blunt the claims of believers in Jesus: they do not keep the Law of Moses, they are sinners who follow a liar, why is their voice credible? Again, while we read a story about events in 30 A.D. we are really in the midst of an angry and crucial argument fully developed in the year 90.

Three final points can be underlined here. First, the story of the blind man begins with a suggestion as to the cause of his blindness from birth: either he was responsible (because of future sins God knows about) or his parents were responsible because of their sins. How many times human beings feel "it's my fault" that this child was born this way, that this child died tragically, that this person is a failure. Jesus refuses to follow that line of thinking; he will not say that the man is blind because of his own sin or his parents' sins. Jesus does not make anyone responsible for this physical evil. He concentrates his disciples' attention on the fact that God can use this sorrowful state to his glory, i.e., to making the person a dignified human being (which is God's greatest glory). The miracle is a moment's expression of the perpetual love which moves God to bring us to our greatest dignity in this life and to the perfect life to come.

Second, the man's blindness suggests two further thoughts to Jesus. Blindness makes him think of night, of death. His mind goes to this further reality: he will work while the light lasts, i.e., he will work for his people as long as life is given to him, until death overtakes him. Moreover, he is the one by whom everyone else can see the truth, the way to the Father. He is the Light of the World. Without him, we remain in the darkest of nights, where we are as good as blind.

Third, at the end of the story, Jesus reveals himself to the cured man as the Son of Man and immediately speaks of judgment. Judgment is a task given to One-like-a-son-of-man, or Son of Man, in the Book of Daniel. Chapter 7 of this Old Testament book speaks of a vision of Daniel in which he sees God, in the form of the Ancient of Days, hand over judgment of the world to the Son of Man. Thus Jesus, who often referred to himself as Son of Man, says immediately that he has been sent into the world for judgment. In John's Gospel, final judgment takes a peculiar twist. One does not wait for the end of the world, the usual time for this judgment. For John, if one now rejects Jesus—that is judgment, a self condemnation which need wait for no future decision. Jesus had expressed himself a bit differently earlier, in chapter 3; there he had said that he comes not to judge, but to save. But then he says essentially what he will say in chapter 9: rejecting him is its own judgment, its own condemnation. Jesus was saddened, frustrated, chagrined over the refusal of the Pharisees in this regard; they claimed they knew what they were doing. One can only conclude, from the believer's point of view, that they were willfully blind.

The blind man's story is wonderful—yet sad, and ultimately upsetting for the continued disagreement over the truth about Jesus of Nazareth.

St. Stephen's Gate

"I CAN SEE THE SON OF MAN STANDING AT
GOD'S RIGHT HAND."
~ ACTS 7:56

The only gate through the eastern wall of today's Jerusalem is found near the northern end of the eastern wall. It has various names. For instance, it received the name of the Lion's Gate after the Six Days War because above the gate are two beautifully sculpted lions who greet visitors entering Jerusalem from the east. At times, the gate was called the Sheep Gate, for sheep were bought and sold nearby. But the gate has also long been called St. Stephen's Gate, for outside this gate is the traditional location of the stoning of St. Stephen (Acts 7:55–60).

St. Stephen is considered the first martyr of the Christian Church; his feast day in the Roman Catholic Church's liturgy occurs on the day after Christmas, a symbol of his nearness to Jesus as the first of his martyred witnesses. The story of Stephen has a number of interesting points for our consideration.

Stephen's Original Ministry
~ ACTS 6:1–7 ~

We know nothing of Stephen's life before we are introduced to him in chapter 6 of Acts; here he, the first mentioned among seven, is chosen to serve in the resolution of a particular problem of food distribution among certain Christians.

The problem was in distribution of food to widows, a charitable deed which Judaism generally had long practiced and which the first Christians, practically all Jews, continued for their own widows. It seems that, by Acts 6, there were two types of widow (indeed of Christian Jew): the widow who was a native of Palestine and whose language, customs, and culture were those of Palestine, and the widow who, though truly Jewish, was a quite recent arrival in Palestine, with a language and cultural background of the Mediterranean area where she had spent most of her life. Given the diverse backgrounds of the widows (and indeed of Jews in Jerusalem) it is not surprising that they divided themselves into two groups along cultural lines. This division apparently led to some imbalance in the charitable help given the widows; without any reason being given, the widows not native to Palestine were to some degree overlooked in the distribution. That men of their own Jewish type were appointed to resolve this problem suggests that somehow the Palestinian Christian Jews were responsible for the imbalance. We must remember that widows would have had an extremely hard time finding work in the public sectors of life, and so were greatly dependent on help from others.

The problem was brought to the attention of the Twelve Apostles who came up with the plan to appoint seven men, not natives of Palestine, to oversee the distribution of food to the needy widows. The Jewish Christians who were not native to Palestine picked the seven men; the Twelve laid hands upon them and thus appointed them to their responsibility. They are to *serve*, and the Greek verb used is *diakonein*; it is easy to see how later generations made a noun from this verb: deacon. Stephen, and his six companions, are often called the first deacons of the Church; they continue to serve as the founding fathers of the newly vitalized diaconate in the Roman Catholic Church and ground the historical basis of the order of deacon which has served Christian churches throughout the centuries.

Of the seven men mentioned in Acts 6 as those appointed to serve, two will play still further roles in the Acts of the Apostles: Stephen and Philip, whose story will be told in Acts, chapter 8.

The Preaching of Stephen
~ ACTS 6:8–7:53 ~

Stephen quickly moved from a rather limited public function in favor of the widows to a fame or notoriety as preacher and defender of Christianity. As we might expect, he specialized in discussion and argument among Jews who, like himself, had spent a good part of their lives outside Palestine and had only recently emigrated to the Holy Land of their forefathers. Stephen was a thorn in the side of those with whom he debated in the synagogues; they finally brought him to a trial where, as in the case of Jesus, false witness against him played a key part.

Stephen gave a long speech at his trial in defense against the accusations Luke reports to us. The accusations are phrased variously, but their essence is that Stephen said that Jesus said he would destroy the Temple and change the customs of Moses. In short, Stephen spoke against God and Moses (Acts 6:14). In thinking about these accusations, we must first ask whether Jesus ever did say he would destroy the Temple and change the customs or laws of Moses.

The distinction should be kept: Jesus never said that he would destroy the Temple, but he said often that the Temple would be destroyed. And though he never said he would change the customs or Laws of Moses, he certainly as a matter of fact adjusted, eliminated, or tightened up various laws of the Israelite tradition. That Jesus in fact changed certain aspects of the Mosaic Law in these ways is interpreted by Jesus as a "making more perfect" the Law Moses received. To put it briefly, Jesus knew that the two central Laws of God are love of God and love of neighbor, as Moses said; what Jesus did was make sure that all the other laws, which are really valid only to the extent that they promote love of God and love of neighbor, did actually support the two central laws. To the extent that they did provide support they were fine; to the extent they did not, they should be dropped or fine-tuned. Since all laws pass before Jesus for inspection, we say that, although Christians obey laws of the Old Testament, we do so, not because the Old Testament teaches them, but because Jesus teaches that they should be obeyed.

One should remember that the Stephen story is being told by Luke about ten to fifteen years after the actual destruction of the Jerusalem Temple. This time factor helps make both Stephen's and Jesus' forecasts of the Temple appear very justified: indeed the Temple was destroyed, as they said!

The speech of Stephen is long; except for Jesus, no one in the New Testament gives a longer speech. The speech does not really deal with the accusation that Jesus said he will change the Laws of Moses; to explain the momentous changes in the importance of the Law for Christians, Luke uses all of the first fifteen chapters, and so the Stephen speech, as long as it is, is really too brief a space for this topic.

Rather, Luke answers the criticism of Jesus in relation to the Temple. Stephen takes his audience through a vast period of Israel's history. He first shows that Israel was founded precisely to worship God in the Temple. He then presents figures of the Old Testament, Joseph and Moses, who speak in some ways of the Jesus to come. He then reverts to the theme of worship and proposes the argument that the worship of the golden calf in the desert occurred because the Israelites had given up on Moses and God and sought other gods to lead them out of the desert. Finally, Stephen points out that the Temple of Jerusalem, as it was conceived by many of his contemporaries was no different from pagan temples Stephen knew in his life outside Israel, temples which contained divinity as though the divine lived in a house made by humans!

All of this background was provided in order to make two points. First, when Israelites thought of God as contained in a little house or temple, they insulted God and misdefined him, and so offered unacceptable worship to God; by falling into this failing they frustrated the very reason for their existing: to worship God (properly) in this Temple. Second, figures of Israel (Joseph and Moses) were images of Jesus; how could Israel reject the one foretold by these figures and so many of the prophets?

Falsely understanding the Temple and God as well, and rejecting Jesus—these two points of the speech form Stephen's counter-accusation. You have displeased God by a blasphemous interpretation of the Temple and by rejecting the only true mediator between God and human beings, the Just One foretold by the Holy Spirit through the prophets. God's displeasure at your hardness of heart and stiffness of neck will bring about the destruction of the Temple.

It should be noted that Luke never depicts the Temple as evil in itself. The Temple can be cleansed, as Jesus cleansed it, and the Temple can be said to be destroyed because "you refused to recognize the time of God's visitation and to accept me," but the Temple, if used rightly, was a credible and holy element in the worship of God. Luke is not contradicting himself when he writes how Peter and John would go to the Temple service to worship the true God; for them, this building remained a valuable means of praising God with all Israel.

Death of Stephen
~ ACTS 7:54–60 ~

Those listening did not appreciate Stephen's counter-accusation, and they ground their teeth in anger. But Stephen really provoked them to violence when he claimed now to see Jesus, the Son of Man (that is, judge of the world), at the very right hand of God! This claim was the culmination of his effrontery: Jesus was not at God's right hand! Stephen was given the punishment which blasphemy deserved: stoning to death. At the death site, outside the northeastern gate tradition says, Stephen conducted himself as Jesus had on his cross outside the city: calm commendation of his soul to the Lord Jesus and a prayer that his persecutors be forgiven (Acts 7:59–60).

Standing by was a young man named Saul—soon to be St. Paul. His holding the coats of those doing the stoning was a sign that he approved of this killing. Within a short time, this Saul, once he has joined the Christians he had learned to despise, will become the major hero of the second half of the Acts of the Apostles.

Jewish Christians of the Diaspora
~ ACTS 8–15 ~

The brief story of Stephen is only one element of a large framework established by Luke in Acts; to this framework we now turn.

The story of the seven deacons (Acts 6) introduces us to a group of Christians of which we had until then been unaware. These are Jewish Christians, but different culturally and linguistically from Christian Jews born in Palestine and native to it, many of whom were the audience of Jesus. With these Christian Jews who were not native to Palestine we have the beginning of that element in Christianity which ultimately decided that Gentile Christians need not embrace many essential elements of traditional Judaism. Thoroughly Jewish, they seem to be the Jews who most warmly welcomed the Gentiles into Christianity, and into a Christianity free from many aspects which many Christian Jews continued to embrace. Many of these Christian Jews, of the same type as Stephen, left Palestine after a persecution against them broke out following upon the death of Stephen. They spread the name of Jesus as they went, especially in what was the third greatest city of the Roman empire, Antioch of Syria. Today, Antioch is considered the most supportive of first-century Christian efforts at evangelizing the Jews and Gentiles of what we call today Turkey and Greece; most likely from it went out the missionaries eager to preach to both Jew and Gentile alike.

It seems clear that Antioch was willing to support a Christianity which, at least for Gentile converts, considered as less important both circumcision and obedience to the total Law of Moses, deemed by much of Judaism as so essential for salvation. Though the Acts of the Apostles explains this changeover from a first Christian community (which held firmly to Jewish laws and practices while believing in Jesus as Messiah) to a later Christian community (which believed in Jesus as savior, but considered much of Judaism as not obligatory, at least for Gentiles, for salvation). Although the Acts of the Apostles describes this changeover as a rather peaceful development, clearly it was not so peaceful for many individual Jewish Christians. These latter continued to think that salvation required Jewish and Gentile Christians to be circumcised and

Jerusalem: warning against Gentiles entering the Temple building

made to obey to the full the Law of Moses. Our Christianity seems logical to us now, without circumcision and many of the Laws of Moses; but what is logical and reasonable now was far from clear-cut to many Jewish Christians of the first century.

It is to present the proper understanding of what faith in Jesus Christ means that Luke describes, in Acts, how Christianity developed step-by-step from the Jewish Christian community gathered after Pentecost to a predominantly Gentile church throughout the Mediterranean Basin, and how God revealed step-by-step the shape of the Christianity he wanted. The ultimate design finally becomes clear; it is worthwhile to realize that it began to emerge for the first time with the appearance of Stephen and those like him. He is part of a vast divine scheme which has given Christianity the fixed shape and form it knows today.

Changing the Customs of Moses
~ ACTS 10:1–11:18; 15 ~

Stephen was accused not only of speaking against the Temple, but also of speaking against the customs or Laws of Moses. His speech explained why it was said that the Temple would be destroyed, but did not really touch on the latter accusation having to do with Jesus' changing the customs of Moses. Why was that latter point ignored?

Although it was ignored in the speech of Stephen, it was far from ignored in Luke's presentation of the development of the early church. Basically, there was need for much preparation on the author's part before he could simply and forcefully answer the accusation. It is finally in chapter 15 that we read the fruit of this preparation: salvation depends only on faith in Jesus, Messiah and Lord; circumcision and obedience to the total Law of Moses are not required for the salvation of the Gentiles (Acts 15:11). But to prepare for this church decision in chapter 15, Luke first introduced concrete examples that God had accepted Gentiles, forgiven them their sins, and given them the Spirit without asking that they first be circumcised and commit themselves to the entire Law of Moses. These examples begin with the conversion of the Samaritans (Acts 8:4–8), develop through the stories of Peter's conversion of the Gentile Cornelius, of the unnamed Christians who win over Jews and Gentiles from Cyprus to Antioch (Acts 11:19–30), and of the many conversions of Gentiles at the preaching of Paul and Barnabas in today's Turkey (Acts 13–14).

Interwoven through this developing form of Christianity is the conversion story of Paul, the one who will be most famous for insisting that Gentiles need not be circumcised and made to keep the total Mosaic Law.

Finally, as preparation for chapter 15 are the first chapters of Acts, where what is required for salvation is vigorously taught: "There is no name under heaven by which a person can be saved except by the name of Jesus" (Acts 4:12). Only with all of this matter in place from chapter 2 to chapter 14, can Luke present so simply and as an easy decision: Christians, especially Gentiles, need not be circumcised and made to keep all the Mosaic Law in order to be saved; belief in Jesus is the one thing required for salvation.

How is it that the Temple accusation against Stephen could be handled in one chapter, whereas the Law accusation needed all of fifteen chapters for its resolution? The best answer lies in the fact Luke wrote his Acts of the Apostles some fifteen years after the Romans destroyed the Jerusalem Temple in 70 A.D. Thus, argument about the Temple was really a dead issue, purely academic now; so it could be resolved in one speech. But the change from Jewish to Gentile church was not resolved for everyone even by the time Luke and Matthew wrote. The problems of relating Christianity to Judaism, of relating a traditional understanding of God's will to the meaning of salvation in Jesus, were difficult to solve. The urgency of the problem, which still agitated certain elements of Christianity, as evidenced in Acts 21, caused Luke to be very thorough in his description of the problem and its solution.

To stand at St. Stephen's Gate, then, is to remember the profession of belief in Jesus, even to the shedding of blood, and to recall the great movement, under the guidance of Jesus and God's Spirit, of which St. Stephen was a first and integral part. We have profited from both his death and from the new understanding of what God requires for salvation, and we gratefully acknowledge Luke's efforts at making clear these moments in his Acts of the Apostles.

The Pool of Bethesda (Bethzatha)

"GET UP, PICK UP YOUR
SLEEPING MAT AND WALK."
~ JOHN 5:8

St. Stephen's Gate is the one gate today through the eastern wall of Jerusalem; it is located at the north end of that eastern wall. If we enter St. Stephen's Gate from the east and proceed no more than a hundred yards, we reach the entry on the right to the compound which contains the Church of St. Anne, and the headquarters of the White Fathers and—most important for our present purpose—the ruins of the famous Pool of Bethesda. In Jesus' time it was called the Sheep Pool because nearby were the sheep market and the Sheep Gate, the one now called St. Stephen's.

Bethesda means *House of Mercy*. Deep beneath a building containing five porticoes or porches were two reservoirs, filled with spring waters from deep in the earth, which fed the Asclepeion or healing baths. Ruins of the building which housed the curative waters are still visible. The building was built as a trapezoid and divided, the north half from the south half, by a wall running east and west. Thus, the building had only four external walls and a fifth within; these walls really formed porches along which the sick could sit or lie. Over the east-west wall a church, whose ruins can be seen, was built in the fifth century.

The waters which served the reservoirs and the pool and baths flowed both before Jesus' time and after; the waters are well attested in ancient documents, which also witness to the occasional worship of deities supposedly healing through these waters. Special moments in the day were those in which the underground springs of water bubbled up through the reservoirs into the pool and baths; these were moments thought to be particularly helpful in the healing process. Whereas Israel attributed the stirring of these waters to the hand of God's angel, other peoples, at various times, praised here the divine intervention of other gods, particularly Asclepius and Serapis, the gods of healing. The Romans under the emperor Hadrian (117–138 A.D.) would eventually build a shrine here to Asclepius, the famed god of cures.

Jesus Healing

The healing of the man at the Pool of Bethesda, a man ill for thirty-eight years, is the second cure told us by John and the third of the signs the evangelist chose to present to his readers. The Gospel narrative stressed three elements: the miracle, the Sabbath occasion of the miracle, and Jesus' reflection of his union with "My Father." Let us look briefly at each of these three elements of the Johannine narrative to appreciate better what happened at the Pool of Bethesda.

The Cure
~ JOHN 5:1–9 ~

The Gospel story gives briefly the few details of the miracle by Jesus. A man, ill for thirty-eight years, lies helpless near the curative waters. Jesus, knowing the man's plight, moves to help him; the man, saying to Jesus that he wants to be cured, does not realize that his cure will come from the power of Jesus. He thinks rather that Jesus will help him to the waters; by himself he never could reach in time the precious moments when the waters bubbled up, "for someone else always gets to the waters before me."

The story is told so as to highlight the helplessness of the man and the initiative of Jesus to offer a cure. The story is also told in such a way that, though the man looked to the waters for cure, it was simply the word of Jesus, that all-powerful word, which would triumph over sickness. The Lord ignores the waters and tells the man to leave, to take his bed and go. Whatever wonder the waters caused in those who witnessed their cures, this wonder is transferred to Jesus, and one looks at him to learn how it is that he has such power over illness and such a will to use that power.

The miracle was astounding, for it was total and immediate: the man got up and with his mat walked away. Moreover, the physical cure is followed by the spiritual encouragement: "Sin no more, or something worse may happen to you." That Jesus would move from the physical cure to concern for the spiritual is typical of him. Given that Jesus saw his adult life as a life calling for repentance and change of life, it is not surprising but to be expected that a miracle story looks to a greater healing, the turning away from sin. Miracles, as they are often presented in the Gospels, are notable invitations to the total restoration, both of body and of soul. The power and authority over evil expressed in the miracles is just a sign of that power and authority which God wishes to use in the more profound healing of the sickness which threatens to separate us from him. The difference between miracle working and spiritual healing lies in the fact that, whereas God can cure physical illness without a person's willing it, he will not heal one on the spiritual level without one's agreeing to it. However powerful his grace, however much he urges and threatens and woos us, God will not take away our free wills. It is precisely this free choice that God so ardently seeks from us.

The Holiness of the Sabbath
~ JOHN 5:16–18 ~

The Gospel expands this marvelous cure to make it one of several acts Jesus performs "on the Sabbath." For the Jews of Jesus' time, there were many activities which over centuries had been evaluated as "works," that is, actions which should not be done on the Sabbath, actions which would break the law that the Sabbath should be kept holy. Healing was considered one of these works; in one story in the Gospels, the people are asked to seek healing on "one of the other days of the week" (Lk 13:14), not on the Sabbath. Jesus, for his part, had his own understanding of the relationship between miracle working and the Sabbath holiness.

On the one hand, Jesus points up the contradiction in the usual interpretation of the law: Jesus cannot work a miracle, but a Jew could water his animal and he could save it from destruction, even though he did these things on the Sabbath. Rather, Jesus thinks, the logic which allowed saving things essential to one's life even on the Sabbath should make logical his saving people from sickness. In all these cases, it should be right to say that God, whose day is to be kept holy, wants works that will save.

On the other hand, one of the main meanings of the Sabbath is that it is a day of liberation (and not only a day of rest to honor God). This meaning of the Sabbath came about as a way of celebrating on the Sabbath the tremendous act of God in freeing Israel from Egypt. When Jesus cured on the Sabbath, he thought he was in the very spirit of the day, for was he not liberating an Israelite from the bonds of Satan who is behind all physical sorrow? How, then, was he wrong for curing on the Sabbath?

Such laws as were made, in order to keep holy the Sabbath, were man-made, in Jesus' view; he claimed to know truly what his Father meant by keeping holy the Sabbath. That is why he could identify himself as Lord of the Sabbath; it is his understanding of how to keep holy God's day that truly reflects God's own mind.

That Jesus continued to work miracles of healing on the Sabbath could only mean that he would eventually be challenged for his disobedience to the Mosaic Law; inevitably, his lack of conformity would be added to other reasons which ultimately issued in a plot to get rid of him.

The charge against Jesus, that he "worked" on the Sabbath, is too widespread an accusation in the Gospels to be doubted as a truly historical difference between Jesus and his contemporaries. It serves to point up the actual area of intense disagreement between Jesus and his opponents: Jesus clearly differed in significant ways about what God's law meant. This claim that he alone understood God's mind best led Jesus to his cross.

Perhaps the dispute over the meaning of the Law seems a scholastic or unimportant exercise, of much interest to experts only. But one must be aware that the Jewish tradition assigned to disobedience to the Law and to false teachers all blame for the major sufferings of Israel's history, particularly the Assyrian (722 B.C.) and Babylonian (587 B.C.) conquests and destruction of Israel and Judah. The Jewish Scriptures are a resounding witness to the belief that Israel's suffering and humiliation resulted from disobedience to the will of God. It is not then surprising that those who felt responsible for protecting Israel from any repetition of its past sufferings insisted on obedience as the hallmark of the true Israelite and the banishment of anyone who tampered with the Law of God and misled the people.

Another example which underlines the importance of interpreting the Law correctly is the community of Qumran, the Dead Sea community so much discussed in the last fifty years. This community separated itself from more normative forms of Judaism precisely because of different interpretations of the Law. This community preferred isolation in the desert rather that association in any form with the sinful authorities of Jerusalem. And over what did they differ? Two issues stand out. First, the calendar which tells when feasts occur was in error, they said, in Jerusalem; God wanted another calendar followed, and thus found feasts celebrated erroneously to be totally unacceptable. Second, the priesthood of Jerusalem was not legitimate; hence sacrifices offered by it were illegitimate. Such was the climate in which Jesus lived; such was the reason why so much of Jesus' life is intertwined with interpreting and teaching God's true will.

Certainly other motivations are cited in the elimination of Jesus: jealousy, stubbornness in refusal to believe the truth, haughtiness, refusal to repent. But deep among all these reasons for getting rid of Jesus was this on-going dispute over who knows what is good for Israel and who is deceiving, what will keep Israel God's Chosen One or will separate God from his people. The healing at Bethesda, then, is not only a wonderful cure, spontaneously done by Jesus because of pity; it is, as a work on the Sabbath, a continuation of the challenge Jesus presented to the official interpreters of God's will: Jesus insisted he knew God's will best—he is the Son of God.

Jesus' Union with His Father
~ JOHN 5:19–30 ~

The miraculous cure at Bethesda gives Jesus the opportunity to reflect on "his work." Jesus' first claim is that he goes on working as does his Father. This statement, by which he implies that he works any and every day, Sabbath or not, for the good of his people as does his Father, incenses some of his hearers, for they see in this comparison of himself to his Father a claim to being God's own Son and the equal of God. More specifically, Jesus claims sonship because he has the characteristic of God: we can tell who is son by looking to see if the person exhibits the traits of one he calls "Father." Such is the understanding of those who hear Jesus claim that he works as does his Father; but is Jesus' work characteristic of God, his Father?

Jesus' lengthy statement bases his relationship with his Father on two acts which reflect how he imitates his Father: the work of giving life and the work of judgment. But these are only two of the works which have been transferred to Jesus because of the filial relationship of Jesus to the Father; indeed, whatever the Father does, the Son does as well, for this is the nature of a son, to be like his father.

Israel expected God to give life and to exercise judgment. Jesus, acting like God, gives life and enters into judgment. One need not wait until the end of time for judgment, because the acceptance or rejection of Jesus makes judgment happen now—that is to say, if I reject Jesus now, do I have to wait until the end of time to be condemned? Have I not condemned myself now?

Through his miracles Jesus gives life; the miracles are the promise of life forever. Union with Jesus is union with the source of life; "I will raise him up on the last day." The miracles give a greater share of life, as they remove the dying inherent in sickness. But the life Jesus wants to give, can give, is the fullness of life; this means life forever, complete life, the total person fully alive.

Israel had identified these two works, giving life and judgment, as characteristics of God. Jesus cites his performing them as arguments that he is from God; he cites his relationship with his Father as explanation of how these works should be understood. Giving life and bringing about judgment should make one think of Jesus as divine; being Son of God, Jesus' work is simply a Son's doing what he sees his Father do—that is how to understand his works.

The Witnesses to Jesus
~ JOHN 5:31–47 ~

Jesus has justified his work of the Sabbath by claiming to work as his Father does and in imitation of his Father and he has claimed that as Son he has been given these two works in particular, giving life and judgment. He then raises the question about witnesses who might justify his claims.

There are five witnesses who testify to his being Son of God. There is John the Baptist, who is described from the beginning as giving "testimony to the truth." John identified Jesus as the Lamb of God and said that he finally saw the one on whom, he had been told, the Spirit would descend. He was not the Light, but he knew the Light was coming; he realized that he, the best man, must decrease while Jesus, the groom, must increase. Jesus could well claim John as a witness to him.

Second, the witness of the cures, healings by Jesus: are they not signs of the life-giving and divine condemnation of corrupting evil? Is Jesus, the one who worked such a cure as the healing at Bethesda, not life-giving? Does he not force one to accept or reject him, does he not force one to judgment? A third witness is the Father himself, whom however no one will hear or attend to who is not first willing to commit himself to Jesus.

Two other witnesses, classical at the time of the writing of the Gospel of John around the year 95, are the Scriptures in general and Moses in particular, the author, it was believed then, of the first five books of the Old Testament. If one is careful, one can realize the immense effort of John and of the writers of the entire New Testament to make emerge from the Scriptures how Moses, the Psalms, the Prophets, and still other pieces of the Old Testament support the faith that Jesus is the Messiah, the Son of God. In these Scriptures is the call to love God; the rejection of Jesus is interpreted now to mean that "you have no love of God in you." Indeed, so strongly is Jesus convinced that he fulfills the hope and promises Moses wrote about, that he can say the rejection of me means "you refuse to believe what Moses wrote."

Jesus' speech here at Bethesda means to explain and defend his work on the Sabbath; it also becomes a summary of the various ways which later Christianity used to defend its belief in Jesus, Son of God. While the speech is heavily defensive and apologetic, it also is filled with a profound understanding of Jesus which is welcome to his disciples and can feed the lives of those already convinced that Jesus is the Son of the Father, the source of their fullest life.

This story leads the reader into the mystery which is revealed in the work of mercy Jesus did for the lame man at the Pool of Mercy, the mystery of Jesus as source of life, about whom each person must decide—the Son of the Father.

The Temple in Jerusalem

"MY HOUSE SHALL BE
A HOUSE OF PRAYER."
~ LUKE 19:45

The term "temple" is used in two senses. On the one hand, temple meant a particular building, the largest and central of buildings all around it. On the other hand, temple meant a large and horizontal, trapezoidal-shaped platform or esplanade, something like the size of a soccer

Jerusalem: model of Inner Court of the Temple

field. This horizontal platform functioned like a flat desktop on which one could safely set various objects. On this platform called temple was placed the building called temple, or house of God.

Many Gospel stories, a number of them from Jesus' life and from the lives of the apostles, take place in the sacred area of the Temple, and in and around the building we call Temple. This temple platform today is heavily protected; it is very dear to many religions. As we enter the platform through guarded gates, we must try to reconstruct the scene of two thousand years ago.

The stone trapezoidal area in which we stand is roughly the same size—again, about like a soccer field—as the Temple area of Jesus' time. If one were to follow the western wall to its middle, then face east, one would be at the place where was the back wall of the central Temple building. This Temple was divided into three rooms; let us look at them from west to east. The westernmost room was the Holy of Holies, or the Holiest Place. It was the private quarters of God; no human being was ever allowed in here except the High Priest of Israel—and he only once a year, on the Day of Atonement, Yom Kippur. At one time this Holy of Holies contained the precious Ark of the Covenant.

The room just east of this most sacred room was called the Holies; here were to be found such sacred things as the table of the twelve breads, representing the needs of the Twelve Tribes, and changed daily; the menorah, a seven-branch candlestick; and the altar of incense. The third room, at the east end of the Temple, was really a large porch-like structure, with the huge altar of sacrifice and the great bowl of washing for priests engaged in this act of worship. This area, where sacrifices were burnt (they were killed elsewhere on the Temple grounds), was open to priests and to the men of Israel. At the eastern half of the third open-air room was the place where the women of Israel would stand for worship of Yahweh.

This entire three-room area was raised up higher than the Temple platform or esplanade. Thus, after reaching the Temple platform, one would have to climb a set of stairs to reach the level of the Temple building. Gentiles were allowed onto the Temple platform, but were absolutely forbidden, under penalty of death, to even begin to climb the steps which bring one to the Temple building. Thus, there is even a geographical indication of how close one can come to God: furthest the Gentile, then the Israelite woman, then the Israelite man, then the Israelite priests and finally the High Priest.

The basic plan of the Temple followed palace architecture of the ancient world: a large area for the king's subjects to gather, in the midst of which was his own house that was made up of a porch area for greeting groups, a middle room for more private meetings, and the private quarters reserved for the king only. The Jerusalem Temple faced east, to greet the God who comes from the east, symbolically in his dawning sun each day, and to recall that it was from the east that Israel's forefathers crossed the Jordan into the Promised Land.

The entire area or platform and the Temple building was under the control and direction of the High Priest, who was assisted by about eight Chief Priests and a Temple police force. All matters of the Temple were attended to daily by priests and levites. The levites, in Jesus' time, were responsible for all the music and the singing at the daily and the special ceremonies, and looked after the cleanliness of the Temple. The ordinary priests executed all other details of the Temple sacrifices. Levites and priests worked in these capacities only eight weeks a year, completing a schedule that allowed each of the Twelve Tribes to take its turn to serve in the Temple. Only the High Priest and the Chief Priests worked in the Temple all year round; the ordinary priest, and the levite, had to have another job to support himself and his family for the rest of the year.

Walls enclosed the entire trapezoid of the Temple area. Roofs were built to reach out from the tops of these walls, and were held up, on the one side by the walls, and on the other by long rows of columns. In this way the walls served to provide porches along the north, east, and south of the Temple esplanade. In these porches one could escape inclement weather. Though the entire platform was open to Gentiles, it seems that the northern half was where one could find the selling of animals for sacrifice and the changing of coins. Coins had to be changed, for one should buy materials to be used in holy ceremonies only with "sacred" money, and secular money, such as Roman or Hellenistic coins with the emperor's head on them, was not fitting money.

The Temple Treasury

In ancient times, many nations kept their national treasuries, as well as their religious treasures, within their well-protected temple areas. The Jerusalem Temple treasury was probably located on the level below the platform we call the Temple esplanade. Individual daily donations, however, were to be made through horn-shaped tubes into strong-boxes in the area where the women of Israel gathered for worship in the Temple building.

Could the Temple treasury be put under the Temple platform? There was a large space under the Temple platform. When Solomon undertook the building of the Temple, he planned that it be on the top of a mountain. But the mountain top was rounded, not flat. He so arranged and sank pylons of such lengths that he was able to lay over these mighty pylons a floor or a platform or esplanade which would hold up the Temple building. Obviously, at its more central point, the platform was only a bit over the rounded top of the mountain, but, looking at the north and south ends of the platform, there was considerable space between the curving mountain and the platform. This considerable space afforded a safe hiding place for the Temple and national treasury.

The Temple Area—Then and Now

Though the Old Testament tells of David's desire to build a house for God, it fell to Solomon, David's son, to actually construct the Temple. This Solomonic Temple lasted from the Solomonic period (about 961–922 B.C.) to its destruction by Babylonian armies in 587 B.C. After Solomon built first a platform to get a flat surface over the curving mountain top of Mount Zion, then he built the Temple building—God's palace—adjacent to his own palace at the south edge of the Temple platform. The Second Temple was dedicated in 515, being rebuilt, after the Babylonian exile, over the ruins of the First Temple. The First or Solomonic Temple was glorious, much more beautiful than what those just returned from exile could afford. It fell to Herod the Great, in 19 B.C., to begin a renovation and embellishment of this Second Temple; no expense was spared, since part of Herod's motivation was to win the favor of the Jewish people, a goal he never achieved.

Having indicated that at the south end of the Temple the distance between the curve of the mountain and the platform was significant, one can then imagine that to reach the Temple platform from the south meant that stairs were provided that led from the mountain onto the platform. Thus, one would go up to the Temple, not only in the sense that one climbed Mount Zion to reach Jerusalem on its top, but also in the sense that from the top one climbed stairs in order to get onto the Temple platform. Into the sustaining wall at the south end were built three gates for entry to the stairs and two other gates for exit from the platform via stairs.

One can imagine that there were several small buildings near the Temple building, for storage and other uses. But, for the sake of the New Testament stories, we should single out the likelihood of a small building just to the south of the Temple building, against the east wall. This was the meeting place of the Sanhedrin, the place, therefore, of Jesus' first trial, before he was taken to Pilate. The placement of the building right next to the Temple of God shows the importance of the Sanhedrin.

This body was the judiciary, as well as the executive branch of Israelite government; it executed the Law of Moses. If it could be said to be also a legislative body, this would mean that it simply applied the Law of Moses to new situations, but often these applications became laws, too. The Sanhedrin (whose name means "to sit together") was allowed to function as long as it did not conflict with Roman control of Palestine, which control meant basically to "keep the civil order, pay taxes to Rome, and provide men for the Roman army." One particular decision Rome preserved for itself: Rome alone would decide who would live and who would die. The Sanhedrin was made up of a High Priest, automatically its President, and seventy others: one group of Elders, one group of Chief Priests, and one group of scribes, i.e., specialists in interpreting the Law of Moses. Men were called Elders here, not because of age, but because they represented old, well-established and wealthy families. One can understand why the governing of Israel was in the hands of the Elders, the High Priest and Chief Priests, and the law specialists. Before them, Jesus, who his detractors said caused civil unrest, would appear.

What do we see on this platform today? Certainly no Jewish Temple; the Second Temple was destroyed by Rome in 70 A.D. and never rebuilt, though obviously the site is extremely precious in Israel's memory. I note only three things. First, the walls surrounding the platform go back to about 1535, when Suleiman the Magnificent had them built. They surely use the old Solomonic walls as their foundations; indeed, the western wall on its western side shows courses of stone which go back that far.

Second, there is the central building of the platform, the Dome of the Rock. This beautiful building dates from 691, though it has often been repaired and also beautified by many gifts. The most recent restoration of the Dome of the Rock occurred between 1958 and 1964. At that time, the roof, which "shines like gold," was applied: it is a special aluminum bronze alloy. Often the Dome of the Rock is considered to be a mosque, but it is not strictly that. Rather it is a memorial over the Rock from which Mohammed is believed to have left this earth for heaven. The Dome of the Rock is the third most holy shrine of the Moslem world, third only to Mecca and Medina. The rock, many think, served not only as the place of Mohammed's departure in the night; it is also considered to be the place where Abraham, except for the contrary command of an angel, would have sacrificed Isaac, his son. This rock is often pointed out as the place where the huge altar of sacrifice of the Jewish Temple was built. One can understand why this place is very sacred both to Jews and to Moslems.

A third, very visible, site on the Temple esplanade stands at the south end of the platform. This is a true mosque, called el-Aqsa, an Arabic adjective which means "the farthest [mosque]." This mosque indicates the "far distance" Mohammed had come from Arabia before finally ascending into heaven. To this day, the el-Aqsa mosque is used on the Fridays, the holy day of Moslems.

To review the Gospel events which are associated with the Temple of Jerusalem, we follow a threefold scheme. First, we consider certain events which occur in the Infancy period of John and Jesus, then we look at one situation taken from Jesus' public life and related by John's Gospel, and finally we consider a series of stories which speak of Jesus' week before his death. After this review, we recall the use made of the Temple area by the early Church.

Apparition of Gabriel to Zachary
~ LUKE 1:5–22 ~

The Angel Gabriel appeared to Zachary, Luke says, at the altar of incense, therefore in the Holy Room, the middle room of the three that make up the Temple building. Zachary was chosen to work here this day during the 3:00 afternoon daily sacrifice for the nation. Here Luke reveals the first element in the actuation of God's plan for the salvation of the world. Zachary is told of the marvelous miracle: that he and his wife will have the power to produce a child. From his earliest moments this son would be filled by the Spirit of God, so that he might become the one to prepare the people for the God who is coming to them, so that he might go before God to prepare his way. John will be his name (meaning "God is gracious"), and he is most intelligible as a new Elijah, that figure who fought so vigorously to keep the Israel of the 850s B.C. faithful to the true God; in the spirit of this great prophet, John will call the people of his time to obedience to God. John himself, a little later on in the Gospel, will broaden his mandate: not only will he call for immediate return to God, but he will prepare for the one who is greater than he, the one who will baptize, not with water, but with God's own Spirit.

Presentation of Jesus and Purification of Mary

In the area of the Temple building reserved particularly for the women of Israel (sometimes called the Court of the Women), Mary was "purified" and Jesus was "presented" to God. What exactly were the *Presentation* of Jesus and the *Purification* of Mary?

The presentation of Jesus involves reviewing briefly the story of the Exodus. At that time, to convince Pharaoh to let God's People go free, God worked through Moses and Aaron what are now famous "plagues"; the last of these powerful acts by God was the killing of every firstborn male, human, and animal, in Egypt. Apparently, this killing was in theory extended to Israelite firstborn, too; but God showed Israel how to avoid the slaughter: if Israel would mark its doorposts or lintels with blood from the lambs cooked for their last meal in Egypt, the Angel of Death would "pass over" their houses and thus not kill their firstborn males.

This "passing over" gave birth to the annual Feast of Passover, and the remembrance of how God kept his People alive. Ever since that fateful night of slaughter and salvation, Israel was to remind itself of God's saving its firstborn males by bringing each firstborn male of every birth into the Temple and offering that child to God. Clearly, though the firstborn animal might be killed as a thanksgiving sacrifice to God, the child was not; he was substituted for by an animal or, if the parents were poor, two pigeons or turtledoves. This presentation of the firstborn male should take place forty days after birth.

But over centuries the presentation of the firstborn came to have another meaning. As Israel settled down to a life of agriculture in the Promised Land, it recognized the central role God played in the annual harvests Israel enjoyed. Israel never forgot that, in strict justice, the harvests of the earth belong to God, for the earth is his, the sun and rain are his, and the successful harvest is heavily due to him. Human beings only enjoy, they do not own; God continues to own his property and its produce. In recognition of this divine ownership and in thanksgiving for the harvests human beings are allowed to keep and use, Israel had a ceremony annually in which the first fruits of the land were returned to God. The first fruits were sacrificed, removed from human use, as a sign of their belonging to God. But Israel understood that the entire harvest really belonged to God; thus, though Israel did not sacrifice the rest of the harvests, it used them with the understanding that they belonged to God and were given to Israel by God for its benefit. But not only were recognition of God's ownership and thanksgiving for his gifts the themes of this ceremony; it was also understood that the rest of the harvest and the rest of the produce of the womb also belonged to God.

In a very similar way, Israel looked upon the fruit of the womb; all life is God's. Life comes from him, is sustained by him, is taken away by him; life is his, he is its Master. The presentation of the firstborn is meant to acknowledge that God is master of every life from the womb; the offering of the firstborn signifies this divine ownership. The offering of the firstborn becomes, then, the offering of all other children from the womb. The firstborn human is not destroyed in sacrifice, but is substituted for by an animal, but the recognition of the true source of this life, and of all other lives from this womb, remains. Jesus, then, is presented in the Temple in accord with these understandings of the ceremony.

Paul will use this notion of the first fruits, when he speaks of Jesus' resurrection. By this reference Paul means to say that Jesus' resurrection was not simply a personal experience. By raising Jesus from the dead, God considers all those united in faith with Jesus to be parts of the same harvest which produced the resurrected Jesus. With his consecration to God we are all consecrated. Just as the rest of the harvest follows naturally after the first successful day, so we follow logically, naturally upon the first resurrection, that of Jesus. Paul says that we are included in his resurrection, as the rest of the harvest is bound to the first moments of the harvest.

Jesus, then, is presented to God in remembrance of the saving of the first born Israelites from the Angel of Death at the Passover. Jesus is also presented to God in remembrance that all that comes from the womb (and all that comes from the earth) is God's; we merely enjoy God's possessions.

For Mary, this day of Jesus' Presentation was also her day of purification. To understand Mary's need for purification, we must look at Israel's Law. In the Mosaic Law, all waste products of the body were considered unclean, and able to make whatever they touch unclean. The term "unclean" was used because it was tied so tightly to the preservation or ruin of health. These flows from the body could harm or even kill others, according to the ancient experiences. Hence one who was unclean should be removed from the community lest he harm others. This excommunication ended by a priest declaring (not healing) the sick person to be well.

The effect of this uncleanness was twofold. First, uncleanness, as a threat to the health of others, also threatened the law that one should love one's neighbor as one would like to be loved. Secondly, if one was unclean, surely one was not worthy to stand before God in worship. Even in Jesus' day, these bodily uncleannesses were considered cause for exclusion from worship of God. Mary, like any mother who has given birth, produced bodily fluids and blood associated with birthing; she, then, was unclean, that is a threat to others' health and unworthy to worship God; at the appointed time, she had to undergo the ceremony prescribed for purification.

Mary's uncleanness does not mean that she was guilty of sin. Mary was not guilty of anything, but she was impure, unclean. Perhaps an example is in order. If you are riding on a train, and the person next to you dies and falls against you, you are, in the eyes of the Mosaic Law, unclean; you must undergo a ceremony of purification. Clearly, you are not guilty of any sin, but a dead body, according to Mosaic Law, was unclean and anything touched by it was made unclean. (Remember that people in the ancient world, even emperors, were to be buried outside their cities, for fear that their uncleanness would cause sickness to others.) Mary, then, needed purification in order to be known as clean and in order to be able to worship God properly.

The more we realize how ingrained in Israelite thinking was the fear of the unclean, the more we can understand how radical was Jesus who claimed that only moral uncleanness could keep one from worshipping God properly. "It is not what [food] goes into a man that makes him unclean or unworthy of God, but what comes out of his heart." In healing, Jesus often touched the unclean. Given the attitudes of his time, his cures had social effects and not just personal benefits: because of his healing, the cured not only enjoyed health again, but could take up again their place in the worshipping community of Israel, something denied many of them all their lives until they met Jesus.

During the visit of Mary and Joseph to the Temple, they met an old man, Simeon. He had gone to the Temple under the inspiration of the Holy Spirit. There he found the Holy Family and, taking Jesus in his arms, praised God for him. This child would be the salvation of all; he would be the glory of Israel and the light to the Gentiles. Simeon, who can die now that he sees Jesus, is understood to represent the passage from the promises and hopes of the Old Testament to their fulfillment in Jesus in a New Covenant. Jesus will bring glory to Israel, for the glory he receives at his resurrection time will be the glory of all those Israelites who, so humiliated over centuries, will have faith in Jesus and so rise with him glorious. For Israel, darkness symbolized the state of the Gentile, for the Gentile knew not the true God or his ways; it will be Jesus who will enlighten the Gentiles so that they can see the only God and become his children.

The Prophetess Anna is then described by Luke as confirming the words of Simeon; indeed, she tells all of those in the Temple area of the liberation that God will now work for his People.

Simeon's words are important, especially for two reasons. First, as with the entire infancy narrative, so his words are meant to prepare for what will happen in the adult period of Jesus' life. Here for the one and only time in these stories is the future mission to all the world announced. Just how Jesus will be a light to the Gentiles is not stated—we will have Acts to explain that—but that he will be their light is an expectation for which the reader is now prepared and eager to see develop. Second, Simeon notes for the first time that the adult Jesus will meet with severe opposition—even Mary will be swept up in it. This harsh con-

troversy is only briefly mentioned here, but we know that it forecasts a
bitterness that indeed is like a sword piercing one's heart.

Jesus Lost and Found in the Temple

The last story from Jesus' childhood that we shall consider is the one told
about Jesus at age twelve being lost and found in the Jerusalem Temple.
This finding probably would have occurred in the Court of the Women or
under the covered walkway along the eastern wall of the Temple platform.

This story is recognized as very important, for it is meant to sum up
the fundamental reason for including the infancy narrative in Luke. To
understand Luke's rationale for the infancy stories we must consider the
first (incomplete) sentence of his major source, Mark. Mark wrote: "The
beginning of the good news of Jesus, Messiah, and Son of God." For Luke,
this brief statement of Jesus' identity, while an insightful profession of
Christian faith, should be developed, not only in the course of the narration of Jesus' public life, but immediately in the infancy period. Luke
begins his development of these titles of Jesus with Gabriel's
Annunciation of Gabriel to Mary. The angel first reveals that Jesus will be
son of David, that is the Messiah of Israel. Then, in answer to Mary's question, the angel says: "The Holy Spirit will come upon you and the power
of the Most High will cast its shadow upon you." This statement leads the
angel to the all-important conclusion: "Therefore, the child will be called
both holy [because of the Holy Spirit] and Son of God [because of the
power of the Most High]." Thus, though God has no sexual intercourse
with Mary, his involvement in the conception of Jesus is such that the
child Jesus will be called Son of God, and will call God his Father. Thus,
while Mark professed Jesus to be Son of God, Luke has explained *why*
Jesus is called Son of God.

Jesus, Son of God, and the Teachers of the Law
~ LUKE 2:41–50 ~

Before allowing Jesus to pass out of childhood, Luke tells a closing story
of his youth which caps the prime element with which we are concerned.
Jesus had been a part of the Passover pilgrimage that so many pious Jews
made annually to celebrate the Feast of Passover in Jerusalem. During

the return home to Nazareth, Mary and Joseph could not find Jesus and so retraced their steps, anxiously searching for the child everywhere they had been with him throughout the Feast of Passover. It was in the Temple area that they found him. While Mary's question to Jesus indicates her worry at his loss, Jesus indicates for his part that he is puzzled at his parents' not knowing exactly where to find him. Where else would he be but in the house of his Father? Is that not where one would first look for any twelve-year-old, in the house of his Father? The story is told clearly to emphasize the logic to be learned well from Gabriel's announcement to Mary earlier. Jesus is Son of God; God is his Father. More to the point, it is the reader who is Luke's concern: have we realized, as we move from the youth of Jesus to his adulthood, just who Jesus is? One is to balance this profound claim about Jesus with the fatherhood of Joseph, but never to forget the words we might still hear in the air, pronounced about 2,000 years ago: God is my Father.

The story of Jesus' being found in the Temple has a secondary purpose which we should consider. Mary and Joseph found their son sitting (usually the position of the teacher, not the disciple) amidst the specialists in the Law of Moses, asking questions and listening; the doctors were, for their part, astonished at his intelligence and his answers to their questions. There is no suggestion here that Jesus was more than a precocious young person, but he was, for his age, astonishing in his ability to deal with the complex Law of Moses. Luke puts enough emphasis on this element of the story to make us ask why. As with much else of these first two chapters of Luke, the small vignette of Jesus among the doctors of the Law is a foreshadowing of the mastery of the Law which Jesus will exhibit as an adult. Again, we gain insight into Jesus from his youth, and insight how Luke meant the infancy stories to enlighten the stories of Jesus' adulthood, crucifixion, and resurrection.

To conclude, a word should be said about what is often sensed to be awkward in the story. How could such a good son as Jesus allow his parents to be so upset? In part, as mentioned earlier, the story is more about the fact that God is Jesus' Father than about the psychologies of the personages in the story. Luke had to show that Mary and Joseph were still struggling to understand fully what we also must struggle to keep clear: Jesus is God's Son. The means Luke chose to underline this essence of Jesus may appear to be harsh, but it does do its job; for the writers of the time, that was accomplishment. In part, however, there lingers about the story a certain distance between Jesus and his parents. This is again a prelude to the adult Jesus. This time it is a matter of recalling his insistence: "If anyone comes to me and does not 'hate' his father and mother . . . indeed his very self, he cannot be my disciple"; to the woman who said: "Blessed is the womb that bore you," Jesus answered: "Rather, blessed are they who hear the word of God and keep it." When Mary and others stood outside a house and asked to see Jesus who was teaching, Jesus answered: "My mother and my brothers are those who hear the word of God and act upon it." These sayings of the adult Jesus simply continue what we find in the story of his youth: there is, without denying love for his parents, a devotion to God his Father which surpasses all other loves and which allows no other loyalties to precede his obedience to his Father. This mindset takes some getting used to, especially since Jesus asks that it be the mindset of his disciple as well. Of course, human beings have often thought just as Jesus described; married people may be said to prefer their spouses to all others. But one must get used to Jesus' way of thinking as a fundamental component of discipleship.

Jesus at the Feast of Sukkoth
~ JOHN 7–8 ~

The fourth Gospel speaks in chapters 7 and 8, of Jesus' visit to Jerusalem for the Feast of Sukkoth, or Tabernacles. Tabernacles, Passover, and Pentecost are the three great pilgrim feasts of Judaism. Tabernacles was an annual celebration, held in the fall of each year in September-October, to thank God for the harvest of what was planted the previous spring. It also means to commemorate the one-time experience of Israel, that for forty years the Israelites lived in huts or tents in the desert, until God lovingly brought them to the Promised Land. As for the harvest aspect of the Feast, we recall that the harvesters, to take advantage of the fullest light in the fall, often during the harvesting lived in tents or tabernacles or booths until all of the produce was safely gathered. These tents help give this Feast the title of the Feast of Tabernacles.

Among the liturgical symbols associated with the eight-day Feast of Tabernacles are water and light. Water is used as a reminder of the crucial need for it, for the water that enlivened the summer crops came from the previous winter's rain, and was kept in cisterns for summer need. There is no rain in Israel in the summer, and so Israel is very conscious of its dependence on bounteous winter rains, sent by God, to whom they are now so grateful as they harvest bountifully. All who live near the desert know the value of water; it is a source of life. And they know their dependence on God for it. As many pilgrims mill about the Temple area during these festive days, they can hear the cry of Jesus, that he will provide the water that will never end, that will sustain life forever. He was speaking, John says, of the Holy Spirit who would descend after Jesus' ascension. It is this Spirit who, like water, will ward off death. The Feast was a fitting time for Jesus to promise this life-giving water.

It was part of the work of the early church to understand as perfectly as possible the relationship between these two divine elements: the Son of God and God's Spirit. Jesus was conceived of the Spirit, and was anointed by the Spirit. As well, it is he who will receive the Spirit from his Father so as to pour the Spirit upon the church which no longer has Jesus with it in a physical sense. The Spirit will, at the direction of Jesus, inspire and strengthen disciples, will live in each one, and will form the bond that will make the church members one in mind and heart. God will raise up the disciples to life, through the life-giving Spirit who gave Jesus life after his death. Indeed, the Spirit will teach all that Jesus and his Father would like the church to know.

Another powerful symbol of the Feast of Tabernacles is light. Given the time of year for this Feast, one is very much aware of the shortening of daylight and the increased hours of darkness. In many cultures darkness reminds one of danger and death, of evil and the fear it creates. In particular, darkness was linked with the night escape from Egypt, a darkness kept at bay only by the guiding light of Yahweh which led Israel from slavery and death. Not surprisingly, at this Feast, at this time of year, Israel reminds itself that God is its true Light. Each day of the feast's eight days, another huge candle was lit in the Temple area. By the eighth night, eight immense candles were ablaze, and ancient testimony said that all Jerusalem could see by their light.

It is against the backdrop of this liturgy that Jesus identifies himself as the Light of the world. Isaiah had given this title to Israel, for it should make clear to the Gentiles just who was the true God and what were the authentic ways of human living. Jesus, at his Sermon on the Mount, told his disciples that they would be the Light of the world, for it would fall to them to make clear the true God and his ways. But here Jesus takes to himself the role of primary light; he is the one who will lead all human beings to God and free them from darkness and the shadow of death. We long to hear again in this sacred place the words of comfort: I am the Light of the world.

Last Week of Jesus' Life on Earth

The third set of events centering on the Temple occurs during the last week of Jesus' earthly life. For convenience sake, let us divide these events into three parts: Palm Sunday, Controversies on the Temple platform, and Prophecy of the destruction of Jerusalem.

Palm Sunday
~ MATTHEW 21:1–9; MARK 11:1–11; LUKE 19:29–38 ~

As Jesus enters the final stage of his journey from Galilee and walks over the top of the Mount of Olives to get a first glimpse of Jerusalem to the west, an enthusiasm and an expectancy grow. From the way he spoke and acted throughout his days in Galilee, was he not the one Israel expected to come to take possession of the Holy City and Temple of Yahweh? Indeed, to declare himself a king, Jesus calls for a donkey on which to ride down the mountain and ascend again up to the southern gates leading into the Temple area. In doing this, he likens himself to the one prophesied by the prophet Zechariah: "Rejoice heart and soul, daughter of Sion! Shout with gladness, daughter Jerusalem! See now, your king comes to you; he is victorious, he is triumphant, humble and riding on a donkey, a colt, a foal of a donkey . . . the bow of war will be banished; he will proclaim peace for the nations" (Zec 9:9–10).

Jesus' act reminds the evangelists of the prophecy from Isaiah: "Say to daughter Sion: 'look, your savior comes. . . .'" (Is 62:11).

Finally, a psalm indicates a liturgical welcome for "the stone rejected by the builders," but made by God the foundational stone: "Blessings on him who comes in the name of Yahweh! We bless you from the house of Yahweh. Yahweh is God, he smiles on us. With branches in your hands draw up in procession all the way to the horns of the altar" (Ps 118:26–27).

The Old Testament texts interpret Jesus' action: he comes to Jerusalem as the Messiah king, representative of Yahweh, and brings blessings and prosperity to his Holy City . As though to carry out the kingly image to its fullest, Jesus is described as coming onto the Temple platform to survey the entire area, before retiring for the evening outside the city. He was the Master surveying his property. We know now, however, that Jesus' kingdom is not one of this earth, as he tells Pilate; Jesus' followers must come to understand in just what ways he was their king and king for Israel and the Temple.

Note the difference between Mark and Luke, who read Mark. Mark says that Jesus entered Jerusalem and the Temple; Luke notes that Jesus entered the Temple. Scholars regard Luke's omission of an entry into Jerusalem seriously. They take as an implication that, for Luke, Jesus has already given up on Jerusalem; he already recognizes it as only the city of death for him. Jesus, then, as far as Luke was concerned, went directly to the Temple area and spent his time there, symbolically leaving the city to its self-appointed fate.

Associated with Jesus' arrival in the Temple area was his cleansing of the Temple. Actually, rather than say Jesus cleansed the Temple—he did not touch the Temple buildings themselves—we should say that Jesus drove out of the Temple area those who, by their changing secular coins for religious money (to buy animals) and by their selling animals for sacrifice, created an atmosphere which harmed the reverent worship of Yahweh, whose presence should be felt "throughout his house and yard." (Indeed, at another time religious authorities moved the selling of animals to the Mount of Olives, precisely to preserve reverence in the Temple area.) Purifying the Temple area had long been, in Judaism, an expectation; it would signal the approach of God for whom all things should be purified. Purifying the Temple itself was an annual part of the Feast of Tabernacles. Many Jews would interpret Jesus' driving out the unworthy businesses as a sign that with the coming of Jesus God himself was near.

Unfortunately, there is no clear way of resolving the apparent contradiction between John and the other three Gospels about the time of Jesus' act. The former, by putting it as early as chapter 2, suggests that it occurred at the beginning of Jesus' life; according to the others, who it must be admitted bring Jesus to Jerusalem, and thus to the Temple, only at the end of his life, the act of purification occurs very late. Telling this story early in Jesus' public life, however, does give the Fourth Gospel the opportunity to speak, right at its beginning, of the destruction of another temple and its resurrection after three days.

Some people argue that Jesus could not have acted in the Temple area as the Gospels indicate. Consider, however, these factors. First, Israelites knew the difference between vandalism and prophetic action; the latter they respected and would allow its extreme gestures within limits. Second, it is hard to imagine that the money-changers and animal-sellers were not back in business soon after Jesus' act. Third, such an act was not inconsistent with Jesus' personality as it occasionally reveals itself. Jesus never physically hurt anyone; but bitter criticism, as well as vigorous prophetic violence, were consonant with his character and his self-understanding.

Controversies at the Temple
~ MATTHEW 21:23–23:39; MARK 11:27–12:40; LUKE 20:1–47 ~

Jesus spent some days in the Temple area before Passover officially began. Stories of his teaching in these days have quite a palpable air of controversy and tension. After these episodes, with their acrimony and bitter challenges and argument, Jesus' newest enemies—particularly the Elders and Chief Priests—resolve to put Jesus away permanently. Mark, who provides the basic outline of these stories for Matthew and Luke, presents these challenges to Jesus as the final challenge of each group which has opposed him thus far: first, the Chief Priests and Elders, then the Pharisees and Herodians, then the Sadducees, and finally the scribes. Let us look at each of these stories for a moment.

The first challenge to Jesus on the Temple platform is the question which goes to the heart of everything: where do you get the authority to do what you do and say what you say? Jesus turns this simple question into his own challenge. He will answer their question if his opponents will first answer his: from where did John the Baptist get his authority? Everyone knew who authorized John to call Israel to repentance; Jesus challenges his opponents to admit it. If they will not see (or admit) God's working in John, what good would it be for Jesus to say that God now authorized Jesus? A stand-off.

A bit later, still in the Temple area, the now-famous question was put to Jesus by Pharisees and Herodians, supporters of Herod Antipas, ruler of the Galilee section of Palestine, and now present for the feast in Jerusalem: "Is it permissible to pay taxes to Caesar or not?" There was no love lost between Pharisees, who wanted to see Herod and all Rome gone from Palestine, and the Herodians, who depended for their livelihood on the continued presence of Herod Antipas—but, because Jesus was a challenge to what each group stood for, they ganged up willingly against him. The Pharisees hoped to hear Jesus say that Jews should not pay taxes to Caesar; he could then be accused of rebellion against Rome. The Herodians hoped to hear Jesus say that the taxes should be paid; he could then lose much credibility among his own Israelites who hated Rome.

Jesus' answer is very clever. He forces his opponents to admit that a coin has Caesar's face and name on it; if this means that the coin therefore belongs to Caesar, then they should give it to him; and if it does not mean ownership, why are his face and name on it? Jesus leaves it to his opponents to figure out if the coin actually does belong to the one whose face and name are on it; if it does belong to Caesar, then they should give it to him. But Jesus, to his liking, extends the argument: give to God what is God's. Israel had always claimed it was made in God's image and likeness, and bore his sacred name. Clearly then Israel belonged to God. Why be so hypocritical, wanting to be free of Caesar and yet not willing to repent and serve God as he should be served? Maybe Jesus is encouraging paying taxes and maybe he is not; he is not clear on that point. But he is clear that we should serve God: give God what he deserves.

A third group Jesus meets in the Temple area is the Sadducees, people he has rarely encountered in his public life in Galilee. Sadducees, like Pharisees, probably trace their roots to a time before 170 B.C. Unlike the Pharisees, the Sadducees believed that only the first five books of the Old Testament, those written by Moses and called Torah, were truly Scripture of God; the rest of the Old Testament was of great value, but the doctrines that made up the Jewish faith came only from the Torah. Limited to these books, and interpreting them conservatively, the Sadducees concluded that there was no life after death; thus, they never believed in an afterlife with God and challenged Jesus for claiming that such there will be. In Acts, a book dedicated to recounting the witness of Christians that Jesus is risen from the dead, the Sadducees are the principal enemies of Christianity.

If we understand how irritating Jesus' profession of a resurrection from the dead was to the Sadducees, we will understand what was the thrust of the rather bizarre case with which they challenge Jesus and try to ridicule the idea of life after death. In the ancient world, continuation of one's possessions in one's family was considered essential, but this continuation should come through a male heir, not the wife or a daughter. If a man died without a male heir, the Levirate (the Latin for brother-in-law) Law said that a relative of the deceased should "marry" his widow, i.e., he should have intercourse with her, in order to raise up the required male heir. The Sadducees now construct a case around the mythic number seven: the widow married her husband, and six of his relatives in an attempt to have this male child. So far so good; no one disagrees. But then the Sadducees get to the point: in the (so-called) afterlife, whose wife will she be, since she was technically married to seven men? If the woman is now in a ridiculous position, it is not the Law, but the insistence that there is an afterlife which has caused it. This would be just one example, the Sadducees are arguing, that proves there is no afterlife; the Law itself militates against such a foolish idea.

Jesus' answer to this problem was twofold. First, we must realize that the need to find a means of continuing the property of the dead man is the result of the man's dying. What if the man lives forever? Such he will do, once raised from the dead. Logically, the man will not have to be replaced by his relatives, for there is no need, now that he lives. Second, in his words to Moses at the burning bush, God identifies himself: "I am the God of Abraham, Isaac, and Jacob," all of whom died hundreds of years before Moses. Is God to be understood as saying he is God of dead men, of men who are no longer alive? Why did God use the present tense, "I am"? He should have said: "I was God of Abraham, etc." if they were no longer alive. No, the words of God himself argue that Abraham, Isaac, and Jacob are alive, that God is God of the living, that there is resurrection from the dead. The beauty of this second argument is that the citation is taken right from the Torah, which the Sadducees used to show that there is no resurrection from the dead! Jesus rather teaches that those who are judged worthy of eternal life will be like the angels, who, unable to die, live forever.

Finally, the scribes approach Jesus in the Temple area to test his knowledge of the Law; this was a professional being examined as only professionals can do it. Jesus is asked: "What is the greatest law?" By this, these scribes (equivalently lawyers of our day who specialize in knowing the entire corpus of law) were asking if there is a law which gives validity to all other laws, if there is a law which all other laws serve; if so, what is it? Jesus answers that there is one such law, to love God with all one's heart and soul and mind and strength; however, though asked to cite one law, he cites two: the second is like the first, to love neighbor as one wants to be loved. This brief reply of Jesus means that all the other laws of Israel made sense, were valid, and could exist because they were simply concrete expressions of either love of God or love of neighbor. Every law should be a particular example of these two great laws; if any law were not, it should be abolished or changed so that it did reflect perfectly how to love God or neighbor.

We note that Jesus could not answer the question put to him by citing only one law; the law of neighbor had to be included, so as to make sense of the entire rest of the laws of Moses. Second, the scribe who put the question to Jesus had only praise for him—a striking tribute from the opponents. Mark here concludes: "And after that no one dared question him any more." Third, the separation of Christianity from Judaism, for decades a most thorny problem and slow process, was grounded in this response of Jesus. All laws were reevaluated against Jesus' central principle, either by him or by his followers under the guidance of the Holy Spirit. All laws must lead clearly to love of God or love of neighbor. In this evaluation of laws, Christianity becomes distinct from Judaism. The Christian church measures God's will by Jesus' teaching that what is truly God's will serves love of God or love of neighbor.

Matthew absorbs these four challenges or controversy stories of Mark into a larger framework, which is characterized by the need, not to contest Jesus, but to prepare for final judgment. It is in this context that Jesus delivers one of his most caustic and bitter denunciations of the Pharisees and scribes that we have on record. Truly, we are at the height of anger between Jesus and his enemies, according to Matthew; the next step can only be the drastic action of capture, trial, and crucifixion.

The testing of Jesus ended; the testing of the enemies did not. Jesus, in his turn, now had a question for them. Tradition had long said that the

Messiah would be the Son of David; fine. But everyone says clearly that the Messiah is to be identified with the second "lord" in the psalm citation: "The Lord Yahweh said to my lord, 'Come sit at my right hand. . . .'" Since David is the psalmist saying these psalm words, he is represented by the "my" in "my lord." Thus, if the Messiah is that second lord of the citation, and everyone says he is, he must be David's lord. Now, how can the Messiah be both Son of David and lord of David? Is that not a contradiction? No one could answer Jesus. In short, the specialists could not interpret Scripture as well as they claimed they could. Indeed, only the Christian knows how Jesus, Son of David, is also Lord of all creation— only the Christian can answer this puzzling question. Only the Christian can explain how David the father is subordinate to Jesus the son, how the resurrection and ascension of Jesus are what brought Jesus clearly to the right hand of his Father and so identified Jesus as lord of David.

Jesus also calls his disciples' attention to a widow's action. She had just put into one of the trumpet-shaped donation receptacles two small coins. What are they worth? Simply as coins, not much. But they are all the widow has. Jesus praises the widow for her gift, worth more than the donations of the rich, for the woman has given all she has. The woman exemplifies Jesus' own giving of himself; he gives all, not just extra that he might have had on a particular day. It is this gift of all of oneself that God deserves. Many scholars think that this story was placed here to introduce the Passion of Jesus, when he will indeed give his all, his entire life, in the obedience God deserves.

Prophecy of the Destruction of the Temple
~ MATTHEW 24:1–51; MARK 13:1–37; LUKE 21:5–36 ~

A short time remains now till Jesus' suffering begins. The time is right to consider the future, the time after Jesus' departure from this world. In a last look around the Temple esplanade before the Passover was to begin, Jesus' disciples praised in wonder the beauty of the Temple and its surrounding buildings. When we realize the limited housing of most Israelites on the land, it is certainly understandable that the gold, silver, precious wood, hangings, marble, and bronze would simply astound the person who had never seen the likes of all this in his entire life.

Jesus' reply to their wonderment and admiration chilled the disciples: "A day is coming when not one stone will be left on another." This gloomy prediction fits into a pattern of Jesus' forecasts about the future of Jerusalem and Israel: Jerusalem will be destroyed, its house (= Temple) will fall in ruins. Jesus' words are not unique. Such words as his were said often in advance of the two terrible destructions of Israel, in 722 and in 587 B.C.

The reaction of the disciples is understandable, even predictable. They want to know when this destruction will happen and what the signs to warn of its coming will be. Jesus' answer does speak of the destruction of the Holy City and its Temple, but it speaks also of the end of this world, as though the entire sweep of history should be considered if one speaks of one element of it.

Interpreters have for many centuries studied Jesus' lengthy reply to his disciples' twofold question: when? what signs? The eternal hope is to uncover from Jesus' words the precise calendar year and even hour of both the destruction of the Temple and the end of this world of ours. All efforts have failed—despite the ingenuity of countless suggestions. This failure in itself suggests that there really is no attempt on Jesus' part to apply clock-and-calendar time to these matters. Jesus used a form of speech usual for prophets: the only certain thing is the assurance that disasters will come whenever they will come because of the hardness of his hearers' hearts. That events appear nearer than they really are is a characteristic of this kind of speech, as is evidenced in many similar speeches over the centuries before Jesus. Further, one can sense, from the way Luke has reworked Mark's rendition of this speech, that Luke feels obliged to lengthen some of these foreshortened periods, precisely to avoid the impression that the speech in Mark gives of the nearness of events.

The usual purpose of this kind of speech in which Jesus here engages is to promote repentance—now! The nearness of events is a major motivation to repent, though one realizes that the disasters predicted need not actually occur soon—but they might. After all, repentance may move God to rescind his decision to destroy the evils before him. Certainly woven into such a speech of Jesus was his awareness of how all contemporary events and attitudes pointed to a deadly challenge to the Romans, the end of which would be destruction—these current events and attitudes would help him see the future very clearly. But his concern was not prediction of time and place; his concern was the sin which would lead to these disasters, if God were not moved to pity.

A sign of Jesus' main interest or concern is very visible at the end of the speech, and fittingly so because the end so often contains the high point of a speech. There we hear Jesus implore his disciples to "watch!," to "persevere!" This ending suggests the interpretation of the speech to be that, whenever the painful events occur, sooner or later, the disciple's proper attitude is watchfulness. Jesus does not give the disciples what they want; they ask for the time of Jerusalem's destruction, but his final word is not about time but about attitude.

In reading Jesus' speech, one notes that, while on the one hand Jesus gives at least some details leading up to the capture and destruction of Jerusalem, on the other hand there are few or no details about the period between the destruction of Jerusalem and the end of this world. The best explanation of this absence of details is that the Gospel writers have to some extent filled the period between the death and resurrection of Jesus and the destruction of Jerusalem with certain details they have come to know as fulfilling Jesus' more general prediction. The Gospel writers wrote at least forty years after Jesus' life ended here: Mark about 70, Luke and Matthew about 85. Mark, the first, fleshed out Jesus' prediction about the destruction of Jerusalem; Matthew and Luke, writing after this tragedy, made Jesus' prediction even more detailed because of what they knew of the period. But Mark, Matthew, and Luke are so much less detailed once they pass their own time of writing; they could only, for the future after themselves, provide the very general description of the end that Jesus gave them.

Jesus' speech has certain words in it which suggest that he saw the tragic future times as part of an immense struggle between God and Satan; we are only the battlefield, as it were, on which these two mighty powers struggle to win. Satan knows he cannot harm God, so he tries to make suffer and turn from God all of those people and the creation that God loves. God's effort is to eliminate all evil and death from his creation. Thus, the vision of Jesus is essentially religious, and understandably calls for the gift of free will choice from free creatures. His discourse to his disciples is, then, on the one hand explanatory (though he gives them few satisfactory answers to their questions), and on the other hand exhortatory. Repentance may avert disaster; in any case, be faithful, watch!

The Early Church

Luke notes that thousands of Jews asked for Christian baptism after Peter's Pentecost speech in chapter 2; by Acts 4:4 the number baptized had reached over five thousand. One place of meeting for many of these Jewish Christians was on the Temple platform. Specifically, they gathered in the portico along the eastern wall; this is the area in which Jesus had taught during his last week in Jerusalem. It is most likely that from this area Peter and John came to enter the Temple and pray at the afternoon services; here Peter gives his famous remark to the lame beggar: "Silver and gold I have none, but what I do have I give you—in the name of Jesus Christ the Nazorean, walk!" The name of Jesus rings out through Acts; it is the name upon which one calls for salvation. Witness to this, particularly that the one we call upon is Lord and Messiah raised from the dead—this is the heart of the Acts of the Apostles.

The Temple, building and esplanade, carries many memories of very important events in the lives of Elizabeth and Zachary, of Mary, Joseph, and Jesus, of the early Christian community. Perhaps a prayer is in order that God show the way of peace to the major religions devoted to this sacred place.

The Upper Room

> "THIS IS MY BODY GIVEN FOR YOU . . . THIS IS
> MY BLOOD POURED OUT FOR YOU."
> ~ LUKE 22:19-20

J ust three minutes' walk from the present Sion Gate, fixed in the southern wall of today's Jerusalem, is the site considered since the time of the Crusades to be the Upper Room (sometimes called the Cenacle). In this simple room, which the practiced eye can see has been used as a

Jerusalem: passage to the Cenacle

mosque, took place three very important events for Christianity: Jesus' Last Supper, his appearances to his disciples after the Resurrection, and the outpouring of the Holy Spirit on about one hundred and twenty of Jesus' followers. How does the New Testament present these events?

The Feasts of Passover and Unleavened Bread

For centuries Jews had been commanded to present themselves for worship in Jerusalem; more specifically, the Law of Moses ordered all Israelite males to come to Jerusalem three times a year, to celebrate the Pilgrim Feasts: Passover (early spring), Pentecost (late spring), and Tabernacles (mid-fall). In obedience to the Law, Jesus goes now to Jerusalem to celebrate the Feast of Passover. This is the feast which commemorates Israel's salvation from Egypt. The blood of the lamb, placed on the door of each Israelite house in Egypt, kept away the Angel of Death sent by Yahweh to kill the firstborn male, human and animal, all living in Egypt. Because of this slaughter Pharaoh let God's people go. When he saw the blood of the lamb on Israelite doorposts or lintels, the Angel of Death "passed over" or "passed by" these houses; thus, Israelite life was saved, and thus the feast to commemorate this saving is called Passover.

We can imagine that compliance with the Mosaic Law to honor Passover meant that Jerusalem would be filled to overflowing with devout and obedient pilgrims, come to celebrate, each in his own family, the dinner which resembled so closely the last dinner their ancestors had before leaving Egypt and slavery forever. We find Jesus, then, directing his disciples to an unnamed friend who would provide Jesus not just with a space for celebration, but with an entire room, an upper or second-story room at that. Only relatively few pilgrims to Jerusalem would have a Passover feast in such privacy as Jesus and the Twelve enjoyed.

The Gospels mention that this particular day could also be called the Feast of the Unleavened Bread. This was the name given to the celebration of the first harvest of spring. It was a time of great joy and gratitude for the winter's abundant rain and growth, and of prayer that the next harvests be generous. The offering to God at this moment was cakes made from the first wheat harvested plus some water; since there was no yeast or leaven added to this wheat, the feast was called the Feast of Unleavened Bread.

Because this wheat harvest occurs in the spring, it was eventually celebrated in conjunction with the Passover. Fittingly, the bread eaten by the Israelites at the first Passover, that night of escape from Egypt, was also unleavened. Thus, with the two feasts coinciding, the bread of the Last Supper was clearly to be bread without yeast. However, the meaning of the bread differs according to the feasts. The newly harvested wheat is offered immediately in gratitude to God, with no human adulteration in it. The Passover bread, the "bread of tears," recalls the haste with which Israel had to leave Egypt and the tearful journey that followed over the next forty years.

Last Supper in Matthew and Mark
~ MATTHEW 26:17–35; MARK 14:12–31 ~

The Gospels of Matthew, Mark, and Luke place the Last Supper of Jesus with his disciples in the context of these two feasts: for these evangelists, the Last Supper is a Passover supper, eaten at the time of the Feast of Unleavened Bread. Because John does not identify Jesus' Last Supper with the Passover (but says that the Passover was to be celebrated in the evening after Jesus died), I will consider his presentation of the Last Supper separately.

The traditional Passover supper involved much more ritual than is mentioned in Matthew, Mark, or Luke. Clearly, these Gospels have chosen to relate only certain moments of this meal, what they thought to be important for their readers.

Matthew follows Mark very closely so that what can be said for the latter can be said for the former. Mark introduces us into the Last Supper at the point where Jesus, well into the meal, abruptly sets a mournful tone by saying that one of his own Twelve will betray him. The reader had been prepared for this betrayal just a few moments earlier in the story which reported that Judas agreed to watch for the moment when he could hand Jesus over to the authorities—when the crowds would not be present to contest this arrest. But for all that, to announce that the betrayer is right here is chilling and saddening for those who love Jesus. The mood is perplexity, sourness, and fear.

As in so many other places in the Gospel story, so here an awareness that "Scripture is being fulfilled" permeates the story of betrayal. All these happenings, even minute details, were in some sense already spoken of by God through his prophets, signs always there for those to read who knew how to read them.

What a sharp turn in mood is established then when the next moment tells us that Jesus' death would be a death out of love for us. Such a contrast between Judas, who sacrificed another human being, and Jesus, who sacrificed himself lest others should suffer! Mark intentionally emphasized this contrast by putting these two persons opposite each other in quick sequence.

By indicating that Jesus' Last Supper is a Passover supper, Mark wanted us to interpret Jesus' death as a death by which believers were freed from ignorance, slavery, and sin, symbolized by Egypt, to reach a state of wisdom, freedom, and holiness, symbolized by the Promised Land. The blood of the lamb, which warded off death for the Israelites, was now Jesus' blood; the slaying of the lamb was the means by which we avoid death and enjoy happiness with God. Thus, what was eaten, the food of the Passover, was now identified as the body of Jesus, the body to be slain tomorrow, to provide the blood which protects us from death. The death of Jesus, then, is not just the death of an innocent treated unjustly, of a martyr to the truth about God and Israel. Jesus is an innocent and a martyr, but he is also the one and only one whose blood sets us free, to live, to reach the land of wisdom, of freedom and holiness, of peace.

When Jesus took up the cup, however, he suggested a further interpretation of his blood. The wine was identified, not as the wine of Passover, but as blood of the new covenant. To refer to blood in this way made one think of the many covenants God had made with his People, and of that new covenant promised by the prophet Jeremiah (Jer 31:31–34; also see Ez 11:17–20). Most directly involved, however, was the act Moses performed whereby he confirmed the Sinai agreement or covenant between God and Israel. In that act, Moses sprinkled blood on the Ark of the Covenant, which represented God and his mercy, and on the people. By this blood the two became faithful, devoted partners. Jesus means to say, then, that by his blood a new covenant is begun, by which again God and his faithful are loyal, devoted, committed partners.

Jesus made clear that his blood was to be poured out, as Mark says, for *many;* this word is an Aramaic idiom and really means for *everybody.* Matthew makes things even clearer: this blood is poured out for the forgiveness of sins, the first step to making us covenant partners with God. By identifying Jesus' blood as that which cleanses us from sins, Matthew reminds us of the many institutional sacrifices, repeated over and over again in the Temple, as petitions for forgiveness of Israel's sins.

St. Paul, twenty years before Matthew's Gospel, had singled out Yom Kippur as an event which his hearers would understand and which would be able to make clear to them the meaning of Jesus' sacrifice. On Yom Kippur, or the Day of Atonement, Israel's High Priest entered the Holy of Holies with the blood of an animal, to sprinkle over the private quarters of God the blood which, all Israel hoped, would move God to forgive all Israel's sins of the past year.

The blood used in this ceremony has a particular meaning. Often one thinks blood represents the death of an animal and that this death is what pleases God. In this ceremony, on the contrary, blood stands for life, and it is life which is being offered to God and which, it is hoped, will please him. Blood stands for life? Yes, in ancient Israel life was thought to exist in two substances, blood and breath; to lose either one, the ordinary person knew, was to lose one's life. The book of Leviticus expressed it simply: "the life is in the blood." Thus, the sprinkling in the Holy of Holies symbolized a rededication of life to God. It was hoped that God in return would shed mercy upon Israel, in a sense renew the dedication of his life for his People. What Paul means, then, by invoking the memory of Yom Kippur is that it is now the blood of Jesus, the dedicated life of Jesus, that pleases God and moves God to lavish his mercy and forgiveness on us; the hope is that the baptized will offer their lives, too, with Jesus' offering, to God, and thus receive in return the dedication of God's life for them.

Particular elements of this Yom Kippur comparison are interesting. On the one hand, Moses, the priest, sprinkled the blood of the sacrifice in the Holy of Holies, specifically on the wooden Ark of the Covenant, which was the chair of God and the box which contained the signs of God's mercy, e.g., manna, the Ten Commandments; from this wood came mercy. On the other hand, now it is Jesus, the priest, who is also the sacrifice and it is his blood which he sprinkles on the wood of the cross, which is the mercy seat of God, from which flows mercy for us all.

Ultimately, the blood of Christ reminds us, in this way of thinking, of our exchange of lives with God.

There is still another suggestion about the meaning of the blood of Jesus and forgiveness of sins; we see this especially in Matthew's Gospel. Jesus can be seen, in his Passion, to be fulfilling the role of the Servant of Yahweh spoken of by Isaiah in chapter 53 so many centuries before the coming of Jesus. This unnamed servant, according to Isaiah, would give his life, like a lamb led to the slaughter, so that we, guilty and deserving of punishment, might go free because of this servant who is innocent and deserves no punishment. It is for our sins that he dies. Mark had earlier noted Jesus' words that he had come like a servant, "not to be served but to serve and to give his life as a ransom for many" (Mk 10:45). In this understanding, the blood of the Eucharist commemorates that bloodshed by which the innocent, in loving God, endured the suffering which really belonged to others. By his blood those who deserve to die go free; he dies for them.

Many, then, are the ways by which one can get at the richness of the sacrifice of Jesus. These ways are so many facets by which to appreciate the jewel we have been given, the Eucharist which we celebrate every day.

As Jesus brought to a close his reflections about this Passover food and drink, now his body and blood, he accentuated again the mournful circumstances of this meal—never again would he eat the Passover meal. Brief is the statement, but it cannot fail to move the disciples and the reader, for by it is signified that the friendship between Jesus and his Twelve, and indeed with so many others, is terminated by futile and destructive anger and jealousy. Their life together as they had grown to know it is finished; these are the last moments of that life.

This dinner does mark an end of life, but Jesus insists that someday he will eat again together with his friends, in the Kingdom of God. There will be reunion and the joys that attend it, a time of complete joy, never to be interrupted again. As St. Paul says, the Eucharist we celebrate recalls the separation from the Lord until he comes again (1 Cor 17:26). The Eucharist reminds us of death, but also of a future life together, and this makes the celebration ultimately a joyous one.

The language of the Last Supper is terse and continues to be intense. After determining the meaning of the bread and wine, the Gospel writer turns to still another and painful moment: Jesus reveals the weakness of Peter and the others, to be revealed soon for all to see at the capture of Jesus. Mark is clever is his presentation of the dialogue now between Jesus and Peter. Jesus quietly insists this his expectation will be fulfilled, while Peter, eventually to claim himself to be more loyal than any of the others at the table, is allowed to have the final word: you will see that I will remain faithful even if it means my death! The last word was Peter's, as though the last word were the truth! Jesus was willing to let actions decide who was right.

We stand in this room, for centuries noted as the Upper Room of the Last Supper. The walls of the Upper Room might yet repeat the words of tragedy and betrayal, of generous giving of life. Here ultimately was the moment of parting, and death was present in the room. It is noteworthy how Mark and Matthew have centered the generosity of Jesus between the hardness of Judas and the selfishness of Peter, as though placed on either side of him they might help reflect even more brightly the one person who spent himself in love in the midst of so much treachery and self-serving weakness.

The Last Supper in Luke
~ LUKE 22:7–28 ~

In his portrayal of the Last Supper, Luke differs from Mark and Matthew both by changing the order of events and by adding teachings of Jesus fitting to this moment. Luke begins the supper with Jesus' words that he had for a long time been eager to celebrate this dinner with his disciples; he had said on an earlier occasion that he had a baptism by which he was to be baptized and how impatient he was until it would be accomplished (Lk 12:50). The baptism for which he longed, his death, was now at hand, and this meal began this baptism.

No more would Jesus eat and drink with his disciples on earth, but just as surely as that was true, it was also true that he would one day eat and drink again with them in God's Kingdom. In this way, Luke from the outset, puts limits to the suffering of Jesus—there will come a time when all of this is over and we will then know only joy and happiness together.

Against this stark, yet hopeful background, Luke sets Jesus' words of consecration; to them, which are so like what we find in Mark and Matthew, Luke adds: "Do this in memory of me." The words justify the unending, weekly practice of Christian communities—in doing with the bread and wine what Jesus did, we recall to ourselves the sacrifice Jesus hoped we would never forget.

Mark had begun his account of the Last Supper with announcement of Judas's betrayal; Luke inserts this element of the dinner here. Having mentioned the presence of the betrayer, Jesus refers to him no more. Rather, Jesus sees this moment as an opportunity for teaching a hard, but precious, lesson. Perhaps what occasioned this teaching is the assumed reactions of the disciples at mention of one of them being a betrayer; their objections would in part be based on the claim that this or that one was "greater" than others and so could not be the betrayer. Whatever the reason for the teaching at this juncture, the teaching itself is clear. If one wants to be "great," and the desire for greatness is not stifled, one must know that, as far as Jesus is concerned, being the servant of others is what makes a person great. The lesson is difficult to learn, for most people think greatness is shown, not by service, but by "lording it over" others. Jesus took these precious moments to say that, as he will show his greatness by serving others, so he expects his disciples to be great by serving.

With perceptive logic Jesus next indicates the reward for those disciples who remain faithful in serving others, in trials—not only the trials to begin this night, but those the disciples would undergo in years to come in serving Jesus and the community. Indeed, in anticipation of their fidelity Jesus now declares them participants in the kingdom to come. With a particularly Jewish imagery, he indicates that this participation is an eating and drinking in the kingdom with him and a sitting on the thrones of Israel as judges of the world. This latter image was meant to recall that one of the ways in which Israel had envisioned its glorification after centuries of humiliation and slavery was its placement as judge over those who had caused it so much suffering, enslavement, and death. This role of judge over one's enemies who had unjustly condemned God's beloved is promised now to Jesus' friends, who, in their turn, will judge justly those who have made them suffer unjustly.

Now Luke has Jesus speak of Peter's imminent denial. Jesus' prayer—that Peter many not fail totally, but, on recovering be a strength to his fellow disciples—is a sign of the preeminent role Luke's Gospel consistently assigns to Peter.

The final teaching Luke gives at the Last Supper concerns the difference the disciples will soon notice after Jesus' departure. Earlier in the Gospel, Jesus had sent his disciples on a preaching tour with the advice not to carry purse or haversack or sandals; they would, in other words, find welcome in their mission (Lk 9:1–6). No more! The tide of favor is against Jesus now, and against those who would represent him; now one should provide for himself and defend himself, for, as Scripture had forecast, "he shall be considered a criminal" (Is 53:12). With Jesus as the criminal, inhospitableness can be an expectation of his disciples.

Luke, then, preserved what Mark had narrated about Jesus' Last Supper, but rearranged things and added elements to teach disciples further lessons which would be very relevant for the near future. The Last Supper, then, increasingly became a moment when Jesus looked more and more to the needs of his disciples in the time when he would be gone. It was natural that the Gospel writers, aware of the situations of their audiences for the next fifty years, should not only tell the story of Jesus' Last Supper, but also orient this farewell moment to benefit their readers. With the good of later Christians in mind, the fourth evangelist devoted the Last Supper to a lengthy instruction for the future. To this Gospel we now turn.

The Last Supper in John
~ JOHN 13–17 ~

If we consider first what the first three Gospels tell us about what happened in the Upper Room that night before Jesus died, we are struck all the more by the contribution John makes to this Last Supper story. Whereas the synoptic report is at most half a chapter in length, John's report extends over five chapters. Most significant, however is the absence from John of the words of consecration of bread and wine. Indeed, should one look for teaching about the Eucharist in John, one would have to turn to a speech Jesus gave in Galilee, in chapter 6. There the emphasis of John is on Jesus' body and blood as food to support our life with God. As food gives life, so reception of Jesus gives life. Finally, we are not certain at all that John regards the Last Supper of Jesus as a Passover meal; more likely it is designed as a friendship meal—John will later indicate that the Passover began only after Jesus' death, implying that the meal after Jesus' death was the Passover meal.

Jerusalem: interior of the Cenacle today

We can only consider here salient elements of the Last Supper event, as John tells it. The five chapters dealing with Jesus' words and actions at his Last Supper can be divided into two uneven parts. First, there are the two accounts of Jesus' washing feet and his announcement of betrayal. Second, from the end of chapter 13 to the end of chapter 17, there is the long discourse of Jesus, punctuated by questions from his disciples, but clearly controlled by Jesus' final thoughts about his disciples and their future needs.

The Washing of Feet
~ JOHN 13:1–17 ~

In reading chapter 13, we are again made aware of two themes constant in John's Gospel, that Jesus was in absolute control of everything that happened to him and that what happened to Jesus brought to completion what his Father had said would happen to his beloved Son. Jesus controls the future by his knowledge, not by his power. Nothing was a surprise to Jesus, in John's Gospel; in this way John argues away the claim that Jesus was ultimately a failure because he was conquered by his enemies, caught off guard, powerless in their grip, abandoned by God. The Gospel writer is at pains to show the correspondence between Jesus' words and actions throughout his public life and the Jewish Scriptures of God, all in the same effort to deny the enemy claim that Jesus' crucifixion was a sign that he was not from God. For John, all argued in favor of Jesus being from God, and he presented the story of Jesus to profess that conviction.

Jesus, aware that he was at the end of his life, taught his disciples, according to John, the same lesson Luke had described: service to others. But unlike Luke, John will have Jesus teach not only by word, but by symbolic act. Jesus does the servant's work by washing the feet of his disciples; it is the greater who washes the feet of the lesser, and by this act of service shows his greatness. Jesus' readiness to be a servant to his disciples helps interpret the death of Jesus as Jesus' greatest service to us. But it is meant not only to help us understand his death, but to help us realize wherein our true greatness lies.

This book does not intend to interpret individual verses; but one verse, John 13:10, is so puzzling that it should be considered. "No one who has taken a bath needs washing, he is clean all over." To understand this sentence, we must realize that here, as so often elsewhere in John, there is more than one level of meaning intended by Jesus. On the one hand, Peter resisted Jesus' washing his feet; this resistance was on the level of natural interaction—indeed, few healthy people want their feet washed by anybody at any time. When Jesus interpreted this resistance as opposition to what Jesus wanted, we are still on the natural level; Peter understood and, in his usual blustering and exaggerated style, showed his willingness to obey Jesus by saying Jesus could wash his feet—his hands and his head as well.

But Peter's willingness to be washed totally, "feet, hands, and head," led Jesus to another thought, which is on another level. Jesus says Peter needs no such total washing, for he has already been thoroughly washed in a bath. We are not now on the ordinary, physical level of washing. This "bath" is the bath of baptism, the bath in which one is totally cleansed and in which one gives oneself totally to Jesus. Jesus is now not concerned about the washing of Peter's feet, as he had been. Rather he wants, in a sophisticated use of language, to say that Peter's total dedication is a sign that he has been "totally washed" in baptism.

But not all disciples can be said to be totally "washed" by a baptismal dedication. There is one, the betrayer, who has not this dedication, who is "unclean." If one has indeed "taken a bath, he is clean and needs no washing," but Judas is not such a one. Subtlely, the reader, baptized, is reminded of the dedication his freely chosen baptism implies.

Peter never left the first or natural level of meaning; he always thought Jesus was referring to plain washing of his feet or his body. Jesus began with that level of meaning, but switched midway to speak of another washing, that of baptism; on this level he declares all of his disciples thoroughly washed, except one. On this level Peter may need some cleansing, given his occasional faults, such as his denial of Jesus, but this partial cleansing does not deny the cleanliness of his baptismal bath; it only suggests the need to perfect the baptismal dedication of the disciple.

Presence of the Betrayer
~ JOHN 13:18–30 ~

The second element of chapter 13 that we wish to discuss is Jesus' announcement of the presence of his betrayer. As in the other Gospels, this is a moment of great perplexity and sadness as each disciple searches for the meaning of Jesus' words. It is to the Beloved Disciple, often interpreted in tradition as John the Apostle, that Jesus reveals the identity of this betrayer. The Beloved Disciple is in the best position to hear what Jesus might say. Since one ate while reclining, supported by his left elbow and eating with his right hand, the Beloved Disciple, placed next to Jesus, needed only to lean backward to have his ear close to Jesus' lips.

Judas is identified; at Jesus' urging he leaves. To mention that "it was night" is unnecessary; we know it is night—unless "night" means not physical night, but the darkness of Satan. With the exit of Judas, Jesus begins to talk about glory, for the Father and for himself. Jesus will be glorified for having been obedient to his Father; the image of the Son of Man is used, that personage from the Book of Daniel, chapter 7, who will be glorified after having suffered great humiliation. God will be glorified for the forgiveness and salvation he will offer as the result of Jesus' obedient death. But John says that Jesus is now being glorified, as if to say that, in some sense, though glory would follow upon the death of Jesus, glory has already begun for him and consequently for his Father. Since obedience is what will bring glory to Jesus, the beginning of obedience, which starts now, can be called the beginning of glory. And Jesus' perfect resignation to his Father leads one to praise the Father, as Jesus does. Indeed, Jesus reminds us of his divinity, as he asks his Father to give him the glory Jesus had before he entered this world. We are reminded of the poem of Paul some thirty years before this Gospel: though he was in the form of God, he did not consider this something to hold onto, but he took the form of a man . . . even to death, death on a cross (Phil 2:8). John reminds us that the frightful events he is about to describe will end in Jesus' glorification, and nothing less.

The foot washing and its teaching is completed, the betrayer is gone, Peter has been warned about his denial. Now Jesus turns to deliver his famous farewell discourse.

Last Discourse of Jesus

In one sense the point of Jesus' long discourse in the Upper Room is simple: Jesus, knowing the grief his death and departure are about to cause, speaks in every chapter to console and encourage his most devoted friends. It is as if Jesus has this one and last chance to say what he can to help his friends through this extremely difficult time. In another sense the speech is difficult: it is hard to grasp fully the degree of intimacy Jesus promised to maintain with his disciples, even though he would be physically absent from them.

The speech can be divided into six parts. First, chapter 14 talks of Jesus' various ways of taking care of those whom he must now leave. He goes to prepare a place for them; if they keep on following him, they will come to the truth and to life because he is in the Father and the Father is in him; they will do greater things than even he has done; he will send another Comforter: I will come back for you; meanwhile my Father and I will dwell in you; the Holy Spirit, the Comforter, will teach you even more than I have taught you; I leave my peace with you. Jesus consoles and encourages his disciples in so many ways to remain faithful to their commitment to him. At the end of this chapter we read words which have raised a question among scholars for centuries. Jesus says: "The betrayer is at hand; let us be on our way to meet him"; yet, his discourse continues for three chapters. Are these three chapters to be understood as additions made by the Gospel writer to Jesus' original speech? Even if additions, they fit very well with the sense of farewell which characterizes these last moments with the disciples.

Second, the first part of chapter 15 brings us the famous analogy: I am the vine, you are the branches. The branch lives by virtue of the life of the vine coursing through it; so it is mysteriously that the disciple has Jesus' life within him, so that he might produce good fruit, good deeds, to the glory of Jesus' Father.

Third, Jesus speaks of the love he hopes will continue to characterize his disciples; the sure sign of this love is obedience to Jesus' commandments. This love will bring them Jesus' joy and they will clearly be Jesus' friends. The Gospel of John does not spend time on detailing Jesus' moral teachings, but rather concentrates its entire attention on the meaning of Jesus. But here there is one general reference to the moral life: Jesus, who just asked that his disciples keep his commandments, mentions that he has only one commandment really, and that is that we love one another as Jesus has loved us. The Old Testament command, love one another as you would want to be loved, is valid, but made even more perfect: love one another as Jesus has loved you. Now I must ask myself, how would Jesus love this person?

Fourth, Jesus now speaks directly to a future obstacle: the world will hate you. Obviously, Jesus is not speaking of the good world God created and called good. He is speaking of that world which has rebelled against God, which lives to adore and serve another god, and wants to destroy him and his. So misguided is this world that it will praise itself for killing the disciples. As with other parts of the New Testament, the claim is being made here that everything in a person's life depends on who his god is; that god will be loved and served, and all that stands to contradict it will be eliminated. Jesus indicates that the disciples will be expelled from synagogues, too. This refers to what we have already heard about in chapter 9, where it was said that the blind man's parents were afraid that if they defended their son, they would be put out of the synagogue. This Gospel is heavily involved in the violent disputes between Jewish Christianity and Judaism as guided now by the Pharisees of 90. It tried to encourage its readers by having them hear the encouragement as given by Jesus himself.

Fifth, Jesus makes a number of comforting statements in chapter 16 which center on his sending the Comforter to continue and develop the guidance to all truth that Jesus had begun, and on further significance of his departure. At the end of this chapter, the contrast again is seen: the disciples claim sure faith, based on clear understanding of the mysteries now, while Jesus can only speak of their imminent lack of courage when faced by trial. He commands: Take courage! Why take courage? because he has overcome those who will make the disciples suffer and so they, too, can be victorious.

Sixth and finally, Jesus turns his discourse into a prayer. He prays lovingly for his own, that God may bestow eternal life on them for they do believe. He asks the Father to protect them now; they are his by virtue of baptism. For them Jesus consecrates himself, that is he accepts his death, his baptism, his obedience to his Father. Jesus then prays for all who will come to believe in him, that they may know Jesus' glory, which should be a comfort and hope for them, and may experience what it means to have "us in them, as you, Father, are in me and I in you," that "I might live in them." In this way, we fulfill our purpose for being, to be in the image and likeness of God.

Jesus leaves off now, to go to face his betrayers and to begin the horrible events which constitute for him his Father's will.

The Upper Room and Further Events Associated With It

Luke and John each tell a story of the risen Jesus' appearance to his disciples in a room, behind closed doors. This room, and its location in Jerusalem, is never specified by either Gospel. The Acts of the Apostles notes that the disciples returned from Jesus' ascension to "the room where they had been staying" and that Pentecost occurred in a house where they were seated. Tradition has put all four of these events in the Upper Room where, tradition also says, Jesus' Last Supper occurred. It is because of this tradition that we now turn to consider these events here.

Resurrection Appearances in Luke
~ LUKE 24:36–49 ~

Luke has three stories about Jesus' resurrection from the dead; it is the last of these that takes place in the Upper Room. In this room Jesus appears specifically to convince his followers that what rose from the dead was not a phantom or ghostly image of himself, but the complete Jesus, the Jesus they had last seen on the cross. To this end, Jesus asks for a fish and eats it; there can be no doubt that the complete Jesus, body and soul, has risen. It is rather clear that this story is apologetic or defensive in purpose. It intentionally means to contradict opinions that said that, if Jesus were risen from the dead, only his soul rose, only his spirit was alive. The insistence is that what you see and hear and touch as the risen Jesus, is Jesus of Nazareth, and not just a shadow of him. So often in ancient literature we hear just this, that persons are alive after death, but only as shadows, as less than what they were as human beings. Luke's story, while it does not explain just exactly what the risen body of Jesus was like, insists that the complete Jesus has risen from the grave.

Also in this third story about Jesus risen, Luke repeats what was a central idea of the other two stories. He, the Messiah and Son of Man, had to suffer and rise, and this necessity is clearly expressed both in the ancient Jewish Scriptures and in Jesus' own three predictions of his death and resurrection. There is a great emphasis in Luke that the reader *remember* what God and Jesus had said about the Paschal event; it is by remembering that one can better see how these moments are only really steps to the placement of Jesus at God's right hand, and to the eventual saving which the resurrected Jesus is to accomplish. Jesus' death will not stop his bringing salvation to human beings!

But if there was a divine necessity that Jesus die and rise, Jesus now informs his disciples that there is a further necessity: in his name must repentance for the forgiveness of sins be preached to all nations, and the Jewish Scriptures had foreseen this development. It falls to the disciples, Jesus says, to be witnesses, that is to bring this offer of forgiveness to all nations, beginning in Jerusalem. But the disciples need to wait for the outpouring of God's Spirit; with the courage and intelligence and devotion the Spirit will bless the disciples, the call to repentance for the forgiveness of sins can begin—in a few days.

However far the Acts of the Apostles takes us in telling about the offer of salvation, Luke's story here shows that all that will happen is rooted in Jesus' words here, in the Upper Room, to his disciples.

The second of Luke's three resurrection stories should be mentioned here. While on their discouraged way northwestward from Jerusalem to Emmaus, disciples meet Jesus. Part of the story is dedicated to Jesus' interpreting the Jewish Scriptures so as to make his death and resurrection intelligible—the Scriptures had clearly spoken of this event, he reminds them, so how can you be surprised or discouraged? But part of the story is arranged to say that the place where the disciple meets the risen Jesus is in the Breaking of the Bread. Luke is thinking now, not of the time of Jesus, but of all time afterward: where is Jesus, my risen Lord? Look for him, meet him, Luke says, in the breaking of the bread, in the Eucharist.

Resurrection Appearances in John
~ JOHN 19:19–29 ~

John, too, recalls Jesus' coming to this room after his resurrection. Like Luke, John has much to tell.

On the day of his resurrection, as John tells it, Jesus appears to his disciples gathered in the Upper Room—an appearance which suggests new qualities for the risen body of Jesus. Jesus' first act in this meeting with all his Eleven is to express his desire that they be in peace. Fear, or lack of peace, had brought them to hide in this Upper Room. What now gives them peace is not the removal of the threat from their enemies, but his showing them his hands and his side: sight of the resurrected Jesus gives peace.

Jesus' second act is to breathe on them, thus giving them the Holy Spirit of God. This brief story enshrines for John the Pentecost more widely known in Christian liturgical life to be found in the Acts of the Apostles. In both cases, John and Acts, the outpouring of the Spirit is attributed to the risen Jesus. In Luke, Jesus will say in the last chapter that, after Pentecost, forgiveness of sins will be offered to the entire world. John is similar here: the risen Jesus, upon giving the Spirit, assures us that forgiveness will reach all peoples through the ministry of the disciples. Note how symbolic Jesus' act is here: the Spirit (which means "breath" in Latin) is communicated by Jesus' breathing on his disciples—as though the Spirit were his own breath. Jesus has always been presented in this Gospel as a source of life; as God had breathed on the dirt and made it live, so now Jesus breathes forth the Holy Spirit to make all people reborn from above, through the forgiveness of sins.

From this meeting of the disciples with Jesus Thomas was absent. His absence gives John the opportunity to teach two vital lessons. First, Thomas confesses Jesus to be "My Lord and my God," clearly names Israel knew for its divine covenant partner. While John never tries to explain how Jesus can be Lord and God (except by such terms as Word of God and Son of God, which are still mysterious), he insists throughout his Gospel that Jesus is precisely this; here is an act of faith precisely because the mind, while seeing the reasonableness of saying Jesus is Lord and God, cannot completely fully explain what it affirms.

It is important to note that the profession of Thomas that Jesus is Lord and God is not the precise conclusion his present experience warranted. That is, Jesus seemed to be offering proof to Thomas that he was risen; Thomas had said, "Unless I can touch the nailprints in his hands, put my finger in them and my hand in his side, I will not believe that he is risen." We are on the level of proving the Resurrection. But Thomas does not say: "I believe you are risen." He leaps far beyond that to say: "My Lord and my God!" This leap John wants to emphasize as completely justified. Jesus had made it clear that first, he has the freedom to lay down his life, and second, he has the power to take up his life. This claim means that he is Lord of life. The actual Resurrection thus shows that he has used his freedom and power to give life; John shows that Jesus is Lord of all life, and gives the final reason to believe that Jesus is Lord and God.

The second lesson John teaches here occurs because John is primarily interested in his reader. This means that his primary interest is not in setting straight historical facts like dates and geography, but in providing, through historical stories, the true and most profound meaning of Jesus. History is used, so as to be able to draw the truth from it; it is this truth that John thinks is so precious and the reason for his labor to write his Gospel. His readers belong in the nineties' A.D. They never met Jesus, probably had never been to Palestine; they belonged rather to the third generation after Jesus' time. It is to these people that Jesus speaks his powerful words: "Blessed are those who have not seen, yet still believe." That is, Thomas had the actual encounter with the risen Jesus to make him cry out that you are "my Lord and my God." Later Christians do not enjoy this experience, yet blessed are they if they still believe. It is the Gospel writer's hope that he has so penetratingly interpreted the events of Jesus' life for his reader that the reader, even though never having met the risen Jesus physically, still believes, with Thomas, that Jesus is "my Lord and my God."

It is not by chance that John finishes his Gospel with this profession of Thomas. (Chapter 21 is believed to be a later addition to the Gospel; yet, chapter 21 is inspired, everyone agrees, and is as much Sacred Scripture as the first twenty chapters.) John began with the profession that Jesus is the Word of God, the Word, through whom all life exists; this Word is God. He now ends his Gospel with a profession drawn from many elements of the life of Jesus, but crowned by his resurrection, that Jesus is my Lord and my God.

Pentecost
~ ACTS 2 ~

Besides tradition's claim that the Upper Room was the place of Jesus' Last Supper and of appearances to his disciples after his resurrection, tradition also locates here the outpouring of the Holy Spirit upon the disciples of Jesus. These disciples, Luke's story suggests, include not only the Twelve; they number about one hundred and twenty men and women in all. This number includes Mary the mother of Jesus, for long not mentioned in Luke's Gospel, but now logically present at the "birth" of the Christian community and its many forms of witness to her son.

That God shares his own Spirit with human beings is the most intimate sharing God has ever offered to his creatures. It was to this eventual sharing that Jesus pointed his life, and it was to pour out this Spirit that Jesus took his place at his Father's right hand. The new intimacy with God through a most profound sharing of his Spirit is really the beginning of that age which, in the language of Jewish hopes and longing, was called "the age to come." Since no more intimate sharing is conceivable, our age is called "the final age," where, as much as possible through this sharing, the sin of Adam which had ruined this age can be replaced by God.

According to the Jewish Scriptures, God created Adam by breathing his Spirit into clay so that it lived. The word *spirit* comes from the Latin word *spiritus* for *breath*. In other words, God gave life from himself to something not alive by breathing life from himself into it. For centuries Jewish prophets foresaw and talked of a new "breathing of God's breath," and saw human beings alive with God's life. Luke, like so many others of the New Testament, knew he was living in this new and final age of God's new, life-giving breathing.

But because Luke had certain limited goals in writing the Acts of the Apostles, he chose to emphasize one effect of this new breathing of God: it would give to human beings the knowledge and courage and prudence to be outstanding witnesses from Jesus and about Jesus, and all that God offers to human beings who believe in him. Thus, the story of Pentecost, while indicating that the long-awaited moment of God's Spirit had arrived, speaks not directly as St. Paul did about how the Spirit comes to dwell in each baptized Christian, but directly about the strength and wisdom certain Christians received in order to be outstanding witnesses to Jesus.

That Luke associated the breathing or outpouring of God's Spirit with the Jewish feast of Pentecost seems quite intentional. Why this association? Pentecost meant two things in Jewish tradition and theology. On the one hand, it was a feast of harvesting. On the other hand, Pentecost recalled the Sinai covenant by which Israel formally was born, when it formally became "my people, and I will be your God." Let us look at Pentecost as harvest.

The plain meaning here is that Israel closed its spring harvest fifty (*pentecoste* means *fifty* in Greek) days after it had begun with the Feast of Unleavened Bread. Again, Israel took time to thank God for its spring harvest, and to pray for a successful fall harvest, particularly for the preservation of water over the summer to this end. From this plain meaning of Pentecost in Jewish life Luke wants to draw a lesson.

Jesus had died and risen fifty days before the Christian experience of the Spirit. Could one not see a link between beginning and ending a harvest, and the beginning and end of Christ's work? In other words, the outpouring of the Spirit is the culminating moment of what the death and resurrection of Jesus began fifty days earlier. The death and Resurrection are completed by the release of the Spirit of God upon the believers.

Just as the death and Resurrection opened up the harvesting of souls, so the gift of the Spirit now makes that harvesting power complete.

But Pentecost in Jewish life referred not only to the fifty days of harvesting and their completion but also, in the centuries near Jesus' time, to Israel's ancient Sinai experience.

Through the centuries Jewish specialists poured over their Scriptures, ever seeking a more profound understanding and a more thorough application of these documents; every possible detail of God's word was to be understood. Thus, in their reading of the Exodus stories, there arose the question of the chronology of the Exodus journey; in particular, how many days after leaving Egypt did the Israelites travel to reach Mount Sinai? The computed time proved to be fifty days. And so, the Feast of Pentecost took on this further meaning: not only did it celebrate the close of the spring harvest, but it also recalled the momentous Sinai covenant made with God through Moses.

Of course, ever since God told Abraham he would have a son, the offspring of Abraham was God's Chosen People. But it was at Sinai that God, through Moses, made this choice formal, as the wonderful phrase indicates: "I will be your God and you will be my people." The giving of the Law, including the famous Ten Commandments, was part of this Mosaic Covenant, becoming for later centuries the hallmark of this covenant. Against this Sinai background, many scholars think that Luke explicitly associates the outpouring of the Spirit with Pentecost in order to suggest that, as Israel was formally born at Mount Sinai and enjoyed the Law of Moses, so the Christian community is born at the outpouring of the Spirit and enjoys the law of the Spirit, as St. Paul calls it. Indeed, the powerful wind and tongues of flame at this gift of the Spirit suggest the circumstances of fire and wind which accompanied God's coming to Mount Sinai to meet Moses. Thus, Pentecost is a word which introduces Luke's narration of the coming of the Spirit, meant to suggest, according to many scholars, that the gift of the Spirit was both completion of the death and resurrection of Jesus (completion of the spring harvest) and source of the birth of the Christian community as God's people (Christianity's "Sinai moment").

But Luke has much more to say about this gift of the Spirit which opens the whole story of the Acts of the Apostles. When Peter heard the suggestion that he and his friends spoke about the wonders God has wrought "because they have drunk too much wine," he embarked on a speech meant to give still fuller meaning to this Pentecost. The first effort of Peter is to explain his and his friends' speech as the result of God's sending his Holy Spirit. To this end, Peter immediately cites a lengthy quotation from the prophet Joel who speaks in the main about cause and effect. That is, Joel promised that there would come a time when God would pour out his Spirit upon his sons and daughters and they would all prophesy. By this citation (from Jl 2:28–32; cited in Acts 2:17–20) then, Peter lays down his first explanation: your hearing us speaking of the wonderful things of God is the result of God's pouring on us the Spirit he promises so long ago, and we are prophesying. Prophecy, strictly speaking, means to "speak on behalf of another"; thus, prophecy may, but need not, speak of the future. The disciples praise God now for his wonders, and begin, like Peter here, to speak on his behalf. Indeed, in accord with Jesus' words in Acts 1:8, the disciples, who had waited for this gift of the Spirit, now with it can be formidable witnesses to speak on behalf of God about Jesus Christ and the Kingdom of God. With the Joel quotation, then, Peter has answered the crowd: it is because of the gift of the Spirit of God that we speak as we do, and that this entire experience, which has attracted you here, has happened. God has once again proven faithful to the promises he made through his prophets, like Joel.

But Peter is not satisfied to give only that part of Joel's quotation that indicated that the Spirit of God has been poured out. He keeps citing Joel so as to include reference to signs and wonders which will happen in heaven and on earth before the final judgment (the Lord's Day) and will end with Joel's famous words: "Then everyone who calls on the name of the Lord will be saved" (2:32). What Peter intends here is to make people think beyond the present moment, the outpouring of the Spirit. He wants them to see that this outpouring is one more step towards the final time, the cataclysmic time, when God will come to judge all the world. And he wants the Jews before him to know that, when that judgment comes, "all who call on the name of the Lord will be saved." Thus, Pentecost is a preparation for the final judgment, for the moment of salvation for those who call on the name of the Lord.

When Joel (perhaps about 350 B.C.) spoke of "calling on the name of the Lord," he obviously was thinking of Yahweh, the God of Israel, the Lord. Peter works a great change here. He so describes the life of Jesus of Nazareth, especially of him risen and ascended to God's right hand, that he can conclude at his last sentence that Jesus is Lord. This term he found in the citation from a psalm in which David speaks of "my lord" who is invited by God (the Lord) to sit next to him to rule the world. This "lord" of David is Jesus the Messiah, since Jesus is the one who has ascended to God; Peter is a witness to this ascension. Thus, Peter, gifted by the Holy Spirit with prophecy, now can tell his audience what Joel's words really mean: "call on the name of the Lord Jesus for salvation."

Peter's words are addressed to Jews in Jerusalem, but the Joel citation, which Peter affirms, speaks of "anyone who calls on the name of the Lord." This citation will be applied to Gentiles, too; Joel's words are broad enough to allow the Christians to conceive this interpretation of them. In this way, Pentecost is a prelude to the offer of salvation to the Gentiles, an offer which will be reported starting with the Cornelius story in chapter 10.

Pentecost also means that Jesus is the one who poured out the Spirit. Peter argues that the Messiah Jesus received the Spirit from his Father and then poured out the Spirit upon the disciples. Joel's quotation never mentioned such a person as the Messiah to pour out the Spirit of God, but the relationship of Jesus to God, his Father, is so clear by virtue of the Resurrection and Ascension that Joel's words should be interpreted this way.

Pentecost, then, does not just evoke the memory of the completion or fulfillment of the death and resurrection of Jesus, nor does it suggest only that the Christian community is being "born" this day through the Spirit. It is a moment which also makes one think of the final judgment and the longing for salvation. It is a moment which, if understood correctly, occurred because Jesus the Messiah poured out the Spirit and which urges us to call on the name of the Lord Jesus for salvation.

Finally, Peter again supersedes Joel. Joel's words, "anyone who calls on the name of the Lord will be saved," mean that the calling on the name and the saving occur at the same time; the saving is the immediate response to the call of the Lord. For Peter, however, complete salvation comes only at the end time, but one calls on the name of the Lord Jesus now. Jesus himself had suggested this when he said, "When the day of judgment comes, you hold up your heads [that is, you need have no fear], for your day of liberation is at hand." He said this to those who were his disciples, who had already "called upon his name." So, for Peter, one calls now in order to be totally saved, liberated later.

With the completion of Peter's speech one might think that the meaning of Pentecost is completely explained. However, this is not so; there is still one element to add. The response to Peter is notable: some three thousand people, Luke says, call on Jesus' name for salvation. This calling is changed to a different key: to "call" really means to repent (of all one's sins and especially of crucifying Israel's Messiah and Lord) and to be baptized in Jesus' name; this repentance and baptism will result in the gift of the Holy Spirit. What follows in Luke's report is a brief description of this Christian community, now with so many new members. The description is of a community which fulfills the Old Testament's law as no other community ever did: this group loves God and loves neighbor. The expression of this love is particularly Jewish, as one would expect of Jewish converts. But the effect of conversion to Jesus is total: they listen to the teachings of those who knew Jesus best, they pray joyfully and share their goods so that no one is needy. It is only with this report of the life of the community converted to Jesus and to his teaching that Luke can end his account of Pentecost and move to another event, that of chapter 3.

Pentecost can be looked at in various ways, then, each way complementing the others. It is a day which begins the witnessing to Jesus; as such it is a day in which the meaning of Jesus is emphasized: he is the source of the Spirit, for he is Lord and Messiah of Israel, and he is the one to call upon for salvation, the one in whose name everyone should be baptized. Indeed, a result of this baptism is that each Christian will receive the Holy Spirit, as Peter and the other disciples did this day.

That 3,000 people are said to call upon the name of the Lord is a reminder of the opening description of Pentecost Day. There we were given a list of the many places in the world from which Jews had come, either to live in Israel permanently or at least to visit for the Feast of Pentecost. Each of these various places in the world spoke its own language. One of the miracles of Pentecost is that, though the disciples spoke their own Galilean dialect of Aramaic, each listener in his own language understood what was being said by the disciples. This description is intentional; it means to show that the one Spirit reached, and will reach, all nations. The universality of Christianity is taught by this image.

And it should be said, too, that all of these conversions were not owed to one person or to just the Twelve; all one hundred and twenty disciples, Mary included, received the gift of prophecy by which they now speak on behalf of God and his Kingdom and his Messiah. The Spirit was for all the sons and daughters of God; thus, upon each of them fell fire, the symbol of the Spirit who, like fire, purifies for life. All Christians serve as witness to Jesus for the entire world; God intends his message of salvation for the whole world.

The Upper Room, then, is filled with memories, all of them so important for Christianity. Great events took place in the room, but continue alive in the hearts and actions of all who are willing to call on the name of the Lord Jesus for salvation.

Via Dolorosa
(The Way of the Cross)

LARGE NUMBERS OF PEOPLE FOLLOWED HIM,
AND OF WOMEN TOO, WHO MOURNED AND
LAMENTED FOR HIM.
~ LUKE 23:27

After Jesus was captured in the Garden of Gethsemani on the lower slope of the Mount of Olives, the Gospels tell us that he was tried by the High Priest Caiaphas and by Pontius Pilate; added to these trials are an informal inquiry held by Annas, former High Priest and father-in-law of Caiaphas, and, according to Luke, a trial before Herod Antipas, Rome's appointed ruler over Galilee and Samaria. Associated with these trials were various abuses Jesus underwent—slapping, spitting, taunting, mocking, crowning with thorns and, eventually, whippings, one of which prepared a prisoner for crucifixion.

In regard to the trial before the High Priest, an old tradition says the palace of the High Priest is under the present Armenian Church of St. Savior, just some yards north of the site revered today as the Upper Room or Cenacle, and very near to the southeastern wall of present Jerusalem. As for most of the other events which marked the hours between Jesus' capture and crucifixion, tradition places them in the area just north of the Temple grounds. More specifically, if we were to proceed a little over a hundred yards westward on the road from St. Stephen's Gate, we would stand near or under an arch which stretches above and over the street; this arch for a long time was thought to be what remains as the spot on which Jesus stood when Pilate spoke his famous words to the crowd: "Behold the man!" The area on either side of this arch and stretching eastward from the arch is the site of the Fortress Antonia, a fort occupied by soldiers and at certain hours by Pontius Pilate during the Feast of Passover.

Very near the arch is a door of the Convent of the Sisters of Sion. Beneath the convent is a smooth pavement which many have identified as a courtyard which had arches at either end, and so was a place of smooth passage; one can see still the marks of carriage tracks, and of striation, which kept the stones from being too slippery for horses. This entire courtyard is called *gabbatha* or *lithostratos*, which means *stone pavement*. At one spot on this pavement we can see ridges and etchings and marks; these have been deciphered to mean a game which Roman soldiers were accustomed to playing, a game in which their prisoner was mocked for his claim to be a king. In this underground area, as we peel off the centuries of later building over this pavement, we have a sense of what the Roman quarters of the fortress may have been like in Pilate's time. The Fortress Antonia, as the Romans called it, sits ominously at the northwestern corner of the Temple esplanade or platform, to remind Jews milling about on the Temple platform that the Romans were watching their every move lest revolt break out. Indeed, if this is the area of Jesus' crowning with thorns, of his scourging, it is also the area of Pilate's

Jerusalem: pavement with traces of the "King's Game"

trial of Jesus and the beginning of Jesus' way to Calvary, due west of here. Thus, here begins the traditional Way of the Cross.

Luke, as mentioned earlier, tells of Pilate's attempt to shift the trial of Jesus (and responsibility for him) to Herod, also present for the Feast of Passover; after all, Jesus was from Galilee, and thus under Herod's jurisdiction. Near the Convent of the Sisters of Sion and near the arch stretching over the road are the supposed ruins of the palace Herod Agrippa used. However, it is more reasonable to look for Herod's Jerusalem residence at a point just south of the Jaffa Gate and on the site pointed out today as David's Tower.

But with the suggestion that the residence of Herod Antipas lay on the west side of old Jerusalem near the Jaffa Gate, we must give fair credit to a position held by many reputable scholars, namely, that here too, near the Jaffa Gate—and not in the area of the Convent of the Sisters of Sion—were the living quarters and praetorium of Pontius Pilate and that here Jesus was tried by Pilate. In this view, Jesus would have been tried, beaten, and led to Calvary from an area due south of the Basilica of the Holy Sepulcher—rather than from the area described above and located due east of the basilica.

Trial of Jesus
~ Matthew 26:57–68; Mark 14:53–65; Luke 22:54–71; John 18:13–24 ~

Shrouded in the secrecy nighttime affords, the High Priest, and his father-in-law, the powerful former High Priest Annas, strove to formulate a charge which could justify the death of Jesus. The High Priest, Caiaphas, had earlier noted the advantage of Jesus' removal: if he did not go, he might so rouse the people looking for political freedom that the Romans would turn their lethal might loose on the leaders of Israel and on their people, and so better that one die, than all suffer.

For many months various religious leaders of Israel had met Jesus, sometimes intentionally, most often in Galilee, but in Jerusalem as well. The gospel stories usually conclude such meetings with the explicit or implicit affirmation that Jesus grew ever more to be their enemy. Matthew and John are particularly willing to provide a picture of intense acrimony between Jesus and other religious figures; the offer of betrayal in Jerusalem was a welcome one to the ears of those portrayed as the harshest of Jesus' critics.

The disagreement with Jesus was grounded in the claim he made, that he knew best of all human beings how to interpret the mind of God; he was Son and knew best what his Father wants of us. Pilate himself realized that Jesus was handed over to him "out of jealousy"; in part this means "out of zeal for the Law," that is for a certain interpretation of the Law, but in part it means "out of anger" that Jesus so berated the authorities, especially those Pharisees he considered hypocrites: "Do what they say, but do not do what they do." It is noteworthy that, once Jesus reaches Jerusalem, the Pharisees and scribes hostile to him are replaced by the more powerful figures of Israel, the High Priest, the Chief Priests and those whose theology these priests supported, the Sadducees.

Given the obvious fact that the Gospel writers were loyal disciples to a Jesus who, they believed, was greater than any human being, it is not surprising that the tragic end Jesus had to undergo should be painted in vibrant colors; the enemy is truly enemy in the retelling of the story. The Gospels know the truth about Jesus, that he was raised from the dead, and is Son of God. To his personal story is added the history of abuse of Christians by Jews between the end of his life on earth and the writing of the Gospels. All of these factors enter into the manner in which the confrontation of Jesus and his opponents is told. One also has to take into account that the Gospels were written for believers, those who already had sided with the authors in faith that Jesus truly represented God and was, in some way, God. Finally, I believe it can be said that, though every Gospel writer thought that what he attested to was absolutely true and thus absolutely invaluable, he had no knowledge that what he wrote would become normative Sacred Scripture for all time. Thus, though he would not have changed his conviction about Jesus, he might have presented his matter slightly differently, if he had known that his audience would be of all time.

Sometimes a sympathetic portrait is drawn of a Jewish religious leader, such as Nichodemus and Gamaliel. Indeed, despite what happened to Jesus at the hands of the enemy, Luke for one is willing to tell how the early preaching of the Apostles considered this animosity to be due to ignorance.

There were more moderate voices and stances regarding Jesus, but certain leaders in Jerusalem pushed these aside in favor of an accusation, known to them as false, that would give legitimacy to their handing Jesus over to Pilate and insisting on the death penalty. In the trial before Jewish leaders, it became clear that the question is that of Messiah: are you, or are you not the Messiah? From Jesus' answer they draw the conclusion that such is his claim. Worse for him is his claim to be Son of God, and to be the one who will come on the clouds of heaven to judge them. Aware, however, that such religious claims meant nothing to Pilate, these leaders translated the entire argument to the political arena, where Jesus clearly made no claims, but where Pilate would enter most willingly. Thus, he heard that the charge against Jesus was that he claimed to be king, that he condemned paying taxes to Caesar. Pilate did not know much about religion or "truth," but he knew about rebelliousness and how to handle people who challenged Rome.

Jesus Before Pilate
~ MATTHEW 27:11–25; MARK 15:1–15; LUKE 23:1–25; JOHN 18: 28–40 ~

Ironically, Pilate sensed that he was being used, but he could not stop the fire and rage roaring against Jesus. History has left a record that Pilate was often a ruthless man; this Jesus situation was no time for an exception to the usual, and to the ruthless it seems satisfactory to calm rage by sacrificing one life. Pilate gave the word and Jesus was taken away to be prepared for horrible crucifixion by the accustomed whipping, meant to blunt the senses and even shorten the life of the crucified—so horrible was this punishment.

Generally, scholars find that Luke has made more explicit than did his source Mark the efforts of Pilate to declare Jesus innocent and to free him; in either case, one is faced with varying degrees of responsibility for the death of Jesus. Certainly, some Jewish leaders kept badgering Pilate for a verdict of death; Pilate's was the only authority that could put one to death, and so the ultimate responsibility is his. If Luke be right that the people (certainly not all of Israel not even all those at the Passover Feast in Jerusalem) were whipped up by their leaders to a fury to ask for the death penalty, the people soon regretted their participation, as Luke indicates: "When the crowd that had gathered for this spectacle saw what had happened, they went home beating their breasts." All the Gospels tell their stories of Jesus before Caiaphas and Pilate so as to emphasize the innocence of Jesus. But they often go beyond just the question of innocence to show that it is the Messiah of Israel, or the Son of Man who will judge the world, or the Son of God who undergoes this trial and its eventual outcome. In the light of Jesus' true identity, the preference of Barabbas, murderer—as revolutionary or thief is immaterial—is all the more poignant and hateful.

John and Matthew have peculiarities to note about the trial before Pilate; to these we turn.

Pilate in John's Gospel

John clearly wants to take up the false accusation made about Jesus that he claimed to be a king. John goes further now than any other Gospel to affirm that Jesus is a king, but his kingdom is not among the kingdoms of this world. Hardly a political figure, Jesus' kingdom exists in any world where his Father and his love and justice rightly play a central role. Jesus can admit to this kind of kingship; it is to admit his identity and to call people to this kingdom that he has come. This kingdom is the truth which sets one free.

Pilate's famous response, "What is truth?" shows how truth is impossible to have apart from Jesus. Pilate knows not the way to Jesus' kingdom, nor how to enter it. Truly an ignorant man, one who could rightly claim that there is no such kingdom as Jesus claims, there is no such truth upon which a person can ground his life. For Pilate, the ignorance of this truth is like death while alive. He has no ultimate reason for living, no hope of living forever.

But Jesus' claim to be a king was not the end of the matter for Pilate. Pilate was particularly shaken by Jesus' claim to be the Son of God. John's Gospel had argued, long before his account of this trial, that Jesus is the Father's Son. Whatever Pilate understood to be the meaning of Son of God, he was afraid as he had not been before hearing this claim. John's Gospel presents for trial the absurdity that not just a king, but a divine person awaits Pilate's decision: Pilate senses that he is now in a world which frightens him.

Pilate in Matthew's Gospel

Matthew's Gospel is based on Mark's Gospel; the former read the latter, then decided to write his own Gospel. As an example of his independence Matthew, at the telling of Jesus' trial, adds to Mark's rendition an astonishing statement not found in Mark (nor elsewhere) that "the people said, 'His blood be on us and on our children.'" What is the meaning and significance of this statement?

As for the trial itself, it had ground down to a slow pace: Pilate did not find Jesus guilty and so had no reason to put him to death, and Jesus' opponents remained adamant, unyielding. Pilate, in a gesture only in Matthew, washes his hands, an act meant symbolically to say that he had nothing to do with this killing, it was not his responsibility—though no one else could give the order of crucifixion! At this point the people speak up to say that they accept the responsibility for this execution, they and their children. That is, if they are right in demanding this death, they and their children will be blessed; if they are wrong about this, they and their children accept the punishment for their injustice. This statement seems to be what moved the process along, for it is immediately after this incident that Pilate gives the order of execution. Of course, the people who shouted out that they would take responsibility for this death did not think they would incur punishment for their responsibility in this death, especially from God who protects the just and condemns injustice.

Important as the people's statement is for the progress of the trial, it is much more important for Matthew's ongoing theological struggle against those of his own time who want to eradicate belief in Jesus. Matthew knows of the events subsequent to Jesus' death. He knows of the resurrection of Jesus, the victory of the preaching about Jesus, and the destruction of the Temple in 70, of the fall of all Israel by 73. To him, the statement of the people at Jesus' trial has its bitter fruit. Because of them Jesus went to death; because of their acceptance of responsibility for this death, they and their children have seen the truth, and the destruction interpreted as punishment for their part in the death of Jesus.

After the statement of the people about responsibility for Jesus' death, the Gospel story Matthew inherits moves swiftly. Actually, the next dramatic intervention by Matthew is his recounting of Jesus' words after his resurrection: "Go now and make disciples of all nations." It is as though Jesus had remained with his own people until the statement of the crowd before Pilate; thereafter, Jesus would, without abandoning Israel, go now to the Gentiles.

And had Jesus preached to Jews only? One remembers the famous encounter with a non-Jewish woman from north of Israel. Her daughter was in dire need; the mother pleaded with Jesus to intervene. It is in Matthew's Gospel that Jesus is shown to be most reluctant. Why reluctant? because, he says, he has been sent only to the house of Israel. He had never given up in his lifetime on his people; only after they give up on him does he go to the Gentiles.

The parable of the vineyard and its hired hands, at the end of Matthew 21, shows that Jesus saw himself as the end of a long line of messengers from God who asked for the good fruit, that is the moral acts in obedience to the Law of Moses. He, the son of the vineyard owner, is killed by the hired hands. What will the owner do when he comes? He will, as only Matthew phrases it, take the *kingdom* (in Mark the *vineyard*) from *you* (in Mark, *them*, the *workers*) and give it to *a people* (the people of Jesus; in Mark, just called "others") who will produce a rich harvest (acts of justice). Added to the image of the vineyard, the son, and the owner is the image of Jesus the stone. Like a stone rejected by the builders but made into the cornerstone of an entire building, Jesus will be rejected, only to be raised up, and on him will be built the people of God.

Such is, in brief, the background which explains the great importance the people's statement to Pilate makes in Matthew's Gospel. Matthew used it as if it were a prophecy of the later destruction he knew had happened; he assigned it as cause of the sufferings of Israel under the Roman army, and in this way argued once again that what was in accord with God's will was that Israel accept Jesus as its Messiah and Lord.

Obviously, a moment's reflection makes one realize that not every Jew was involved in the trial of Jesus or approved of the statements made there. This realization should put severe limitations on any thought that "all Israel is responsible for the death of Jesus." One must be more perceptive in one's interpretation of Matthew and in one's assigning responsibility for Jesus' death. The price of a lack of correct perception is, we know, incalculable.

The Brutal Hours

One should recall the painful humiliations and physical sufferings of Jesus during the miserable hours associated with his trials. Ridicule and mocking were meant to cause Jesus mental anguish; brutality is the final boiling of a long-cooking anger. Slappings and the crowning with thorns are other dehumanizing forms of pain. Finally, there are two scourgings indicated in the Gospels. The one, occurring before the final decision made about Jesus, is meant to satisfy the crowds and stop them from asking for death. It was the usual kind of punishment for disturbing the peace, a warning to cease upsetting authority and civil order. The other, occurring after the decree of death, is meant to weaken the prisoner. Crucifixion was a terrible punishment, which often lasted for days before death mercifully came. With a certain humaneness, the Romans wanted, after affixing a person to the cross, to dull the pain and to bring the end more swiftly; to accomplish these goals, a whipping, usually with thongs with metal pellets fixed into them, was ordered before the procession to the place of crucifixion. What a form of mercy!

Jesus Before Herod
~ Luke 22:8–12 ~

The trial of Jesus before Herod should be considered under the title of "humiliation." As mentioned earlier, Pontius Pilate sent Jesus to Herod Antipas, son of Herod the Great who plagued Jesus' childhood in Bethlehem. Pilate did not want to deal with Jesus; once he learned that technically Jesus belonged to Galilee and was in Jerusalem only for the Feast, he said Antipas should decide his case, he is a citizen of Antipas. Jesus, however, once arrived before Herod, offered the ruler no cooperation. Soon the trial before Herod was allowed to turn into a buffoonery, with Jesus being dressed in colors meant to taunt him for pretending to be a king. Pilate tried to use this foolishness as a further argument with the Jewish leaders that "no one finds fault with Jesus." Later, the Acts of the Apostles will underline the fact that, while up until now Pilate and Herod were enemies of each other, from this trial they became friends in their opposition to God's Messiah.

Jesus Carries the Cross
~ MATTHEW 27:31–33; MARK 15:20–22; LUKE 23:26–32; JOHN 19:17–18 ~

In the process of crucifixion, the prisoner must carry his cross, with the bill of charges visible to all, or at least the crossbeam which will be attached to the vertical beam already awaiting the prisoner's arrival. Jesus, then, begins his walk to Calvary, the place of the Skull, outside Jerusalem's walls, on the city's northwest side. The Gospel tells of two events along the way.

Jerusalem: Fourth Station sculpture of Jesus carrying his cross

Simon of Cyrene
~ MATTHEW 27:32; MARK 15:21; LUKE 23:26 ~

Among the crowd watching Jesus was Simon, a Jew from Cyrene, a city on the north coast of Africa. The Roman soldier's demand that Simon help is mute testimony to the weakness of Jesus, who could not move even the equivalent of three city blocks without significant help. That the Roman soldier could simply command someone other than the prisoner to carry the crossbeam is a concrete example of something Jesus had mentioned in his Sermon on the Mount. Jesus had said that, "if you are pressed into service to go one mile, offer to go two." This example of love of enemy was based on a law which allowed a Roman soldier, while on duty, to force any bystander to help him for the distance of a mile to execute his duty. So it was that the order given to Simon, to help the prisoner complete a walk which was three-fourths of a mile, was legitimate, though a sure reminder of Rome's domination over all Israelites.

This Simon was the father of two sons, Rufus and Alexander. Rufus was most likely the Rufus to whom Paul sent his best greetings in Rome and whose mother, Paul wrote, was "like a mother to me." Cyrenians, together with Alexandrians, formed a synagogue in Jerusalem, after being set free from an imprisonment in Rome which began about 63 B.C. Thus, it is thought that this bearer of the Lord's cross had relatives in the Christian church of Rome who were known to Mark and to Paul; that is why Mark—and Matthew and Luke followed him—immortalized Simon's special act and his name.

Jesus and the Women of Jerusalem
~ LUKE 23:27–31 ~

Along the route to Calvary Jesus met certain women. The custom of the time was that women would weep and lament on behalf of the prisoners going to death; these were not followers of Jesus, but pious women of Jerusalem. Their public expression of grief was meant as a comfort to the condemned.

The sight of these weeping women brought to mind the terrible tragedy which would visit Jerusalem for its rejection of Jesus. Sympathetic as they were for Jesus, they should think of the time to come when they will be weeping for themselves. How fortunate they will be not to have children, for the grief of those who do will be magnified as the women realize what is in store for their children as well as for themselves. More merciful would it be if the mountains fell upon them and the hills covered them; better that than what is in store for them when the Roman armies come.

One should remember that the prophet Hosea had used the same imagery of mountains and hills when he described the punishment to fall on Israel for refusing to obey God's will (Hos 10:8): better that the mountains and hills cover us than face the punishment God will send for worshipping false gods. The rejection of Jesus, then, is another act against the good God, and the punishment for this will make death under falling mountains and hills appear the easier, the preferred death.

If, indeed, the sight of Jesus' suffering brought the women to lament and wail (this is the time of the green wood), what would be their weeping for themselves (the time of the dry wood). If the women weep when it is not their own punishment for which they weep, what will they do when it is time to pay the price for the rejection of Jesus?

Jesus might appear ungrateful to the women for their attempts to console him. But his attitude here is instructive for understanding many episodes in his life. Much as he might appreciate sympathy and concern, the picture shown us by the Gospels is rather his concern that people attend to the one thing Jesus thinks crucial in their lives: repentance, change of mind and heart and life, for the forgiveness of their sins and reunion with their God. At this moment, before the women, Jesus will not let his death be seen as the great tragedy. Rather, the great tragedy is the suffering the women and their children will undergo; it is about this and other, greater tragedies that Jesus always feels compelled to warn. To him his life is secondary to the salvation of others.

Jerusalem: a narrow street today

The northeast district of old Jerusalem has traditionally served to recall the painful events of Jesus' trial before Pilate, the abuses he suffered, the carrying of his cross to Calvary, at the northwest corner of the old City. It is not difficult to understand the people who took part in these terrible hours. Fear, jealousy, anger, preservation of what they thought to be the truth of the Law—all this moved certain leaders of Israel to eliminate Jesus. Pilate, a man used to cruelty when solving problems, found the death sentence a small price to keep the peace he thought would please his superiors. Peter, one is not surprised to find, did not have the courage to profess his discipleship; what makes this a particularly painful act is his claim that he would be more loyal than all others. Perhaps the most difficult person to understand in all this is Judas. If money was his only goal, by his own hand he threw his profit away. He had responded at one time to the ideal of leaving all to follow Jesus. This all ended in suicide. His is not a story beyond human experience; it is just that he is ultimately an enigma—most of all for his not having learned, in his following Jesus, how Jesus forgives even the most heinous sins. To doubt God's mercy is to fail to understand the truth about God. Jesus came only to give life; mercy was his sole intention. Why assume anything different?

These scenes ending in the Way of the Cross tell the Gospel reader about Jesus and his friends and enemies. They tell us something about sin, as well; as such they speak directly and forcefully to every reader.

Basilica of the Holy Sepulcher

CHRIST DIED FOR OUR SINS,
WAS BURIED, AND WAS
RAISED TO LIFE ON THE THIRD DAY.
~ 1 CORINTHIANS 15:4

Within the Basilica of the Holy Sepulcher are two areas of great importance: the place of Jesus' death and the place of his entombment; as far as science can judge, these are the sites of Jesus' death and burial. The basilica's obvious deterioration cannot diminish the realities it contains. The visitor may feel disappointed at the state of the basilica, but here, more than anywhere else, we must distinguish between the events which happened here and the sights and sounds we must contend with. The visitor must use imagination to the full here!

Upon entering the basilica we notice stairs on the right. These steep, small stairs lead up to a level at a height of about fifteen feet; at this height is a chapel divided into Orthodox and Latin parts, with three altars. At the base of the altar farthest to the left (the Orthodox Altar of the Crucifixion) is a hole, encircled by a star. By reaching through this hole one reaches down to rock, the rock which held in place the upraised cross of Jesus crucified.

On descending from the chapel over the rock of the crucifixion, we pass a large stone slab, revered as the site of the thirteenth station of the cross, where Jesus is first in Mary's arms, then is washed and prepared for burial. Then we round a wall of paintings and go to the center of the rotunda. A look upwards gives us a view of the large cupola of the basilica; beneath the cupola and in the center of the round floor is a marble monument, like a little house, with many lamps and candles in front of its entrance. This monument contains within it the shelf on which the body of Jesus was laid to rest, until he could be finally buried after the Sabbath, as the Gospels tell us. To reach this shelf, we pass through the low doorway of the monument into a first chamber, then through a second doorway into the second and final chamber. Here, under a marble slab to protect it, is the shelf on which the body of Jesus was laid after his death.

If we could imaginatively take down the entire basilica with its monuments and paintings and statues and lamps and mosaics and altars and sacristies and pillars, and remove the flooring of stone, we would stand between two places not more than thirty yards apart, with dirt and rock and grass under our feet and the open air all around us. Such was the original state of this area before Jesus died and was buried here. Indeed, there was nothing of any significance here, except other burial tombs; the place in 30 A.D. could be described simply as a garden lying outside the city walls of Pontius Pilate's Jerusalem.

This garden area was once a quarry. One piece of rock, about fifteen feet in height, was left by stonecutters because it was rock of poor quality—perhaps because it was broken by an earthquake or cracked during quarrying. This rock stood out in this "garden" space and gave the effect of a skull rising out of the earth. Hence it was called in the languages of the time *Golgotha*, *Kranion*, and *Calvary*—all of which mean *skull*.

Unprotected, uninhabited, a scroungy garden and former quarry, here was a suitable place for the crucifixion and burial of criminals.

Such then were the two sites, of death and entombment, before Constantine built the basilica in 335 to protect them. So many changes have occurred over the centuries since that it would take a particular and long study to explain how things evolved from a simple garden place to what we have before us today. One should note that today's basilica includes, at the far end from the tomb of Jesus, a chapel marking the area in which, tradition says, Constantine's mother, St. Helena, found the cross on which Jesus died.

Between the burial of Jesus and the building of this basilica, the Romans twice destroyed Jerusalem; the second time in 135, the emperor Hadrian built an immense Temple of Venus, together with a statue in a large park-like area with buildings, and surrounded it all by a wall, covering exactly the area revered as the place of Jesus' death and burial.

Constantine's architects would have had a large job on their hands as they replaced one massive shrine with another. Indeed, some of the remains from the Roman shrine were used to build Constantine's basilica.

Jerusalem: Basilica of the Holy Sepulcher

Today's basilica is a place where three communities—Greeks, Orthodox, and Latins—have rights and allow other Christians to have liturgies here. The Latins, that is, Roman Catholics and Uniates, both represented by the Franciscans, the Greek Orthodox, and the Armenian Orthodox have residences here, control certain chapels, and succeed one another, by turn, at night and by day in praying their own forms of liturgy. Others—Copts, Syrians or Jacobites, and Abyssinians—are also allowed a presence and times for their liturgies, much more limited than those of the first three mentioned. It is important to realize that each group has rights, often in history defended by blood; because of the history of Christian struggles associated with contrary or contradictory beliefs, there is at best reluctant cooperation among them. The standoff which characterizes the uneasy existence of the six religious groups accounts in the main for the present condition of the basilica, for its disarray, and its varied forms of religious art, prayer, decoration, and dress.

Death of Jesus
~ MATTHEW 27:33–66; MARK 15:22–47; LUKE 23:33–56; JOHN 19:17–42 ~

The details reported about the last hours of Jesus are not many. He reached Calvary, with Simon carrying the crossbeam Jesus was too weak to carry. Jesus was stripped of his clothes, a particularly painful moment since his blood had clotted in many places that caused the cloth of his garments to stick to his skin.

The Roman executioners enjoyed whatever they could salvage from his clothes. Jesus was nailed to the crossbeam; this meant nails through his upper hands and a nail through his crossed ankles. Then his arms were tied for good measure, lest his weight pull him off the nails. Also to lessen the pull of gravity, Jesus was fitted on to a small seat which had been fixed onto the vertical beam already set in the rock. Thus, Jesus was raised up to arrive at a certain degree of sitting, crucified. Here he was offered a drugged drink, to alleviate his pain. Here he died, and here he was taken down to be placed, according to Christian tradition, in his mother's lap before cleansing and burial.

The New Testament encourages us to think of the death of Jesus in three major ways. First, his death took away our sins. Second, his death was a martyrdom of the just at the hands of the wicked. Third, Jesus was offered as a model for his followers at this crucial moment of life. To these three considerations we now turn for a moment.

Removal of Sins

St. Paul is the one who presents this understanding of Jesus' death most thoroughly, so it is to him that we turn for enlightenment here. Without explaining each step in his own arriving at the belief that Jesus' death removed sin, Paul consistently explains Jesus' death this way and thanks God profusely for this unique gift. The removal of sin is indeed a gift, for it depended on God's decision to send his Son to make up for sin, and it depended on the Son's free choice to do this act. We could only wait upon their freedom. Once we realize that Someone who owed us nothing has given us everything, we can breathe a sigh of great relief, for we realize what our fate would have been, had he not intervened. Paul offers us in particular four metaphors or analogies which help clarify what God has worked for us in Jesus and they have become part of our religious language and liturgy.

Reconciliation

Paul called Jesus' death a reconciliation. This human experience, which he counts on our understanding and perhaps having experienced, first knows of an initial union between two people, then the painful separation of one from the other, finally a joyous reunion which ends the tragic separation and brings back the freshness and happiness of friendship again.

This sequence of moments Paul applies to our relationship with God. At first, we were his friends, as Genesis points out when it describes Adam as one who "walked in the garden with God in the cool of the evening after work." This intimacy was broken by Adam's disobedience and its brokenness continued because of our own sins. At a third moment, while we were still his enemies, God sent his Son to die for us, thereby proving his love for us, and, for his part, bringing about a reconciliation. It falls to us to complete the reconciliation by dying to that which caused our share of the ruptured relationship. This reconciliation is unusual. Usually, it falls to the guilty party to initiate the reconciliation, but in this case it is God who, in the death of the Son of God, buries his justified anger with us and seeks our love by offering his, at a time when we had not yet begun to look for reconciliation with him.

Redemption

Another way of looking at what Jesus accomplished on the cross is to consider it as redemption. In Paul's time as in ours, redemption meant buying something back for a price, something which originally had belonged to its rightful owner, but somehow had fallen into the possession of a foreign owner. In Paul's wider Mediterranean world, the most common experiences of redemption were those of slaves who could, for a price, buy back their freedom from their owners. In the more limited world of Judaism, there is a very famous experience described in the Old

Testament as a redemption: it is the Exodus, God's acquiring a people for himself from the foreign owner, the Pharaoh of Egypt. In this case, God is not described as paying a price, but the sense of acquisition, so much a part of the term redemption, justifies the Old Testament in description of the God taking back his people from an owner not either their natural owner or master.

In applying the term redemption to what Jesus accomplished for us, Paul builds on the Jewish Scriptures which describe how thoroughly creation, and human beings in particular, belong by their very nature to God: he is our natural master. But Jewish belief also held that in some ways Satan was allowed control over God's world, and through circumstances Satan became thereafter, because we freely chose him, the new master of human beings. It is God who on his own intervenes to buy us back, and the price he pays, as we play out this analogy, is the blood of the Son of God. We become God's again, if we accept him as our rightful Master, but we can do this only because his Son first paid the price to free us from the evil master to whom we had, freely and foolishly, committed ourselves.

How one reaches the point where he willingly chooses such a master as Satan is difficult to explain and anyway is a story unique to each of us. Sadly, many people learn only much too late the real meaning of being slave to Satan, slave to their own destruction and to causing it in others. But Paul insists that now, in the death of Jesus, God frees us from being helplessly mired in slavery to Satan, and asks us to accept this freedom.

Occasionally, this analogy seems rough-edged because we do not like to consider ourselves slaves. But the service of great masters, God or Satan, is our lot for that is what is meant by being creature. We have no third choice, that is, we cannot declare ourselves free from mastery. The only choice given us is to choose our master. Perhaps we should not be told this, but should simply try to live as "free." I am sure that, eventually and painfully, we will become very conscious, if honest with ourselves, that willing it or not we serve a master. Jesus' preaching pleads with us to serve the only Master natural to us, the only Master who can bring us complete happiness forever. We become free of one master, then, by accepting what Jesus did on the cross, but only to accept another—the only true Master, our Creator.

Atonement/Expiation

Paul suggests that we look at Jesus' death as an atonement or expiation for our sins. For Jews, and for other religions of the Mediterranean of Paul's time, sacrifices in a holy place were a way of life. There were many purposes for which one offered sacrifice; not the least of which was to seek forgiveness of sins. The most famous communal Jewish sacrifice for sins was that of Yom Kippur, which means *Day of (Yom) Atonement (Kippur)*. It is particularly to this sacrifice for sins that Jesus' death on the cross is compared. Let us consider the essence of the Yom Kippur celebration.

On one day a year, and this one day only, the Jewish High Priest of that year entered the holiest room of the Temple, the private quarters of God. In that room, from the time Solomon constructed it until its destruction in 587 B.C., was the famous Ark of the Covenant, a box of precious wood and metal, in which could be found the Ten Commandments and manna and the rod of Aaron by which he and Moses worked miracles before Pharaoh. These possessions made one think of the Ark as a seat of mercy, for these elements show God's mercy to Israel and remind Israel of that mercy.

The box of the Ark is also fashioned in such a way that it has the appearance of a chair or seat. At the two back corners are fixed figures which look like protecting angels, hovering over God who is imagined to be seated here. Thus, the Ark is the throne of God, and the seat of his mercy, in the midst of God's people, Israel.

After Solomon's temple was destroyed, eventually another temple was built, and dedicated in 515 B.C. by those who had returned from the Babylonian exile. Here there was the Holy of Holies again, but the Ark of the Covenant had not been recovered; either it was destroyed or lost. The Yom Kippur ceremony continued through the centuries to Jesus' time, but now the High Priest went into an empty Holy of Holies. Even so, the annual ceremony was performed, which involved the sprinkling of blood.

Some distance from the Temple building itself, an animal was killed and a bowl was filled with its blood. With the bowl of blood the High Priest entered the Temple, to make his way to the Holy of Holies. Once inside this room, he sprinkled some of the blood about the room. In ancient times, when the Ark was there, he would sprinkle the blood on the Ark. Then the High Priest exited this sacred room to go to the people awaiting him outside. There he would sprinkle the people with blood from the same bowl.

What is this ceremony all about? It is ancient Jewish teaching that in the blood is life. This was an observable fact, since the letting of blood, like the loss of breath, signifies the diminution and eventually the loss of life. Because God is the only one who can give life and take life, he alone can take the blood of a human being; murder, then, is wrong, killing belongs to God.

It is this blood which is a key to understanding Yom Kippur. Notice that it is not the death of the animal which is done before God; in fact the animal is intentionally killed quite a distance from God's dwelling place, for God takes no pleasure in death. It is the life of an individual, symbolized by blood and offered to God, which pleases God. It is this offering of one's life (and not of one's annihilation) that is understood in Israel to be a rededication of oneself after the sins of the past year. This rededicated life is poured on the Throne of Mercy, and the sprinkling of blood upon the people is understood to be God's rededicating himself to Israel after forgiving all Israel's sins. Thus, Yom Kippur is an atonement because it is a rededication of life to God; God, in turn, shows his mercy to Israel.

Paul saw in this contemporary event of his Jewish tradition a way of explaining what Jesus did by his death. Just as the animal of Yom Kippur is sacrificed to gain its life, so Jesus is now the sacrifice. He, too, is the priest who performs the sacrifice, for it is his free will that allows his death. It is his blood, his life which stands for the rededication of all peoples. Jesus' dedication is for certain, ours waits upon our free will. Jesus' total and pleasing self-giving occurs now, not on the wooden box of the Ark of the Covenant, but on the wood of the cross. There, on that wood, sits the Lord of mercy, Jesus himself acting for God; from him flows that mercy, that rededication on God's part which frees us from our sins and allows us to be one with God again. Atonement is often "spelled" AT-ONE-MENT; we are one again with our God. In a real sense, Jesus' self-dedication is a dedication of all the world to God, a plea for and an assurance of forgiveness; still, nothing takes place without our freely embracing it, wanting it, without our rededication to God.

Justification

A fourth way of understanding the effect of Jesus' death is contained in the word justification. This word was used particularly in Paul's major letters, to the Romans and to the Galatians. There is a long history behind this word. The Old Testament very often describes as "just" the person who pleases God, who can stand before God, who can enter into his presence. The goal of the religious person was to be considered by God as "just"; it is, of course, sin that makes one unjust before God, that destroys the union between the creature and his creator. Paul, like so many other Jews, longed for justification, cried that God would make him just. It is Jesus' death which Paul identifies now as the means by which the justice for which he sought was now possible for him; because of Jesus' death Paul could enter to live with God forever.

Behind the words "just," "justice," and "justification" stands a human experience, known in all times of human history. The context is a courtroom, the place where one is declared just or unjust. I can imagine myself to be the prisoner, brought before the judge for serious crime. All around me, and I myself, know that I am unjust, and deserve punishment; it will be a punishment which will deprive me of certain of my precious citizen's rights. For some reason unexplained, the judge decrees that I, whom he knows to be guilty, am innocent, just. I walk out of the courtroom, free and able to enjoy all my rights as a citizen, even though everyone knows I am guilty.

Using this analogy of an improbable courtroom scene, Paul underlines the fact that God, though he knows I am sinner, declares me innocent, considers me to be just. What I deserve, I do not get; what I do not deserve, I receive. Though Christian baptism involves more than just accepting God's declaring me innocent and just, I realize that my new self, pleasing to him, begins with his loving declaration, because of Jesus' death for me, that I am in God's eyes just. The gift of the Spirit of God helps me change to be a just person; with the Spirit I must cooperate. But I always remember that the beginning act by which God was pleased with me was not mine, but Jesus' death for me.

Such then are the metaphors or analogies Paul used to help us understand the effects of Jesus' death for us. One's acquaintance with Christianity is evidence of the immense contribution these four metaphors—reconciliation, redemption, atonement/expiation, justification—have made to the Christian understanding of God in Jesus. It is not going too far, though, to say that, as these metaphors or analogies help one's understanding, so also they should cause joy and peace. For these experiences all result in our enjoying a future which was far beyond our grasp, our hope. What we could never have had by ourselves is now given to us as a gift. Thus, the death of Jesus is a source of immense relief, joy, and hope for an everlasting life which we did not deserve; one might even say we were not even looking for it, so lost were we. And now we are found; we were dead and now we are alive.

Associated with the four metaphors just described is the figure, often used in the New Testament, of the Suffering Servant of Yahweh; this figure is described in Isaiah 52–53, and is applied to Jesus in his death. The Isaian figure is one who, like a lamb, goes silently to the slaughter; he also is an innocent person, who takes upon himself the punishment which others deserve. When he accepts what is their punishment, they go free; he alone is left to die. This image of the Suffering Servant helps fill out the image Jesus used so often of himself, that of Son of Man. The Son of Man image was instructive, for it described someone who, after suffering humiliation, would be glorified and become judge of the world. So did Jesus see himself. But the Son of Man image does not express why the Son was humiliated or what was achieved by this humiliation. It is by joining to this image the image of the Suffering Servant, so visible in the Christian Holy Week, that one sees that the suffering and humiliation of the Son of Man was undergone in order to free others, the guilty, so that they need not suffer the punishment they truly deserve. No wonder, then, that the news Christian missionaries wanted to tell the world can be called "Good News!"

Unjust Crucifixion of the Just Man

One can hardly overestimate how basic to the Gospels is the theme that Jesus was unjustly condemned to death; even though the Gospels are written to believers, the authors feel greatly obliged to show the injustice of what happened to Jesus. Probably this sense of obligation comes from the fact that, if there was anything that made belief in Jesus difficult in the first century A.D., it was his humiliating death in utter weakness. So much is Jesus' innocence a structuring element of the Gospels that, though it be an exaggeration, the saying of the nineteenth century contains some truth, that the Gospels are nothing more than a story of Jesus' death with a lengthy introduction.

Jerusalem: Calvary Crucifix in Basilica of the Holy Sepulcher

From the beginning of every Gospel it is clear who Jesus really is; it is clear that he comes from God, is Son of God, is conceived from the Holy Spirit of God, is the Word of God made flesh—and the Word is God. These preludes to the Gospel are followed by many episodes which in part show that Jesus' teaching is not only profound and correct, but is the clearest expression of the mind of God; no one, he says, can know the Father in this way except the one who is his Son. The miracles of Jesus show not only an endless power, but a mercy which is God-like and a control over Satan that means, as Jesus says, the kingdom of God is here. All of these elements of Jesus' public life, together with his integrity and his own prayerful, pious life—all this is argument, subtle or no, stored up against the day when Jesus will be put on trial, against the day when Jesus will be judged just or unjust.

But not only are the Gospel narratives sources for helping one to see Jesus' holiness and innocence. The stories of Jesus' trial(s) make abundantly clear how unfair and cowardly was the decision to put him to death. In ordinary life, one can only shrug one's shoulders at the claim that a person was treated unfairly by two of the highest authorities in the land; such is our trust of judicial authority. The Gospels tell the true evolution of the charges against Jesus and the eventual condemnation to death. The retelling of his last hours shows how the fateful decision was anything but just.

Behind this imagery of the just man being put to death by the iniquitous lies the wisdom literature which Jews knew very well as part of their Sacred Scripture. The figure of Jesus was placed against this literature, which spoke so eloquently of the pious Jew who suffered for his goodness at the hands of his own brethren. These latter are even said to want to put the just man to the test, to see if his so-called holiness is genuine or not, to see if God is on his side or not. The impious are tired and angry from hearing the just person calling them to obedience to their God; the test they impose will show, they think, that this thorn in their sides, is a charlatan. Let us put this so-called just man to the test!

The just man of Wisdom literature (see especially the Book of Wisdom 1–3) certainly is a helpful image by which to explain to Jews what really was going on in the trial of Jesus; other literature of the Mediterranean knew of the struggles of the just against the unjust, and so Christian Gentiles, too, were aware of this kind of image. Indeed, it is the hope of the Gospels that, even if we are not conscious of their preoccupation with this theme, we will subconsciously and through their efforts know certainly that Jesus is the innocent man ragged to death by the unjust.

Jesus as Model

Jesus is a model for his followers. Often enough the various writings of the New Testament speak of the sufferings and trials which Christians have endured, are enduring, and will face for their belief in Jesus. Some of the New Testament writings point up in particular the anguish and suffering of the missionaries of the Christian message. Mark's entire Gospel is thought to be heavily motivated by a desire to help Christians in Rome face persecution and martyrdom. Certainly, the bulk of the Book of Revelation is aimed to give Christian readers the strength to exit this world victorious over the deadly attacks of Christ's enemies. Whether it be individual phrases, particular stories, or entire works, the New Testament is concerned to urge Christians to determined fidelity, intense dedication, and public profession of faith in Jesus Christ.

In presenting Christ as one to follow into death, the New Testament offers a number of reflections. One of the most vivid remembrances is that of Jesus on the cross, asking his Father "to forgive them for they know not what they do." Forgiveness had been an exhortation of Jesus to his followers; now, on the cross, he gives them example in the most trying of circumstances. Jesus on the cross also commends his soul to God; the Christian is often tried because it is so hard to see the meaning of suffering for happiness, but Jesus calmly expresses his trust in his Father, that he will bring him through this suffering to eternal life. In this trust Jesus is a model for his disciples.

Jesus had always trusted in his Father's wisdom and love; it was, he knew, with him always. Thus, in the time of suffering, he knew he was not forgotten or lost, that there was purpose in his suffering, understood at least by his Father. In his agony he prayed to be spared his crucifixion, but he repeatedly asked that his Father's will be done, for he knew that by this wisdom and the love behind it he would enjoy eternal life. Nothing but his Father's wisdom and love, even if it involved the most painful and unintelligible suffering, would bring him life. In Jesus' admission of this truth he was a model for his disciples. If anywhere, it is here at Calvary, that Jesus' calling God his Father means so much. The suffering asked of me is asked by my Father. Let me, his child, trust in his wisdom and his love; they, and they alone, will bring me to my resurrection to eternal life.

When I sit in the Basilica of the Holy Sepulcher and realize that here is the place where my Savior died for me, the confession of Paul overwhelms me: "he gave himself for me; while we were still God's enemies, God gave his Son for us." Death is never pleasant. Here was death. It was a death for me.

And, though it might seem to complicate things a bit, we should always remember that, though we can say that Jesus offered himself to God to make up for our sins, it is truer to say that God the Son offered himself to God the Father. It was God, then, who died for me; to say that

Jesus took my place and suffered what I deserved is to say that God took my place, that God (the Son) offered his human life to God (the Father).

It was a death for me, but a death that was necessary only because of me. Such is the particular unpleasantness of this death. The only lessening of my humiliation for being the cause of this death is the memory of how much God loved me, that he would even go to a terrible death for me, if that would help me. I caused a very unpleasant scene here; but I know from it how sure is the love God has for me.

Jesus Risen
~ MATTHEW 28:1–10; MARK 16:1–8; LUKE 24:1–12; JOHN 20:1–18 ~

Not far from Calvary, the place of ignominy and intense suffering, is the site of glory and eternal joy, of hope for all of us for everlasting life. Jesus was hastily taken from his cross and wrapped in cloth; the intention of those who did this was to lay him to rest on this Friday before sundown or six o'clock, when the Sabbath began. Having accomplished this much, they would then rest on the Sabbath until it was over at six o'clock Saturday, then wait to return to the tomb at the first light of Sunday to complete the anointing and wrapping of the body for burial. Thus, the discovery that the tomb was empty occurred "on the third day" (Friday Jesus was buried, Saturday was a day of rest, Sunday was the day of discovery). On the third day, too, disciples heard the marvelous words: "he is risen, he is not here."

The Resurrection as Apologetic or Defense

As the Passion stories were protective of Jesus' innocence before all authorities, so the resurrection stories are filled with reasons to justify belief that Jesus is risen from the dead. For everyone, proofs were required; no one knew in advance that Jesus would rise from the dead, and so various elements are called into play to help all, but especially the reader, to believe firmly that the resurrection truly happened. The emptiness of Jesus' tomb is one of these elements; another is the call to remember what Jesus had promised about resurrection and what the ancient Scriptures had said in this regard; a third is the divine messenger(s) sent to assure disciples that Jesus is risen. Luke explicitly says that the risen

Jesus appeared to his disciples often over forty days to convince them that he was risen. Parallel with this effort to justify faith in the Resurrection is the continual picture of disciples who do not, cannot believe in it. They are in a sense negative examples, to spur the reader to surer faith as the reader sees how wrong these nonbelieving disciples really are. Everything is made to assure the reader that faith that Jesus is risen is justified.

Resurrection as Fulfillment of the Old Testament

One of the strongest arguments of the New Testament that Jesus is risen comes from a careful presentation of this event against the prophecies and other writings of the Old Testament. Nothing, of course, could be second to actually seeing the risen Jesus, but this kind of proof was reserved for a relatively small number of people, all of them disciples. Next to this kind of proof was the witness given by those who did see Jesus to others; the witness of these people throughout the Mediterranean was an indispensable component of the missionary effort.

The missionaries, especially in their efforts among Jews throughout the world and Gentiles devoted to the Jewish religion, made great use of the Old Testament as a buttress to their witness of Jesus risen. One gets a clear sense of the importance of the appeal to the Old Testament from Acts of the Apostles 17:2–3, where it is said that "Paul, as was his custom, on three successive Sabbaths explained to them the pertinent Scriptures, making clear that the Messiah had to die and rise from the dead; he then made clear that this Jesus 'whom I announce to you' is that Messiah." Thus, Paul strove to show both what the Scriptures said was the true identity of the Messiah and that Jesus fulfilled this definition of Messiah. Notable in this definition is the death/resurrection, an element most Jews had no idea was part of the definition of the Messiah. There are two concrete examples of how the Christians argued from the Scriptures; admittedly, in our day one does not often use the Old Testament to try to justify belief that Jesus is risen, but, as the passage in Acts above indicates, the argument was crucial for the New Testament times, and so we spend a moment on the matter.

Peter, with his Pentecost speech, wanted to prove that Jesus was Messiah and Lord of Israel; a secondary goal was to argue that it was

Jesus who had just poured out the Spirit upon his disciples. To prove that Jesus is Messiah and Lord of Israel, Peter did not have recourse to Jesus' public life. Rather, he combined citations from three Psalms and the Second Book of Samuel to argue his point. First, Psalm 16 is clear that David or one of his descendants would never see corruption. About whom could Psalm 16 be speaking? David? Solomon, his son? Any other of the ancient kings of Israel? If not one of these, then whom? There must be someone, for God does not prophesy in vain. Peter proposes the right candidate. Psalm 132 and 2 Samuel 7:12–13 are clear that David would have one particular descendant who would rule on his throne; everyone knew who this was: the Messiah, Son of David par excellence. Now it seems only logical to conclude that Psalm 16 must have been speaking about that particular descendant of David who is the Messiah, showing that he will never see corruption. In short, Peter links up Psalm 16, with its promise of never seeing corruption, with the Messiah, the one spoken of in Psalm 132 and 2 Samuel: the Messiah. Thus, Peter shows, Scripture, if understood properly, argues that the Messiah, about whom Scripture speaks, must rise from the dead, and will never see corruption. And who has risen from the dead never to see corruption again? Peter can say it is Jesus, "of him risen am I an eyewitness." Scripture, then, surely argues that Jesus is the Messiah of Israel.

In a similar way, a Psalm, this time 110, says that "my (= David's) Lord will be invited to sit at God's right hand." Who is this lord of David? Most likely it is the Messiah. But has the Messiah moved to God's right hand? Again, eyewitness concludes the argument: Peter has seen Jesus ascend and so can witness that the one Scripture expects to sit at God's right hand, the Messiah and David's Lord—this is most logically Jesus of Nazareth.

In this way Jesus can be called Messiah and Lord, the terms or concepts drawn right from Old Testament texts themselves. And to boot, it is the Messiah at God's right hand—who else?—who receives "from his Father the Spirit which Jesus the Messiah then pours out." Since Jesus is now clearly the Messiah and at God's right hand, Peter can say that Jesus is the one who poured out the Spirit this day.

The argumentation is a bit tortuous, but clear enough. When one gets the hang of it, the process is relatively simple. Let us look at one other example, drawn from Paul's speech to the Jews of Antioch (in present-day Turkey).

Paul's goal in this speech is to claim that Jesus, who had died about fifteen years before, will today give forgiveness of sins and justification to Paul's audience. Paul's first point is to argue that death was not the end of Jesus. Does Scripture support this point? To show that God planned a resurrection from the dead, Paul cites Psalm 2: "You are my Son, today I have begotten you." The crucial word is *begotten;* usually thought to pertain to actual conception of a child or to inaugurating the reign of a king, the idea here is, Paul says, that God begets by giving life after death; can this "giving life" not be a begetting? Now, there is a right expectation of a begetting to new life, but will that life endure? Add Psalm 16, which says that God's Holy One will not see corruption. Thus, the Son, the Holy One of God, is not only newly alive, but has a life which will not see corruption. He is alive forever, and so can provide good things to the Jews of Antioch, even fifteen years after Jesus' death. But will this Holy One provide "holy things"? If he is the "Holy One," it is logical to expect him to provide "holy things." But does Scripture say he will? Isaiah 55 quotes God as saying that he will give to Israel the holy things promised to David. How will God fulfill his promise? By having his Holy One, who is newly alive and will never see corruption, dispense the holy things promised us. Finally, what would be a holy thing promised us if not justification and forgiveness of all our sins? All of this argumentation depends, of course, on whether or not Jesus has been raised. Enter Paul's eyewitness; he has seen Jesus risen. Thus, Scripture again combines with eyewitness to argue that Jesus is risen and is Israel's salvation.

The arguments are plentiful that the Scriptures spoke about the resurrection of the Messiah; eyewitnesses speak truthfully that Jesus is risen. He must be Israel's Messiah. But the New Testament has other things to say about the meaning of Jesus' resurrection. Let us consider these.

Resurrection as Vindication

A theme taken up by more than one writer of the New Testament is that Jesus' rising from the dead is sure proof that Jesus was never guilty of any of the things he had been accused of; rather, the Resurrection, which occurs through the power of God, shows that Jesus must have been pleasing, very pleasing to God. Thus, while other events of Jesus' life argue that he is from God, the Resurrection, which is owed solely to divine power and divine choice, argues best of all that Jesus is "from God." If God gives life and thus destroys death, he gives it to "his own"—Jesus, to whom God gives life, is one of these.

Resurrection as Restoration of God's Saving Plan

Another way of understanding the resurrection of Jesus is that it is a crucial moment which sets in motion again the mission for which Jesus was sent. Jesus' mission began when he returned to Galilee after he was baptized or anointed with the Holy Spirit at the Jordan and passed forty days in the desert. This mission, to ask people for repentance and return to the one true God, was of its nature to continue to all people everywhere. Jesus' death in Jerusalem had every appearance of terminating that mission, especially since in it his opponents seemed so totally victorious. Death's sealing off the mission was final. The only proper answer to this violence was the divine giving of new life to Jesus, so that the mission can continue. And so it happened. As Acts says: "Jesus was raised up so that he could bring forgiveness of sins to Israel, light to all peoples." In this way, too, the Resurrection is a pivotal moment in human history.

Resurrection and the New Life of Human Beings

If the death of Jesus wipes away our sins, the resurrection of Jesus risen determines a new life for us. We can express this idea in two ways. In one sense, it is his resurrection that is said to give us our resurrection; moreover, his look of immortality, glory, exaltation, incorruptibility, perfection—all of these will define what we shall be. In another way, if we have been baptized, we have committed ourselves to a new look, to look like Jesus. This new look is nothing less than a new way of life. It contradicts the choices we had been in the habit of making: choices of hate and harm, choices that make ourselves and others a little less alive. We now live as people who give life, not take it away, by love for others, by helping another to live the best, most dignified life. Jesus is our model for this new life, which is committed to him in baptism and lived in response to his example, his teaching, his inspiration, and his strengthening of our wills.

The Necessity of the Resurrection

The resurrection of Jesus was an absolute necessity; it had to happen. Indeed, if Jesus is divine, how could his resurrection be anything less than necessary? What other ending could there be for the Word that is God?

Also, as we have noted, God often said through prophets that the Messiah had to rise from his painful death. So, if God said this about his Messiah, it had to happen. Similarly, if Jesus said the Resurrection had to happen, it had to happen.

But there is another reason for Jesus' having to rise from the dead. His love for his Father made this resurrection a necessity. Love, we know, creates life; that is our human experience. To God's love we owe creation and all its good; it was God's love, behind his power, which brought all to exist and to live. Thus, when God the Father asked human death of his Son, and Jesus God's Son, out of love for his Father, gave his life, the only outcome of this mutual love was life. Love made life necessary. Jesus' putting his hand in the hand of his Father and undergoing death—the Father never loosened his grip on his Son and within three days brought him to life, forever. The irony is that we think God's plan to give life is thwarted by death; as St. Paul suggests, God does save us from death, not from dying, but from that power of death which is to keep us dead. In God's raising us from death, death loses all its power, its hold on us, forever. Death, it can be truly said, is dead, because life is now unending. And love is the force that inexorably brings this victory about.

The resurrection from the dead means that Jesus continues to live. A number of stories in the Gospels show that the risen Jesus is identical with the crucified Jesus. But the fuller teaching suggests that the resurrected life is an absorption of the human into the divine in a way that we do not experience it here on earth. Many religions of ancient times thought of people living after death, but the living was only a shadow of what they knew human life on earth to be like. For the Christian, the life after death is not that; it is a life-with-God, a life-absorbed-into-God. Without having experienced it, we cannot explain it, but we know it is true, for we will live, the New Testament tells us, by the life, not of our parents, but of the Holy Spirit of God. Thus, we will be vigorous, uncorruptible, perfect, as much in the image and likeness of God as is possible.

Jesus risen is noted for certain particular things. He sits at the right hand of his God; this is the royal position, and signifies not only his kingly control of the world, but that he will be judge of the world. Also, he is described as the High Priest, who once presented to God the perfect sacrifice by which we are all cleansed from sin and now prays unceasingly for us. Moreover, Jesus risen received from his Father the Holy Spirit whom he then poured out upon all his disciples; every baptism and confirmation is simply the continuance of this one outpouring described as Pentecost in Acts. Jesus risen continues to act in this world, responding to prayer, healing and curing, causing peace, guiding his mission to call all to repentance for forgiveness of sins, the repentance which leads to life.

We should give more than passing recognition to the fact that, in the resurrected life, we will live by the life of God's Holy Spirit. On earth we know how human beings are conceived, but we do not explain why they have life at conception. Since God is life, and all life flows only from him, somehow he enters into the aliveness a human conception enjoys. Clearly, this life, which in a real sense is independent of parents, is limited by the circumstances of this world; the person who enjoys this life will, nonetheless, die, even if his life be God-given. But what happens when there is no human conception? And there is no more human death? The New Testament professes that we live, not by the human life-principle we experience in this world with its eventual participation in corrupting death—we live by the life of God in God's world, without human parentage. We live, more exactly, by the life of God's Holy Spirit. It is a more divine life we live when risen.

This Spirit we already possess, by virtue of baptism. Already we begin to live this divine life which is independent of this world and its corrupting death. We will die, but only to let this burgeoning life from the Spirit totally dominate us, totally fill us, so that we live solely by this life, and by no other, limited life-principle. Jesus is the first to enjoy this life; we follow right after him.

The Risen Jesus at Emmaus
~ LUKE 24:13–35 ~

Only once is this story told in the New Testament, but it has lasting and powerful significance. The risen Jesus meets two of his disciples on their way to the town of Emmaus. They are leaving Jerusalem, and they do so because, though Jesus might have proved to be a prophet, his death has proved him to be nothing more. The disciples explain what they have understood of Jesus, but do not recognize that it is Jesus to whom they are speaking. In response to the disciples, Jesus does two things, as Luke portrays it. First, he explains the ancient Scriptures, in how many ways they spoke of him and of his death and resurrection. Then, once Emmaus is reached and all three go in for a dinner, the two disciples finally recognize Jesus when he breaks the bread for them. Many scholars realize how the structure of Luke's story is a major teaching of the Gospel. Basically, Jesus' response to the doubts of the disciples is the interpretation of God's word and the breaking of bread. This is teaching that, if one wants to understand Jesus and meet him, the Christian does so in the Eucharist, where the word of God is heard and explained and the breaking of bread brings again all the meaning of the Last Supper, followed by communion with Jesus. Luke's point is to show his Christian readers how they, now fifty years from the time Jesus was on earth, might still nourish their faith, make it more understandable and meet the risen Lord Jesus.

The Resurrection of Jesus as Our Hope

One need not live long to know what death is, to want to avoid it, escape from it; we want to hold on to life. We sense that we are made to live. The New Testament, apart from the occasional miracle, offers no respite from the unstoppable grinding of life into death. But it is only the New Testament that offers the supreme hope that we will live, after death, forever. What happened to Jesus will happen to us and this belief replaces the fatalism of death with an exuberant joy, which nothing will ever take from us. The resurrection of Jesus offers us hope most of all because the gift of new life to Jesus flows from God's love. Ultimately, our hope is in this love; no matter how frail I am, his love will bring me to eternal intimacy with him.

Jesus' Resurrection

A last note about Jesus risen. All that has been said so far is directed to the meaning of the Resurrection for us. But there is another consideration to offer: what did the Resurrection mean for Jesus? For himself, it was fulfillment, unimaginable joy and perfection, forever. Great saints have encouraged Christians to think of this aspect of the Resurrection—to be glad for Jesus, not only for ourselves. Friends are glad for the joys of their dear ones; no difference here. Only it is true that, like Mary Magdalene, Jesus may have to ask us not to hold on to him, but to let him pass from the privileged moment of his stay on earth to his heavenly place next to his Father. Though far from totally absent from us, we do feel his absence, but we rejoice in his success and with fervent hope that we shall see him again one day, for unending days.

We have every reason to rejoice for ourselves and for Jesus. Everyone benefits from love unhindered by evil of any kind; we sympathize fully with the love of God for Jesus and of Jesus for God. We can only be grateful and joyful as we place ourselves before the tomb of the Resurrection. We know that we too shall rise, that nothing will keep us from enjoying the love of God. We have a grasp on how much God loves us, for he has placed us with Jesus; Jesus is risen, we also shall rise. Alleluia!

Glossary

BETHLEHEM: city from which David came; the city's name means House of Bread (perhaps intending to mean House of the god of Bread). Bethlehem is only six miles or so south of Jerusalem.

BYZANTINE: a style of architecture, and indeed a culture, springing out of the city of Byzantium (= Constantinople = Istanbul); Byzantium had replaced Rome, from the mid 300s A.D., as the major governing force of the Mediterranean world. This city was overcome by the Moslem Arabs in the 600s A.D.

CAESAR AUGUSTUS OCTAVIAN: Roman emperor from Jesus' birth to the year 14 A.D.; he is the one who commanded that all people be registered in their family towns for a census, and so Joseph took Mary to his family town of Bethlehem, where was born Jesus.

CAESAR TIBERIUS: Roman emperor from 15 A.D. till Jesus' death; it is this person who appointed Pontius Pilate to rule Judea and its capital, Jerusalem.

CRUSADES: a series of Christian attempts, from 1090s to 1290s A.D., at repossessing the Holy Land, with little lasting success.

ELIJAH, ELISHA: powerful prophets of the 860s–840s B.C. in northern Israel; Jesus was often likened to them. Elijah, who never died, was expected by the prophet Malachi, dated somewhere around 450 B.C., to return to prepare Israel to meet its God.

ESDRAELON, PLAIN OF: vast plain that runs northeast to southwest through the center of Galilee.

EUCHARIST: a word coming from the Greek word meaning "to thank." It early signified the Christian service in which prayer, readings with comment, the representation of the Last Supper, to commemorate and make present again the death of Jesus, and Communion were major elements.

GABRIEL: one of the angels (with Michael and Raphael) who stand always before God; also one who was chosen to announce at times the plan of God for salvation.

GALILEE: equivalently the top one-third of Israel. Both Jews and Gentiles lived in this territory at the time of Jesus' living there.

GOSPEL: a particular presentation of the salient moments of the life of Jesus of Nazareth which will accomplish the goal for which the Gospel was written; each Gospel is the result of preachings and a preaching itself.

HEROD: Herod is the name of a non-Jewish man who was appointed by Rome in 40 B.C. to rule all of Israel or Palestine; in 37 B.C. he actually took command of this territory and ruled till his death in 4 B.C. Among his many accomplishments, he embellished the Temple in Jerusalem and built the Mediterranean seacoast city of Caesarea; he is the Herod who ordered the killing of the Innocents in Bethlehem, and after his death Joseph returned from Egypt with his family. Three of Herod's sons inherited his name and his kingdom; two of the brothers are noteworthy:

HEROD ARCHELAUS: ruled the bottom 1/3 (Judea with Jerusalem) of Israel or Palestine, till 6 A.D., when Rome removed him because of his harsh rule and replaced him with Procurators or Governors; it was this Herod that Joseph avoided when returning from Egypt—Joseph preferred to live under Archelaus' brother:

HEROD ANTIPAS: ruled the top two-thirds of Israel till removed in 39 A.D. He had John the Baptizer beheaded and put Jesus on trial at the urging of Pontius Pilate. Herod Antipas abandoned his wife for Herodias, who had a daughter, Salome, by her former, abandoned husband; this Salome requested the head of John the Baptist, because he had publicly criticized Herod Antipas and Herodias for their sinful marriage.

JERUSALEM: city conquered by King David and made the capital of Israel's heart and government. Here was the first Temple of God, that of Solomon, and its successor, by Zerubbabel; the latter is the Temple, embellished by Herod the Great, which Jesus knew.

JOHN THE BAPTIZER: son of Zachary and Elizabeth (somehow related to Mary), he was conceived miraculously about six months before Jesus was conceived. John seems to have been raised and educated among the religious communities strung along the Jordan River; he preached repentance for Israel and baptized as a gesture that showed repentance. He never became a disciple of Jesus, but testified that one greater than he was to come—and asked Jesus if he were that person.

MATTHEW, MARK, LUKE, JOHN: names of authors assigned to the four Gospels. Matthew and John were disciples of Jesus and sources for their Gospels. Mark was a companion of Peter and Paul and author of his Gospel. Luke was a companion for some parts of Paul's life and the author of his Gospel and the Acts of the Apostles. Mark's Gospel was likely the first, written about 70 A.D., and read by the authors of the Matthean and Lucan Gospels. John's Gospel was written about 95 A.D., perhaps with some knowledge of Luke's Gospel. John the Apostle is also traditionally the source for the 3 Letters of John and the Book of Revelation (or Apocalypse).

MESSIAH: means "Anointed One." Anointing with oil was an ancient act by which a person was made king. Hence, Messiah is, in the thoughts of many generations, to be a king, who will provide for all his subjects the safety, prosperity and life all hoped for. He was thought by many to be a descendant of King David. By Jesus' time, this figure was expected to be holy and wise, as well as all-powerful. Further, when he came to exercise his Messiahship, this age would pass away, and a new age, without death, would begin.

PHARISEES: a group of pious Jews begun perhaps about 185 B.C. These people were consumed with obedience to the law of Moses; they never numbered more than 8,000 at any one time, but tried to influence Jewry away from any meaningful contact with non-believers and forced the revolt in 66 A.D. which brought the Romans to destroy Israel. Their interpretations of the law often put them at deadly odds with Jesus. The Pharisees supported the belief in resurrection of the dead, and so in some sense supported Christianity; on the other hand, the resurrection should take place for all at the end of the world, not for one just after his crucifixion. Not all Pharisees were against Jesus.

PONTIUS PILATE: appointed Procurator or Governor of Judea from about 26 A.D. until 35 A.D., when he was banished from office for poor governance.

SADDUCEES: traceable to the about 180 B.C., these Jews believed in no resurrection from the dead, no afterlife. They opposed Jesus strenuously on this point. They had influence with the upper classes, and so had influence over Jesus.

SAMARIA: in Jesus' time, the middle one-third of Israel or Palestine wherein lived these non-Jews who had a history of antipathy and fighting toward Jews, particularly toward Jerusalem considered a threat to Samaria. Samaritans actually considered themselves the true descendants of the Patriarchs and worshipers of the God of Moses.

SANHEDRIN: name of the highest ruling body of Israel, which numbered seventy men plus the High Priest, its President. The seventy were made up of Elders, Chief Priests, and scribes. The scribes were specialists in knowledge of the Law of Moses and subsequent bodies of traditional law. Chief Priests, numbering seven or eight in any given year, assisted the High Priest in his Temple duties;

they were appointed by the High Priest and, unlike ordinary priests, practiced their priesthood all year round. Elders were members of old-time, aristocratic, wealthy, influential families. In the Sanhedrin were all the judicial, executive, and legislative powers; as long as the Sanhedrin did not contradict Roman law, the Romans let the Sanhedrin rule Israel. The High Priest, often considered to have prophetic powers, was President of the Sanhedrin, responsible for the operation of the huge Temple complex, and prime representative of Israel to Rome. Rome insisted on appointing the High Priest and on deciding if any Israelite should be put to death. Most likely most scribes were pharisaic in outlook, while most Elders and Chief Priests and High Priests were Saduccean in outlook.

SATAN: initially the one who reminded God of how evil and unfaithful to him were human beings; from this unpleasant role, Satan developed into the full-fledged enemy of human beings, bent on their complete destruction. While God held final sway over his creation, Satan was considered to have major influence in this age of ours, to be able to say "all these kingdoms are mine," and even to take possession of human beings. It will be the Messiah who finally will defeat Satan, purge his influence, and restore all things to their original beauty forever.

SCRIBES: nowadays called lawyers, because, while they did not try cases, they were extremely knowledgeable about all the Laws of Moses (612) and all subsequent laws derived from the Mosaic Law. They may not have been as devoted to the law as were the Pharisees, but they challenged Jesus' knowledge of the law vigorously and to the death.

SYNAGOGUE: wherever nine good men could be gathered, a synagogue could be had. It was a place of reading sacred texts, of meditation and pious conversation. Each Saturday, a ceremony was held, in which prayers, readings, and comments on the readings took place. The synagogue was not a place of sacrifices. The one and only place of sacrifices was the Temple in Jerusalem.

TESTAMENT, NEW AND OLD: literature which is centered on agreements or covenants or alliances the God of Israel made, on the one hand, with Israel, and, on the other hand, with the followers of Jesus.

YAHWEH: the proper, personal name of the one true God, the God of Israel. "God" is the general name applied to all divinities. The ancient Jewish equivalent or substitute for Yahweh is "Lord."

Bibliography

Aharoni, Yohanan, and others. *The Macmillan Bible Atlas.* New York: Macmillan Publishing Company, 1993. A most valuable, clearly written, and diagrammed presentation of lands, cities, and periods of the Bible; an admirable blend of archaeology and history.

Doyle, O.F.M., Stephen. *The Pilgrim's New Guide to the Holy Land.* Wilmington, Del.: Glazier, 1985. A prayerful guide with hymns, concerned with equipping the pilgrim with religious helps to appreciate the sites of the Holy Land.

Hoade, O.F.M., Eugene. *Guide to the Holy Land.* 7th edition. Jerusalem: Franciscan Printing Press, 1973. A lengthy and time-honored guide to the Holy Land, a major guide for many, many years.

Kopp, Clemens. *The Holy Places of the Gospels.* Translated by R. Walls. New York: Herder and Herder, 1963. For many years, the trustworthy guide to New Testament sites with respect to history and geography.

Mackowski, S.J., Richard. *Cities of Jesus.* Rome: Pontifical Oriental Institute, 1995. A lively discussion of how to evaluate the historical correctness of sites in the Holy Land. Fr. Mackowski has also written an excellent scholarly discussion: *Jerusalem, City of Jesus.* Grand Rapids, Mich.: Eerdmans, 1980.

Miller, J. Maxwell. *Introducing the Holy Land: A Guidebook for First-Time Visitors.* Macon, Ga.: Mercer University Press, 1982. The book admirably fulfills the promise of its title.

Murphy-O'Connor, O.P., Jerome. *The Holy Land: An Archeological Guide from Earliest Times to 1700.* 3rd Edition. New York: Oxford University Press, New York, 1992. A scholarly presentation of the Holy Land's archeological problems, proposed solutions, and the effect of these solutions on understanding the Bible.

Page, Charles R., II, and Carl A. Volz. *The Land and the Book.* Nashville, Tenn.: Abingdon Press, 1993. Fine, brief summaries of the archeological and historical facts associated with both Old and New Testament biblical sites, as well as a good short history of the biblical land up to the present. Meant to be an introduction—historical, cultural, archeological—to the world of the Bible.

Recommended Bibles:

Many people have their own preferred Bibles, but the following can be recommended for their readability, their professional accuracy in translating from the original biblical languages, and their helpful notations:

New Jerusalem Bible. New York: Doubleday, 1985.

New American Bible. Collegeville, Minn.: Liturgical, 1988.

New Oxford Annotated Bible. New York: Oxford University Press, 1992.

Important
Periods and Dates

ABRAHAM, ISAAC, JACOB: approximately 2000 B.C.– 1700 B.C.

EXODUS FROM EGYPT: about 1250 B.C.; about 1200 B.C. Israelites under Moses enter the Promised Land.

DAVID: King Saul ruled 1020–1000 B.C.; he was succeeded by King David, who ruled all Israel 1000–962 B.C.; David was succeeded by his son, King Solomon, 961–921 B.C.

TWO KINGDOMS: at Solomon's death, Israel was divided into two countries. The North, two-thirds of the original Israel, was called Samaria, Israel, and the Kingdom of the North; the South, one-third of the original Israel, was called Judah and the Kingdom of the South.

ELIJAH AND ELISHA: about 860–840 B.C., in the Northern Kingdom

EXILE OF NORTHERN KINGDOM: this Kingdom was conquered by Assyria and its people sent into Exile in 722 B.C. According to Jewish history, the northern two-thirds of the Promised Land was populated with foreigners, soon to be known, even in Jesus' time, as Samaritans; these people built a Temple to the God of Moses just 35 miles north of Jerusalem

ISAIAH: prophesied from 722 B.C. in the North; and afterwards in the South

EXILE AND RETURN OF SOUTHERN KINGDOM: 587 B.C. the South is conquered and sent into exile by the Babylonians

JEREMIAH, EZECHIEL, DANIEL:	Jeremiah prophesied before and during the South's destruction; Ezechiel prophesied during its exile; Daniel lived during the exile, though much of his book describes events in the centuries afterward. In 538 B.C., after the Persians had conquered the Babylonians, King Cyrus of Persia allowed Jews to return to the South and to rebuild it; they began with Jerusalem.
BUILDING OF SECOND TEMPLE:	begun in 515 B.C.; this temple not as elaborate as the first one, built by Solomon. This second Temple is the one Jesus knew and which Herod the Great tried to improve.
ALEXANDER THE GREAT:	the Persian empire ruled its "province" of Judah till Alexander the Great, 333–323 B.C., conquered all and ruled all of Palestine. Many Jews took on Greek culture and ways.
EGYPTIAN/SYRIAN DOMINANCE:	Alexander's kingdom was divided into four parts; from 323 B.C., the Egyptian sector ruled Palestine, till eventually about 200 B.C. the Syrian section took over Palestine. During the Syrian dominance, a revolt began under the Maccabees; their victory in Jerusalem, in 164 B.C., is called Hannukah, and began the freeing, part by part, of Palestine from foreign rule. Alongside the Maccabees, it seems Pharisees and Sadducees fought. It is this string of liberating victories that eventually brought Jews to live in large numbers in the North again, e.g., Galilee and Nazareth, while few Jews, if any, lived in the central section of Palestine, Samaria.
ROMAN CONTROL:	in 63 B.C. Pompey the Great took over Palestine for Rome; Jews finally left Palestine before Rome ever gave up control of the Land.
THE HERODS:	in 37 B.C. Herod (called "the Great"), a non-Jew, began his rule of Palestine, which had been given him by Rome. He died in 4 B.C., and his kingdom was divided among his sons Philip (till 34 A.D.), Antipas (till 39 A.D.), and

Archelaus (till 6 A.D.). Jesus was born before Herod the Great died; Jesus' public life ended under Antipas (Philip had nothing to do with Jesus).

PONTIUS PILATE: when Archelaus was removed from ruling Judea, he was replaced by Roman Procurators or Governors. One of these was Pontius Pilate, who ruled 26–36 A.D., and saw to Jesus' death in 30 A.D.

DESTRUCTION OF PALESTINE/JERUSALEM: during the war by Rome from 67–73 A.D., Jerusalem (with its Temple) was destroyed in 70 A.D.

NEW TESTAMENT WRITINGS: extend from 50 A.D. to 120 A.D.; all Paul's letters were written before any of the four Gospels (70–95 A.D.) was written.

CONSTANTINE: Roman rule continued and Palestine became more and more Romanized; the crushing of a second Jewish revolt in 132–135 A.D. finally drove most Jews out of Palestine for centuries. Around the time of this second rebellion Hadrian made Jerusalem a Graeco-Roman city and built, on the presumed site of the crucifixion, a Temple to Juno, the chief goddess of Rome. It was with his victory in 312 A.D. that the Roman emperor, Constantine, after allowing Christianity to be an officially recognized religion (indeed, his preferred religion), built three basilicas in Palestine to honor famous Christian events on sites discovered by his mother, Helena: the Crucifixion/Resurrection, the Birth of Jesus, and the Ascension.

ISLAMIC CONTROL : when the power of Rome moved to Byzantium in the latter 300s A.D., Palestine was under Byzantine control; Christianity had always existed in some form in Palestine, but flourished under Constantine and the Byzantine emperors. But by 638 A.D., the forces of the new Moslem religion conquered Jerusalem (and Byzantium as well) and, within 50 years,

	built what we know to be the Dome of the Rock, which sits above the old Solomonic Temple.
CRUSADES:	in 1071, a new force, the Seljuk Turks, conquered Palestine and Syria, and, though the Moslems before them had allowed Jews and Christians to live together peaceably in Palestine (as long as they paid taxes), the Seljuk Turks harrassed them to the point of exasperation. In 1095 A.D. the call for a freeing of Byzantium and of the Holy Land was made. Seven Crusades in all happened, three of which were crucial for Palestine. The entire Crusade period came to an end in 1291 A.D. Moslem forces eventually regained control of the Holy Land.
SULEIMAN THE MAGNIFICENT:	in 1517 the Ottoman Turks took control of Palestine. One of the most famous acts at this time was the building of what are the present walls of Jerusalem; Suleiman did this building on top of remains of an earlier crusader wall.
MODERN TIMES:	in the 19th century, the Zionist movement urged Jews to repatriate to Israel; in the same years, Arab groups urged the same for their people. Turkey still had control of Palestine, till it made the mistake of supporting Germany in the First World War. Turkey lost control of Palestine, in favor of the British, who governed it till they could no longer withstand the pressures of native groups for independence. In 1948, Israel was declared an independent state, though Arab states refused to recognize this declaration. Intermittent wars have raged over this territory; the war of 1967 saw Israel take command of the Golan Heights, the West Bank, Gaza. To this date, there is still discussion about the eventual disposition of these lands occupied since 1967, but no discussion anymore about the sovereignty of the Israeli state, the first free Israeli state since Rome's conquest in 63 A.D.

Index of Subjects

Index of Biblical Texts

Ps 132 272

2 Sam 7:12-16 8, 272

Wis 1-3 268

Zec 9:9-10 209

Acknowledgements for Illustrations

Raymond V. Schoder, S.J. Collection, Loyola University Chicago Archives, E. M.
Cudahy Library, for photographs on pp. 5, 23, 33, 81, 102, 109, 127, 134, 141, 145,
149, 166, 185, 195, 228, 253, 259, 267.
Mark J. Link, S.J., for photographs on pp. 50, 86, 175, 219.
Ruth E. McGugan for photographs on pp. 8, 30, 41, 44, 90, 105, 159, 245, 255.
Amelia Janes/Mike Gallagher, Midwest Educational Graphics, L.L.C., for maps facing
title page and on pp. 2, 100, 164.

Also from

Loyola Press

THE GIFT OF PEACE
Personal Reflections
by Joseph Cardinal Bernardin

"In this gem of a book, reminiscent of the best of Henri Nouwen, Bernardin stresses the importance of regular prayer, the need for loving human relationships and the profound peace that comes from trusting God even in the worst of times."
—Publishers Weekly
ISBN: 0-8294-0955-6; $17.95 hardcover

CHRISTIANITY AND HUMANISM
From Their Biblical Foundation into the Third Millennium
by Timothy G. McCarthy

"If you are looking for one book to solve the problem of widespread religious illiteracy, this is it . . . in this book McCarthy does justice to the questions, the doubts, the fears of real people today and he does this by devoting a good portion of his work to scripture— what it is, and how to read and interpret it."
—National Catholic Reporter
ISBN: 0-8294-0913-0; $26.95 hardcover

THE DISCERNING HEART
Discovering a Personal God
by Maureen Conroy, R.S.M.

"I know of no recent treatment of Ignatian Discernment which analyzes so extensively the historical, personal, and practical aspects of discernment and which opens the Rules of Discernment in a popular mode for spiritual directors as does Conroy's book. Young spiritual directors who want an easy yet thorough lesson in Ignatian Discernment have an unparalleled tool here."
—Presence: An International Journal of Spiritual Directors
ISBN: 0-8294-0752-9; $13.95 paperback

Available at your local bookstore or order directly from Loyola Press.
Send your check, money order, or VISA/MasterCard information (including $4.50 for
shipping one book, $5.00 for two books, or $6.50 for three) to:

LOYOLA PRESS, ATTN: CUSTOMER SERVICE, 3441 NORTH ASHLAND
AVENUE, CHICAGO, ILLINOIS 60657
800-621-1008